Contemporary Literature and the End of the Novel

D1744862

Contemporary Literature and the End of the Novel

Creature, Affect, Form

Pieter Vermeulen

First published 2015 by
PALGRAVE MACMILLAN

Palgrave Macmillan in the UK is an imprint of Macmillan Publishers Limited, registered in England, company number 785998, of Houndsmills, Basingstoke, Hampshire, RG21 6XS

Palgrave Macmillan in the US is a division of St Martin's Press LLC, 175 Fifth Avenue, New York, NY 10010.

Palgrave is the global academic imprint of the above companies and has companies and representatives throughout the world.

Palgrave® and Macmillan® are registered trademarks in the United States, the United Kingdom, Europe and other countries.

ISBN 978-1-349-49030-1   ISBN 978-1-137-41453-3 (eBook)
DOI 10.1057/9781137414533

A catalogue record for this book is available from the British Library.
A catalog record for this book is available from the Library of Congress.

Typeset by MPS Limited, Chennai, India.

For
Mats and Stine,
affective agents
no novel
can contain

Contents

Acknowledgments

I am finishing this book as I am about to return to the Department of Literary Studies at the University of Leuven, the place where it was first conceived four years ago. I spent these four years first as a postdoctoral researcher at Ghent University's Centre for Literature and Trauma (LITRA), and then as an assistant professor in Stockholm University's English Department. I owe it to the inspiration, provocation, and generosity of the intellectual communities in these different places that writing this book has been a more exciting and fulfilling experience than I had imagined. In Stockholm, I had the good luck to encounter a head of department committed to providing a welcoming and supportive environment for young scholars; apart from Claudia Egerer, I especially want to thank Stefan Helgesson for his intellectual and professional generosity, and Bo Ekelund, Charlotta Palmstierna Einarsson, Irina Rasmussen Goloubeva, Paul Schreiber, and the other members of the literature section for continuous support, friendship, and dialogue. In Ghent, I wish to acknowledge the support and kindness of Stef Craps and Gert Buelens. In Leuven, Ortwin de Graef and Arne De Winde played a quietly enabling role in thinking through the stakes and challenges of this project when I started to conceive it.

Several parts of this book began or developed as presentations, lectures, or workshops. These parts, and indeed the book as a whole, owe a lot to discussions in Copenhagen, Durham, Linköping, Leuven, London, Odense, Stockholm, Uppsala, Urbana-Champaign, and Zaragoza. I have to thank Lucy Bond, Rick Crownshaw, Kristina Fjelkestam, Danuta Fjellestad, Kasper Green Krejberg, Jessica Rapson, Michael Rothberg, Peter Simonsen, David Watson, and Helena Wulff for the opportunities to share some of the work that went into this book.

In the last few years, much of my thinking on the ethics and politics of the novel form intersected with that of Arne De Boever, and I am grateful that these intersections invariably served as encouragements. Reading through the manuscript one last time, I was reminded how many of my ideas were triggered by wonderfully suggestive posts on Michael Sayeau's blog, *Ads Without Products*, which not only reads the right books, but also asks the right questions.

Most things I think I know about the relations between affects, creatures, and forms, and about the exhilarating messiness of living,

I would never have dared to imagine without my two children, Mats and Stine. If this book time and again emphasizes how some affective charges escape emotional codification only to bloom into something too awesome to name, that is their fault. And as they are, strictly (or ontologically) speaking, partly *my* fault, dedicating the book to them seemed the right thing to do. I share this *felix culpa* with Mirjam, who has always been there in the turns and twists of what I am ridiculously proud to call "our life."

Stockholm, May 2014

Parts of Chapter 1 appeared as "The Critique of Trauma and the Afterlife of the Novel in Tom McCarthy's *Remainder*" in *Modern Fiction Studies* 58.3 (2012): 549–68; parts of Chapter 2 appeared as "Abandoned Creatures: Creaturely Life and the Novel Form in J.M. Coetzee's *Slow Man*" in *Studies in the Novel* 45.4 (2013): 655–74; a shorter version of Chapter 3 was published as "Flights of Memory: Teju Cole's *Open City* and the Limits of Aesthetic Cosmopolitanism" in *Journal of Modern Literature* 37.2 (2013): 40–57; a number of paragraphs from the coda, finally, are reused in "Don DeLillo's *Point Omega*, The Anthropocene, and the Scales of Literature," published in *Studia Neophilologica*. I am very grateful to Teju Cole for permission to use one of his photographs for the cover of this book.

Introduction: After-Affects

Genre dying into form

In his famous 1967 essay on "The Literature of Exhaustion," the American postmodernist John Barth declared that "the novel's time as a major art form is up" (71); English novelist D.H. Lawrence's 1923 essay "Surgery for the Novel—Or a Bomb" visited "the death-bed of the serious novel" and diagnosed the patient as "senile precocious"—a condition only "a convulsion or cataclysm" could hope to cure (152); already in the 1760s, when the English novel was at best a few decades old, Lawrence Sterne's *Tristram Shandy* was "the first novel about the crisis of the novel" (Alter 39); and even the second part of *Don Quixote*, published in 1615, already encoded the death of the genre that its first part had inaugurated ten years before (Reed 270–72). The temporal distance between these four moments may begin to suggest the vast scope that a literary history of the end of the novel would have to cover. To make matters worse, declarations of the death of the novel are inextricably connected to the dialectic of creativity and destruction that propels modern literary history. When Barth wrote "The Literature of Replenishment" as a follow-up to his declaration of exhaustion in 1979, he looked back on more than a decade of vibrant postmodern production; two years after stopping just short of euthanizing the novel, D.H. Lawrence hailed it as "the one bright book of life" ("Why The Novel Matters" 195); the Russian formalist critic Viktor Shklovsky, for his part, argued that *Tristram Shandy*, far from rendering emerging novelistic conventions obsolete, was in fact "the most typical novel of world literature" (170); and of course, *Don Quixote* is widely recognized as the original modern novel (Schmidt), not least in Barth's later essay, which celebrates it as an inexhaustible source of imaginative "refreshment"

1

(205). When declarations of the end of the novel so often tend to shade into moments of productivity and innovation, the history of the end of the novel becomes almost co-extensive with modern literary history as such.

This book offers no such literary history. Instead, it tests the paradoxical productivity of the idea of the end of the novel in a significant sample of contemporary fiction, and discovers that these fictions dramatize the end of the novel in order to reimagine the politics and ethics of form in the twenty-first century. These fictions not only update the enabling role that statements of the end have played in modern literary history, they also interrogate the role that the novel form can play in contemporary media ecologies. In light of the spectacular rise of digital media, it is unsurprising that rumors of the end of the novel are as alive as ever; what is more peculiar about the present critical climate is the currency of claims that the novel form has historically exercised a momentous cultural power. Assessing the state of contemporary novel criticism, Mario Ortiz-Robles helpfully summarizes some of its axioms: "We now quite commonly hold that the novel participates in all sorts of social processes, helping to found the modern nation, to consolidate overseas empires, to advance industrial capitalism, to enforce sexual difference, and, more generally, to produce and police the subject" (2). The novel is assumed to have inculcated and sustained a particular distribution of interiority, individuality, domesticity, and community—a constellation that has defined modern life. The strongest statement of the intricate relations between literary form and these modern forms of life is perhaps Nancy Armstrong's assertion that "the history of the novel and the history of the modern subject are, quite literally, one and the same" (*How Novels Think* 3).

Contemporary fiction's dramatization of the end of the novel conveys a sense that neither these modern forms of life nor the novel's cultural power are quite what they used to be. Instead, it paradoxically draws on the novel's perceived impotence as a resource for figuring forms of life that cut across the distinctions between individuals and communities, between the self and the social. This imaginative work exercises a far weaker cultural power than the one the novel is assumed to have had in the past, yet it is precisely because it suspends particular assumptions of agency—or even wishful ascriptions of "aggrandized agency" (Anderson 46)—that it can attune the remainder of the novel to unregimented forms of life and to affective intensities that escape the emotive scenarios that have traditionally animated the novel. Following (and quoting) Adorno, Sianne Ngai has argued that "bourgeois art's reflexive preoccupation with its *own* 'powerlessness and superfluity in the empirical world' is precisely what makes it capable of theorizing social powerlessness in a manner unrivaled by other forms of cultural praxis" (3). The novels in this study theorize powerlessness (in Ngai's words) and imagine weak forms of affect and life (in my slightly more upbeat phrasing) by dismantling the "strong" affective scenarios that have allowed the novel to exercise its cultural power, and by elaborating less robust assemblages of life, affect, and form in their wake. These novels explore the notorious elasticity of the novel form in order to move beyond a particular hegemonic instantiation of that form: the unusually powerful version that criticism and theories of the novel assume, and that these novels identify as a distinctive codification of emotive experience.

Whether the novel is best thought of as a genre, a form, or even a mode is, as Fredric Jameson has remarked, the object of a "long-standing and desultory debate" (*Antinomies* 138–39). At the heart of that debate is the novel's famous capaciousness and elasticity: its capacity to infuse everything it contains with what Jameson calls, following Roland Barthes, "a novel-ness that extend[s] down into the very pores of the language and the individual sentences" (161). The novel seems to lack the specificity and solidity we expect of a fully fledged genre, if we understand genre, with Gérard Genette, as the intersection between a particular mode of enunciation and particular thematic elements (61–62), or, with Tzvetan Todorov, as a historically realized "codification of discursive properties" (162). The texts we recognize as novels, it appears, do not have fixed themes or discursive elements in common. In that respect, the novel must be distinguished from genres such as the romance and detective novel, which are not only marked by certain types of event, but also by "their ordering, emphasis [...] and the perspectives from which the events are viewed" (Malik). Lacking "a set of stable thematic preoccupations, habits of address, or social functions," then, the novel is less a particular genre than "a certain formal possibility" (Kurnick 228). Even if a particular constellation of conventions and expectations arguably allowed the realist novel to achieve generic stability for part of the nineteenth century (Jameson, *Antinomies* 3), we can better account for the variability and adaptability of the novel, or indeed for the dissolution of that generic formation, by considering it as a form rather than a genre.

In this book, I will consistently refer to the novel (as) form, and underline that the flexibility of that form gives contemporary literature the freedom to evoke as well as frustrate generic expectations. The novels in this study exploit that formal license by departing from a particular, and partly fictional, conception of the novel as a homogenous, clearly codified genre in order to explore what forms of life and affect emerge after the dissolution of that genre—a dissolution that these novels explicitly stage.

These novels ascribe to the novel (as) genre the now obsolete power to choreograph the distribution of modern life into individuals, families, communities, nations, and empires; their declarations of the demise of that cultural power serve as so many scaffolds for their explorations of different forms of affect and life and for their interrogations of the ethics and politics of form. By evoking a particular understanding of the novel genre in order to measure their difference from it, these fictions in a sense conspire with criticism and theory of the novel to construct a genre they declare defunct; as Todorov notes, "[t]he fact that a work 'disobeys' its genre does not make the latter nonexistent; it is tempting to say quite the contrary is true" (160). This intricate process of construction and dismantling is at the heart of *Contemporary Literature and the End of the Novel*. The different chapters and the coda each foreground one postmillennial novel: Tom McCarthy's *Remainder*, J.M. Coetzee's *Slow Man* (together with his *Diary of a Bad Year*), Teju Cole's *Open City*, Dana Spiotta's *Eat the Document* (which I read alongside Hari Kunzru's *My Revolutions* and Russell Banks's *The Darling*), and James Meek's *We Are Now Beginning Our Descent*. Five novels, and five ways in which the novel genre dies into form.

Fictions of agency

So what is the structure that these novels reconstruct only to go on to disassemble it? What, in other words, is the cultural power that the novel genre is presumed to have enjoyed? How is it supposed to have organized the distribution of modern life into the meaningful and the meaningless and into individuals and aggregates? The power that novel theory and the fictions in this study ascribe to the novel has at least two dimensions: an emotive one that I discuss below and an epistemic one. This epistemic dimension presents the novel as "the genre par excellence of cognitive mapping" (Kurnick 229). As Alex Woloch notes, the novel genre has traditionally been praised for "two contradictory generic achievements: depth psychology and social expansiveness, depicting the interior life of a singular consciousness and casting a wide narrative gaze over a complex social universe" (19). The novel is uniquely capable of simultaneously affirming "the importance and authenticity of ordinary human interiority" and elaborating "an inclusive, extensive narrative gaze" (19). The novel, that is, asserts the value of individuality as a social force by drawing interiority and the social into the same fictional universe. Arguably the most ambitious statement of the codependence between the individual and the social is Georg Lukács's theory of the novelistic "type," which holds that particularly significant characters can embody vital social forces. In my fourth chapter, I show how Dana Spiotta's *Eat the Document*, as well as Hari Kunzru's *My Revolutions*, sabotage such a significant articulation of the individual and the social by removing their protagonists (late 1960s or early 1970s political activists) from society and forcing them underground. In both novels, this disabling of the "type" serves as a strategy to explore new—and less epistemically robust—ethical and political possibilities for the novel form.

The sabotaging of the logic of the type, and of the meaningful articulation of the individual and the social that it promises, is not the only strategy that contemporary fiction uses to explore the demise of the novel's epistemic privilege. Another procedure that I trace in this book is the refusal to endow characters with the kind of psychological depth that novels, on many accounts, have the power to mine in particularly significant ways. Disallowing characters a meaningful interiority, then, is also a way of denying, and creating a space to rethink, the mandate of the novel. Mark McGurl has recently argued that the current renaissance of zombie fiction responds both to an impatience with fleshed-out character and to the realization that the novel "may have outlived its life as a key cultural form"—that it has, in fact, become a "zombie genre." It is afflicted by the declining credibility of "deep, psychologically complex fictional characters, the kind we find at the center of realist novels like *Pride and Prejudice*." The novel, for McGurl, "is neither alive nor dead but undead" ("Zombie Renaissance"); in the terms I use in this book, it is obsolete as a uniquely authoritative genre, yet it survives in formal attempts to imagine a consciously diminished version of that lost agency. In my first chapter, I argue that Tom McCarthy's *Remainder* constitutes one such attempt; it inhabits the undead zone in which the novel, according to McGurl, finds itself, through its outright refusal to render the combination of reflexivity and emotion that we know as interiority. If the experimental psychological realism that we associate with some instances of high modernism surrenders the social half of the novel's double epistemic mandate only to confirm its psychological half, *Remainder*'s studied indifference to both halves marks a radical break with that mandate.

The novel's famed epistemic capacity to shape the domains of the psychological and the social into meaningful forms is intimately connected to its "commitment to everyday life" (Woloch 19). In his classic *The Rise of the Novel*, Ian Watt seconds Erich Auerbach's claim that the novel affords everyday life a seriousness that was traditionally confined to tragic events (79–80). The novel, Watt writes, differs from other forms "by the amount of attention it habitually accords both to the individualisation of its characters and to the detailed presentation of their environment" (18). Watt's choice of the term "individualisation" over "individual" points to an aspect of the novel's epistemic prerogative that has remained implicit until now: for the novel to valorize everyday life, it needs that life to change and develop. Michael Sayeau notes that "the novel is conventionally a model of individual and social dynamism, in which initial situations are pushed into evental action and change, thus revealing dynamic truth" (183). If, according to Watt, the novel brings the contingencies and banalities of everyday life into a literary frame, "the ordinary or uneventful" is only allowed entry "under the condition that it is structurally determined as the subsidiary backdrop against which significant, revelatory action can occur" (Sayeau 32). Stories in which nothing happens, therefore, or in which a character refuses to be transformed, constitute massive challenges to the meaning-making mandate of the novel; alternatively, they generate creative spaces for imagining life and affect differently. In my second and third chapters, I focus on two contemporary novels that resist meaningful change in very different ways. J.M. Coetzee's *Slow Man*, which I discuss together with his *Diary of a Bad Year*, features a protagonist who stubbornly refuses to act, change, or even desire change. In Teju Cole's *Open City*, a catalogue of events, experiences, and encounters refuses to congeal into the protagonist's meaningful transformation or psychological development; things do happen, but they fail to matter. Sayeau notes that "[t]o start a story is to enter into an implicit contract with your listener or reader that, at some point soon, something will happen and this something will be meaningful" (29). *Open City* and *Slow Man* are aware of the terms of this implicit contract, but they decide to overwrite them in their attempts to make room for unexplored forms of affect and life.

The first, epistemic, dimension of the novel's presumed cultural power depends on a second one: its capacity to engage its readers on an emotive level, and to instill particular habits of feeling. Genres are defined by particular modes of emotive address, if we understand genre, with Lauren Berlant, as "a loose affectual contract that predicts the form that an aesthetic transaction will take" ("Intuitionists" 847). Just as the novel traditionally promises its readers meaningful events as well as serious depictions of social and/or psychological life, it serves as "an aesthetic structure of affective expectation" (Berlant, *Female* 4)—an implicit contract that prescribes a particular kind of emotive engagement. The novels by McCarthy, Coetzee, Cole, and Spiotta foreground two interrelated aspects of that promise, precisely by refusing to honor them: desire and identification. Desire has long been recognized as a key element in the organization of novel plots, perhaps most notably by Peter Brooks and René Girard. For Brooks, for instance, the heroes of the nineteenth-century novel can be seen as "'desiring-machines' whose presence in the text creates and sustains narrative movement" (39). Even for critics like Leo Bersani who see narrative as the *repression* rather than as the *organization* of desire, desire is a key element in the interaction between novels and their readers. Whether it is conceived as an "unending process of displacements and substitutions" (Bersani and Dutoit qtd. in Clayton 43) or as "a plastic and totalizing function" (Brooks 37), desire is what keeps readers riveted to novelistic narrative.

As Teresa de Lauretis has shown, the traffic of desire between reader and narrative is closely related to the power of the latter to solicit identification—to make readers (desire to) identify with the desire of characters (de Lauretis). Here, we can appreciate the intricate connection between the novel's emotive powers and its epistemic force: its capacity to shape meaningful events and evoke psychological depth makes characters available for identification, while it is the power of identification that grant these formal features the power to choreograph the distribution of modern life into the meaningful and the meaningless, as well as into individuals and communities. When the novels in this study then present their readers with characters without psychological depth or without significant desires, they deliberately sabotage the genre's cultural power, while they at the same time make room for affective registers that cannot so easily be codified through desire and identification.

Emotion, literature, affect

If, as we have seen, genres function by soliciting readers' emotive expectations, the novels in this study activate generic expectations only to frustrate them. This approach allows them to morph into zones where *unexpected* feelings can emerge. Throughout this book, I code the difference between codified and cognitively available feelings, on the one hand, and intractable and unrepresented intensities, on the other, by borrowing the terminological distinction between *emotion* and *affect*. I am aware that the vocabulary for mapping emotive domains in cultural and social theory is notoriously slippery, and that the distinction between emotion and affect is complicated by their contiguity and even overlap with terms such as passion, feeling, mood, and sensation. Still, theorists of affect have, under the influence of the work of (especially) the psychologist Silvan Tomkins and the philosopher Gilles Deleuze, begun to separate the domains of affect and emotion: while affects are non-cognitive and non-representational intensities that take place outside of consciousness, emotions emerge when such intensities are narrativized, named, and represented as part of individual experience. Affects are non-subjective, asignifying forces that are "narratively delocalized" and "disconnected from meaningful sequencing" (Massumi 25); emotions, for their part, are "the conventional, consensual" absorption of affect "into function and meaning" (28). Affect, in other words, never belongs to an individual subject, but is rigorously presubjective (Abel 6). Affect dissolves the self-contained interiority of the individual and opens it to new connections and recombinations.

Affect's refusal to be contained by individual subjects makes it a crucial resource for the fictions I discuss in this book. When the novels in this study annul the emotive scenarios that underwrite the novel's cultural power, they make room for unrecognized and unowned affects that operate outside of "the subjective domain of consciously codified emotion" (Greenwald Smith, "Postmodernism" 428). Their formal departure from the generic codes of the novel simultaneously undo the alliance between feeling and individual, and make it possible to imagine forms of life that cannot be contained by conventional emotional scenarios. As Vilashini Cooppan notes, "[e]ven when captured as emotion, affect lingers on beyond the point of capture, opening itself to potential liberations, escapes, and freedoms" (56); it is a dynamic principle that "passes through but also beyond personal feelings" (Terada 109), and that allows contemporary fiction to explore *impersonal* feelings that more capriciously and less predictably circulate across the divisions separating individuals and communities.

It is important to dissociate my emphasis on the interactions between emotion and affect from versions of cultural and social theory that tend to reify affect as the material substrate of human behavior. Especially prominent in posthumanist thought, and often inspired by a desire to escape the trappings of the so-called linguistic turn, this tendency upholds affect, life, and the body as the neurally based, realist foundations of knowledge (Colebrook, "Calculus" 144); affects, on this account, are blissfully untainted by signification, intention, and mediation, and instead present "a set of innate, automatically triggered brain-body behaviors and expressions" (Leys, "Turn to Affect" 465). Affects then function as a biological bedrock that is, in Brian Massumi's phrase, *"resistant to critique"* (28). The main problem with this strict separation between affect and consciousness is that it allows invocations of affect to claim a privileged access to the material determinants of culture, and to immunize themselves from critique. Such rigorously undialectical mobilizations of affect underwrite an uncritical posthumanism that fails to account for the ineluctability of consciousness, cognition, intention, and narrative in the understanding of contemporary life (Vermeulen, "Posthuman Affect").

If the presumed autonomy of affect is unhelpful for a proper understanding of contemporary life, it is decidedly unworkable for a study such as this that aims to understand the reimagining of life through literary works. *As linguistic constructs*, literary works cannot dwell in uncodified affect; literary works are "linguistically based and therefore inevitably codifying" (Greenwald Smith, "Postmodernism" 431), even if, *as aesthetic operations*, they simultaneously generate affects that cut across these codifications. Literary works are defined by a restless interplay between emotional codifications and affects that inevitably escape them; even if they attempt to control unruly affect and contain it as individual emotion, affect always exceeds these efforts. Affect in literature is then not a fatefully pre-linguistic and pre-conscious substance, but an effect of the inability of literary works to fully contain the intensities they irresistibly unleash; rather than a warrant of knowledge and readability, as some versions of posthumanist theory would have it, affect is a placeholder for *unreadability* (Colebrook, "Calculus" 144). It serves, in Rei Terada's helpful formulation, "as nonsubjective experience in the form of self-difference within cognition" (3).

Affect as self-difference within cognition: this is very different from the materialist fantasy of a world "independent of signification and meaning" (Leys, "Turn to Affect" 443). Cognition, consciousness, representation, and narration generate their own affective surplus; as Michael Clune has noted, current research on human consciousness makes clear that we don't need to invoke the nonconscious to "stir up" our understanding of consciousness, as consciousness itself "is the great destabilizing factor in our intellectual world" (35). This becomes especially clear in my reading of Teju Cole's *Open City*. This novel presents a highly self-conscious and erudite first-person narrator, who painstakingly captures and filters the events and encounters that make up his everyday life. This conscious registration of life at the same time functions as a strategy of emotional neutralization. Paradoxically, the very success of this neutralization effort conveys the narrator's dissociation from his world, which asserts itself as an awkward, uneasy feeling that the narrative cannot control. In *Open City*, affect's capacity to escape containment depends on the work of consciousness and cognition. This is a dynamic that a position insisting on the autonomy of affect cannot account for. Indeed, a coherent account of the workings of affect needs to locate affects' emergence in what William Egginton calls "the thorough interpenetration of bodies and mediation," which generates "paradoxes of mediation" that in turn assert themselves as affects (25). As part of the same dynamic, neither affect nor consciousness can be understood separately from each other, as consciousness is "itself a powerful motor of affective life" (31).

The friction between emotional codification and affective solicitation marks all literary works, not just the novels in this study. What sets these apart is their decision to evoke the emotional codifications that they take to underwrite the former cultural power of the novel and to generate affect through their dismantling of those generic codes. Importantly, this emotive scenario in which clearly identified emotions are suspended does *not* lead to an outright *absence* of emotion, but, as in the example of *Open City* above, to a less comfortable and less tractable affective dynamics "taking place outside of sensory and emotional codification" (Greenwald Smith, "Organic Shrapnel" 163). Sianne Ngai has called such an affect that usurps upon the elision of a familiar emotion "a second order feeling": it is "a meta-feeling in which one feels confused about what one is feeling [...] the dysphoric affect of affective disorientation—of being lost on one's own 'cognitive map' of available affects" (14). The affects generated by dismantling the novel genre, in other words, are inevitably "after-affects"—byproducts of complex interactions between processes of literary mediation rather than substances that literary form cannot touch. Crucially, this sense of emotive disorientation, this second-order feeling that is generated by the absence of emotion, need not only be a negative experience; as Rachel Greenwald Smith underlines, such trackless affect can also be valorized as "something transformative," and as a change "in physical sensation, in corporeal orientation" that marks the site for the emergence of novel possibilities ("Organic Shrapnel" 163).

Focusing on this—and only this—emotive scenario allows me to sidestep the methodological difficulty of locating and tracking an unruly affective movement that by definition "eludes language and its naming of things" (Jameson, *Antinomies* 29); throughout the book, I have resisted the temptation to specify the affects produced through the formal operations the novels use to loosen emotional codification; I stop at deliberately vague assertions that they are at times dysphoric, awkward, and uneasy, and at other times excessive, even farcical. As the different chapters together make clear, these affects are best considered as underdetermined and open-ended—as potentialities that communicate both a sense of powerlessness and an opportunity for novel combinations, connections, and assemblages to emerge.

Affect, in this book, serves as the name for *formal operations that aim to undo emotional codification*. To the extent that such codifications are assumed to have buttressed institutions such as the family, the nation, and the individual, their formal dismemberment points to modes of life that cut across such institutions of modern life. Life, here, should not be thought of as a biological substrate that precedes mediation; just as the *after-affects* I trace are generated through complex mediations, so new figures of human life are marked by their inability to fully surrender their humanity. These figures can neither coincide with familiar forms of life, nor can they simply escape these forms and become rock, or stone, or tree. At the end of my first chapter I turn to the work of Lars Iyer, in which I unearth a form of "farcical" life. In my second chapter, I further elaborate this mode of what we can call *non-non-human* life in the late work of J.M. Coetzee, in which I locate figurations of what Eric Santner has influentially called "creaturely life." In one of several excursions in this book to classic texts of novel theory, I also turn to Erich Auerbach's account of "creatural realism." Tracing the place of creatural life in Auerbach's genealogy of the novel, and its surprising subterranean afterlife in Ian Watt's *Rise of the Novel*, I theorize the creatural dimension of the life that emerges through the disassembling of codified emotion in Coetzee's novels. As the coda to this book makes clear, this form of *non-non-human* life is a promising figure for reimagining human life in the anthropocene—a period term that, as I explain, redefines the human as a geological force without dissolving its intentionality and responsibility. The novels in this study cannot conform to the expectations of the novel (as) genre, but neither do they escape the novel form; in a comparable way, creatural life can neither coincide with available forms of life nor abandon human life entirely. This is the zone in which contemporary fiction contributes to the reimagining of life and experiments with the ethics and politics of form. The three terms that make up the subtitle of this book—creature, affect, form—can stand as the provisional coordinates of that uncharted zone.

Scope and scale

Contemporary Literature and the End of the Novel interrogates one particular strategy through which contemporary fiction rethinks the ethics and politics of literary form as it grapples with new modes of life and affect. Through this strategy, the works I discuss mobilize the conviction that the novel can no longer assume its authoritative cultural role for the exploration of a weaker aesthetic mission, which is more attuned to forms of life that are no longer sovereign and centered, and to forms of affect that are not yet codified and controlled. Even if they lack the capacity and confidence to articulate a clear response to the ethical and political challenges they intuit, their formal experiments at the very least affirm the urgency of imagining such a response. I propose that (non-emotional) affect and (non-non-human) creatural life can be vital resources for thinking such a response.

Even if the scope of this study is much more modest than theirs, this combined sense of the exhaustion of old forms and the intimation of a new ethics and politics of form tallies with the conclusions of two extraordinarily wide-ranging studies of postmillennial writing: Peter Boxall's *Twenty-First-Century Fiction* (2013) and Caren Irr's *Toward the Geopolitical Novel* (2013). Boxall organizes the disparate set of concerns that animate contemporary fiction around that fiction's commitment to register and figure a new temporal awareness; informed by "the perception that the narrative mechanics which have allowed us to negotiate our being in the world, to inherit our pasts and to bequeath our accumulated wisdom to the future, have failed" (217), the impressively varied set of fictions he analyzes "is involved in the reimagining of the relationship between time, narrative and embodied subjectivity" (123). Boxall's argument makes clear that my insistence on the novel form, affect, and different modalities of life resonates with a broader attempt to "imagine ethical, political and embodied life" (123) in early twenty-first-century writing. The specific trajectory that I trace gives phenomena that Boxall's study only intuits their specific names; when he describes a recurrent "negotiation of political and biological subjectivity after the lapsing of certain forms of humanism" (123) that takes a variety of forms in contemporary fiction, I show how a smaller set of fictions recognizes that altered subjectivity as creatural life or as human life solicited and distorted by the anthropocene.

Boxall's *Twenty-First-Century Fiction* not only shares its wide scope with Irr's *Toward the Geopolitical Novel*, but both studies also convey a sense that contemporary fiction is as yet more concerned with voicing the urgency of new ethical and political coordinates than with confidently fleshing out such an updated imaginary. For Boxall, contemporary writing *"prepares* the narrative conditions in which the new, the future, might come to expression" ("Late" 681, italics mine). In her study of over a hundred recent American fictions, Irr identifies a renewed political impulse, even if, she admits, that impulse has not yet congealed into firm ideological commitments; contemporary writing is still moving *toward* the geopolitical novel, and its tentative achievements constitute a provisional "matrix of possibilities" that counts as "a proto-political orientation" (3). I share Irr's diagnosis of the inchoate and open-ended nature of contemporary fiction's ethical and political work, even if I arrive at that diagnosis through a methodology that is very different from hers, in at least two related ways. First, while I locate contemporary fiction's innovations in its strategies to undo generic determination, Irr emphasizes how responses to current global challenges have taken shape in emergent genre norms such as those of the genres she identifies as the digital migrant novel and the Peace Corps fugue. These new genres aim to sidestep the perceived limitations of older models and consist in "new motifs, characterizations, conflicts, and modes of resolution" (10) that recur across a number, often dozens, of novels. Such larger developments remain undetected in my focused readings of a smaller set of novels, and they are rendered visible by Irr's principled commitment to a version of distant reading (13). Irr resists "the hagiographic tendencies of close reading," noting that it "rarely provides illuminating accounts of the underlying genre norms" (13). The flip side of such resistance, I argue, is that it misses what my readings foreground: the paradoxical productivity of a self-conscious refusal of genre in contemporary fiction's "proto-political" experiments.

I have introduced Boxall's and Irr's books not only because they allow me to situate *Contemporary Literature and the End of the Novel* in the field of twenty-first-century fiction studies, but also because they demonstrate that it is possible to map contemporary literature without overplaying the importance of what until a few years ago, when I first started thinking about this book, still seemed like inevitable reference points: the aftermath of postmodernism and the events of September 11. Especially in the field of American literature, questions of whether "post-postmodernism" (Timmer) or "late postmodernism" (Green) were appropriate terms to capture the widely felt decline of the postmodern, and of how to locate the work of the likes of David Foster Wallace and Jonathan Franzen in relation to postmodernism, seemed urgent until not too long ago;[1] what Boxall, Irr, and other recent studies of contemporary fiction show is that an account of the present as the period after postmodernism unhelpfully obscures influences, challenges, and precursors that are at least as important for current literary practices.

One of the premises underlying this book—that formal innovations shape a reimagining of agency and subjectivity—is at least as much a modernist notion as a postmodernist one (J. Ryan). David James and Urmila Seshagiri have shown that much innovative twenty-first-century fiction attempts to "move the novel forward by looking back to the aspirational energies of modernism" (93). In the works I discuss, modernism appears in the different guises they distinguish: "[a]s a historical antecedent, a cultural trope, and an archive of stylistic and technical possibilities" (93).[2] In my readings of McCarthy and Coetzee, the very different modernisms of the *nouveau roman* and of Hugo von Hofmannsthal are crucial reference points; in my chapter on Spiotta, I emphasize that the dialectic of realism and modernism (as filtered through Lukács) persists in contemporary efforts to reimagine political agency; and in my discussion of Cole's *Open City*, I read the novel as a critical revision of modernist cosmopolitanism. When Michael Sayeau writes that modernist narrative eschews "unalloyed novelty" and instead "ironically undercut[s], erode[s] from within" obsolete narrative structures (39), this accurately describes the anti-generic thrust of the fictions in my book. Because of these echoes and affinities, it does not seem too far-fetched to characterize the key gesture of the novels in this book—staging the demise of an obsolete model in order to inhabit its aftermath—as faithful to a modernist impulse.[3]

Like postmodernism, the traumatic legacy of September 11 has by now turned out to be a less compulsive intertext for postmillennial literature than it seemed only a few years ago. If the subtitles of prominent studies of fiction after 9/11 cast that date as a decisive rupture in the history of "the novel" (Versluys), of "the literature of terror" (Randall), or even of "American literature" (Gray), the traumatic impact of that day has increasingly become less a unique reference point than "one element among many" to which contemporary literature refers (Keniston and Quinn 3). As we can see from our present-day vantage point, 9/11 was followed by global events that had very different evental structures: while September 11, as Roger Luckhurst writes, "was a punctuating event that [...] was strikingly easy to narrate within the paradigm of trauma" ("In War Times" 721), the subsequent wars in Iraq and Afghanistan, but also developments like global warming and the financial meltdown, lack the readability and narratability of 9/11, and require different strategies of engagement for which no narrative templates were available. In that sense, September 11 has morphed from a uniquely significant traumatic event into one of several global events, phenomena, and developments that have inflected contemporary ethical, political, and aesthetic paradigms (Gasiorek and James 610–11).

While *Contemporary Literature and the End of the Novel* is careful not to reaffirm September 11 as a master signifier, it reflects the altered perception of its literary impact in different ways. In my first chapter, I read McCarthy's *Remainder* as an (only partly successful) attempt to move beyond the ethical pieties that beset conventional trauma fiction, and to reduce trauma to a non-emotive narrative grammar. As I show, this attempt to elide emotion ends up generating dysphoric, secondary feelings. This shift in *Remainder* from the particular emotive scenarios encoded in trauma narratives to a more capricious range of unregimented affects captures the changing textures of literature after 9/11—from the overwhelming traumatic impact of the events of 2001 to a more disparate and varied engagement with a multiplicity of global forces (Greenwald Smith, "Organic Shrapnel" 161–63). The other novels discussed in the book all touch on this multiplicity: the chapter on Coetzee by reading *Slow Man* together with *Diary of a Bad Year*, which explicitly addresses postmillennial political events in essayistic form while simultaneously producing a form of creatural life that opens these reflections to a broad range of affects; *Open City*, for its part, is mostly set in post-9/11 New York, yet it carefully connects these events to a more encompassing history of violence; *We Are Now Beginning Our Descent*, which I discuss in my coda, discovers traces of that history in the campaigns in Afghanistan and Iraq, and it brings that history under the rubrics of the creatural and the anthropocene.

Even if contemporary fiction has been increasingly successful in situating the impact of 9/11 in broader ethical and political forcefields, the (political, aesthetic, commercial, and psychological) pressure to consecrate 9/11 is itself a literary historical fact; in the immediate aftermath of the events, literature that wanted to resist that pressure often had to make a point of bracketing that context. In my fourth chapter, I analyze a curiously underresearched subgenre that emerged in this direct aftermath: novels that deal with the inactive afterlives of activists from the 1960s and 1970s. I show how Dana Spiotta's *Eat the Document* and Hari Kunzru's *My Revolutions* return to memories of activism and life underground in order to raise questions of ethico-political agency while holding the impact of September 11 on such questions in abeyance. Both novels decline to refer to 9/11; both their stories end in the late 1990s and suspend the question of the relation between their narratives and the early twenty-first century. In the last section of that chapter, I finally turn directly to criticism of post-9/11 literature in order to argue that that suspension of the present is part of these novels' point: by bracketing the direct impact of contemporary terror, Kunzru and Spiotta can leverage the end of the novel—in their case, the Lukácsian historical novel—as a paradoxically productive site for their explorations of the contemporary possibilities of the novel form. My decision to only engage the context of 9/11 *after* having attended to those explorations is a way of acknowledging that such a suspension of direct historical referents plays an enabling role in fictions of inactive activists. I strengthen that point by contrasting Spiotta's and Kunzru's novels to Russell Banks's *The Darling*, a novel that also mobilizes the conceit of the terrorist-gone-underground, but that does opt for a Lukácsian typical character who directly confronts, rather than suspends, historical forces. While this allows Banks's novel to embody the global and transcultural perspective that many critics of fiction after 9/11 have called for, the novel fails to register the unregimented and intractable forces that cut across the extension from the local to the global, from the domestic to the transnational.

Throughout the second half of the book, starting from the chapter on *Open City*, I emphasize that the affective work of contemporary fiction does not so much point to the need for a more global *scope* in addressing current ethical and political challenges, but rather to the need to imagine a radically different *scale*. If non-emotional affect cleaves categories such as the individual, the nation, and even the human, my reading of *Open City* makes the point that neither can it be contained by cosmopolitan models. While *Open City* is widely received as a successful cosmopolitan performance, it subtly indicates the insufficiency of the empathy and curiosity promoted by aesthetic cosmopolitanism. Through its careful manipulation of tone and its portrayal of a narrator who remains disturbingly unaffected by his many aesthetic and transcultural experiences, the novel indicates the limited purchase of empathetic transcultural encounters and so suggests the need for the novel form to also engage the limits of the human. In my coda, I relate this concern with nonhuman scales to theoretical interventions by Mark McGurl (on the "posthuman comedy"—works that intimate the nonhuman vastness of geological and biological time) and Dipesh Chakrabarty (on the anthropocene, which exposes humanity as a geological force). This shift from a difference in *scope* (from the domestic to the transnational) to a difference in *scale* (from the human to the nonhuman) is dramatized in James Meek's *We Are Now Beginning Our Descent*. Meek's abandoned, disgraced, and multiply shamed protagonist is inevitably reminiscent of Iyer's "farcical" and Coetzee's "creatural" characters. By returning the critique of cosmopolitanism in Cole, Spiotta, and Kunzru to explorations of different forms of life and affect in McCarthy and Coetzee, Meek's novel demonstrates the impossibility for the novel form to domesticate the affects that it engages, and the critical urgency of attending to the transformative potential of not-yet-codified affects.

The novel, in theory

A final note on method. My readings consistently put the novels in dialogue with both canonical and contemporary works of novel theory and criticism. This choice is informed by an awareness that the idea of a singularly influential novel genre on which these fictions depend is less a historical reality than a construction that is, while not without factual basis, at the same time a theoretical, critical, and literary fiction. I therefore directly engage critical and theoretical discourses that construct that fiction, as well as interventions that deconstruct it. I don't invoke these texts as authoritative statements. Heeding David Kurnick's insight that "if the novel isn't a genre, novel theory decidedly is" (229), I apply as much pressure on these theoretical and critical interventions as on the novels themselves. The result of these confrontations between novels and theories is that several self-declared detractors of the form find themselves captured by it, while some of the main advocates of "the novel as modernity's pre-eminent sense-making form" (Kurnick 229) end up intimating forces that the form cannot contain.

In my first chapter, I situate Tom McCarthy's invectives against middlebrow fiction in the context of Lars Iyer's "Literary Manifesto after the End of Literature and Manifestos" and David Shields' much-discussed anti-novel manifesto *Reality Hunger*. While only Iyer's text has made its peace with the inevitability of "the end of literature" as the only possible context for residual creativity, Shields' and McCarthy's statements find themselves perpetuating the life of the novel form they aim to bury once and for all. In their works, affect is produced by the impossibility of burying the undead corpse of the novel. In my last chapter, I show how Mark McGurl's defense of genre fiction (at the expense of literary fiction) as the appropriate form for evoking the vast as well as infinitesimal scales that shadow human life can be read against the grain as a plea for the literary novel. In my third and fourth chapters, I read the work of Cole, Spiotta, and Kunzru against contemporary accounts of transnationalism and cosmopolitanism to show how these works sidestep the parameters of those discussions and intuit unsettling affects that escape the spectrum from the domestic to the transnational. In all these cases, the novels end up distorting the messages that the critical and theoretical interventions think they are delivering.

Contemporary Literature and the End of the Novel also revisits some of the classic texts that elevated the novel to its status as the quintessential modern form. In my reading of fictions of the inactive afterlife of activism, I show how two distinct phases in Georg Lukács's reflections on the novel—his early *Theory of the Novel* and his later defense of realism—are telescoped into a surprisingly coherent account of the role of different media in the novel's contemporary questioning of its own residual agency. If the early Lukács diagnoses the novel with an endemic nostalgia for the epic, Spiotta's *Eat the Document* refracts that dynamic to imagine an *analog* aesthetic for contemporary fiction. According to this aesthetic, which is also at work in *Open City*, the novel functions as a recording device inscribing—rather than actively shaping—the real. This minimal gesture of rendering and keeping things "legible" constitutes an act of realism that, unlike Lukácsian realism, allows contemporary fiction to register forms of life and affect that it does not yet understand.

These unruly forms of life also emerge in my readings of Ian Watt's *Rise of the Novel* and Erich Auerbach's *Mimesis*, one of Watt's insistent intertexts. Restoring that intertext makes it possible to see that Watt's account curtails Auerbach's genealogy of the novel by excising Auerbach's *creatural* realism—a realism that, like that of the novels in this book, attends to forms of life emerging in the interstices of obsolete forms, such as the novel, that can no longer house them. The unleashing of creatural life in contemporary fiction, then, makes it possible to reread Watt's history of the novel as an attempt to domesticate creatural life and to transform it into the modern individual subject. I make this point through my reading of Coetzee's late fiction, and I return to it in my reading of *We Are Now Beginning Our Descent*. Meek's novel articulates creatural life with war, which adds another twist to our understanding of Auerbach, who famously wrote his *Mimesis* during World War II in Istanbul, and of Watt, who spent that period as a prisoner of war in the East: it shows the close affinities between creatural life, unruly affect, literary form, and war. This revisionary account of the history of novel theory is not much more than a subplot in this book; foregrounding it would risk forgetting that it is only enabled by a reading of the postmillennial fictions that by right take up most of the book. These fictions demonstrate that, if the contemporary novel makes its mark on the history of the form, it cannot but affect its theory.

1

Persistent Affect (Tom McCarthy, David Shields, Lars Iyer)

> *I wonder about those who proclaim cities, authors, theo-retical approaches, bands, history over. Does it make the pain stop?*
>
> —@NeinQuarterly

Burying the novel

Declaring the end of the novel has proven to be a productive gesture in modern literary culture. Consigning old literary forms to the dustbin of history is often the rhetorical flip side of the inauguration of new literary dispensations, and the novel's popular and middlebrow success has made it an obvious target for such declarations of redundancy.[1] Especially modernist statements of the death of the novel tend to function as "deck-clearing statements," stating "the irrelevance or immi-nent demolition of an old form in favor of some particular alternative within sight" (Greif 12n2). Take, as an example of such a double-sided performance, T.S. Eliot's famous delayed review of Joyce's *Ulysses*. While "*Ulysses*, Order, and Myth" (1923) applauds *Ulysses* for imagining an alternative to the novel, it locates the diagnosis of the novel's deformi-ties somewhere else:

> the novel is a form which will no longer serve [...] the novel, instead of being a form, was simply the expression of an age which had not sufficiently lost all form to feel the need of something stricter. Mr. Joyce has written one novel—*The Portrait*; Mr. Wyndham Lewis has written one novel—*Tarr*. I do not suppose that either of them will ever write another "novel." The novel ended with Flaubert and

with James. It is, I think, because Mr. Joyce and Mr. Lewis, being "in advance" of their time, felt a conscious or probably unconscious dissatisfaction with the form, that their novels are more formless than those of a dozen clever writers who are unaware of its obsolescence. (Eliot 177)

The novel form has become obsolete because the conditions for its continued "service" have disappeared: it could only "serve" in an age that still had form. Only Lewis and Joyce "felt" the insufficiency of the novel form in a formless age, and articulated their intuitions by writing a "more formless" novel—effectively demoting the novel to the status of an anachronism that only survives, in Eliot's review, between quotation marks.

Joyce's *Portrait* and Lewis's *Tarr* play a curious role in Eliot's argument. Both are written *after* the novel is said to have ended "with Flaubert and with James," yet the fact that they express a feeling of dissatisfaction with it still somehow indicates that their authors are "in advance" of their time. If Flaubert and James thought they had killed the novel, Lewis and the early Joyce prove that the victim has survived and is as yet merely undead. In this book, I will mainly be interested in the ways in which contemporary novels address the awkward persistence of the novel; I will read novels that do what Eliot has *The Portrait* and *Tarr* do. We can begin to appreciate the differences between the present moment and Eliot's confident modernism when we recall that *The Portrait* plays a merely diagnostic role in Eliot's essay; it is only *Ulysses* that will deliver a cure for the defects of the novel that *The Portrait* had expressed. If the novels of Lewis and the early Joyce are credited with the power to voice a feeling of dissatisfaction, this feeling is hygienically separated from a very different one: a feeling for "the need of something stricter." Eliot's essay famously identifies this "something stricter" as a different literary approach: Joyce's (and Yeats's, and, obviously, also Eliot's own) "mythical method" (Eliot 178). Unlike Lewis's and the early Joyce's diminished novels, this new and stricter method need not occupy itself with registering dissatisfaction; instead, it can be dedicated to the momentous task of "making the modern world possible for art" (Eliot 178).

Eliot's intervention relies on a neat division of labor between the novel, which can do nothing more radical than record dissatisfaction, and the mythic method, which gives shape to an alternative "order and form" (Eliot 178). Significantly, Eliot does not classify *Ulysses*, in which he finds the mythic method on display, as a novel, and instead consistently refers to it as a "book." Eliot's own career as a poet–critic is enabled by a comparable generic division of labor: the demise of the novel form is registered in a critical essay, whereas his pursuit of a stricter poetics takes shape in the genre of epic poetry (*The Waste Land* was published eight months after *Ulysses*). Eliot's critical endeavor hardly affects his creative one, and this means that the dialectic of poetic individuation, in which "the past [is] altered by the present as much as the present is directed by the past" (Eliot 39), can run its course in Eliot's poetical project.

Eliot's poetry need not occupy itself with the awkward persistence of a form that James and Flaubert have, it seems, failed to end once and for all. Importantly, this generic logic is only possible because poetry, for Eliot, holds sufficient symbolic capital to enable the overcoming of the novel, and to decisively move beyond the hesitations and frictions reflected in *Tarr* and *The Portrait*. The contemporary declarations of the end of the novel that I am interested in lack confidence in a radical alternative to the novel; unable to imagine a creative space that is not affected by the novel, they are inevitably afflicted by its uneasy persistence. Both in Tom McCarthy's novel *Remainder* (2005) and David Shields' book-length manifesto *Reality Hunger* (2010), dissatisfaction with the novel feeds into an imagined alternative, yet that alternative is still shaped by the strictures of the novel. If Eliot can bury the remains of the novel outside the domain of poetry, McCarthy and Shields, in their very different ways, only have those remains to bury the novel with; the decidedly compromised result is, in McCarthy's words (borrowed from Laurence Rickels), an "improper burial" ("Technology"). Of course, McCarthy is not only one of our most vitriolic critics of middlebrow fiction; he is himself an increasingly celebrated novelist, whose third novel *C* was shortlisted for the Man Booker Prize. His debut novel *Remainder* is an attempt to embody a clean break with "the middlebrow commercial novel" (McCarthy, *Transmission*), and especially with its most recent incarnation: the trauma novel. As my reading shows, *Remainder* converts McCarthy's programmatic declarations of the end of the novel into something much less heroic: a protracted attempt to bury the novel that cannot help but reanimate it, and that ends up transmitting weak, dysphoric, and uneasy affects. *Remainder* conveys a range of affects that can neither be conflated with the traditional emotional repertoire of the novel nor with the studied affectlessness of McCarthy's high-minded programmatic declarations.

On the strength of my analysis of *Remainder*, I turn to David Shields' manifesto *Reality Hunger*, which has become an almost compulsory point of reference in discussions of contemporary literature. The occasion for much pre-publication hype and post-publication online debate in 2010, Shields' book confidently presents itself as "the *ars poetica* for a burgeoning group of interrelated (but unconnected) artists in a multitude of forms and media [...] who are breaking larger and larger chunks of 'reality' into their work" (3). The urgency of this self-assigned task derives from Shields' impatience with the form of the novel, whose moves he finds "unbelievably predictable, tired, contrived, and essentially purposeless" (118). A combination of confession and collage, *Reality Hunger* practices what it preaches: the double need to "smuggle more of [...] reality into the work of art" (3) and to sound the death knell of the novel form. But as is the case for *Remainder*, *Reality Hunger's* death knell cannot avoid sounding a lot like a novel; indeed, the "novelistic" shape (200-odd pages sustained by one confessional voice) of Shields' self-designated manifesto belies the clarity of its programmatic intent, and ends up reanimating the form it intends to bury. My reading shows that Shields' text can only achieve the reality-effect it aims for by extending its gesture of dismissing the novel until its very last page. The real interest of the text lies in the unpredictable affects produced by its imperfect and protracted attempt to move beyond the novel, rather than in the alternative artistic practice that it officially proposes. A testimony to the difficulty of making a clean break with an inadequate form, *Reality Hunger* ends up playing the role of Joyce's *Portrait* and Lewis's *Tarr* in Eliot's essay on *Ulysses*, and discovering that there is, as yet, no radical alternative to embrace.

What do we make of the continued solicitation of a form that refuses to be buried? Even if Shields believes he has an alternative for the novel—a form he calls the lyric essay—he is, like McCarthy, drawn back to the remains of the novel as part of a literary project that is, again like that of McCarthy, dedicated to a retrieval of reality, which the conventionality of novelistic realism is supposed to have obscured. At the very least, this situation points to a mode of survival that is not marked by self-determination, self-control, or emotional composure, but that is instead awkward, dependent, and compromised. While this diminished form of (after)life lacks both the heroic decisiveness of Eliot and the significant and transformative emotional experiences customarily associated with the novel, it points to the contemporary novel's surprising relevance as a catalyst for imagining new forms of affect and life. One such form, which I call "creatural life," takes center stage in my reading of J.M. Coetzee in the next chapter; in the last section of this chapter, I anticipate that mode of life by extending my reading of contemporary intimations of the end of the novel into a discussion of the work of the British novelist Lars Iyer. Iyer's 2011 "Literary Manifesto after the End of Literature and Manifestos" differs from the work of Shields and McCarthy in that it refuses fantasies of decisive change and embraces the reality of belatedness. Iyer does not declare the end of the novel; for him, we are witnessing the end of the whole regime of literature. Such untimeliness does not call for an illusory move beyond literature, but rather for the more minimal task of finding "ways to address this lateness" ("Hot Tub"). Removed from its traditional position of authority, literature can now dedicate itself to an exploration of the unheroic and pathetic dimensions of life—what Iyer calls "gloomy, farcical" life. In his own trilogy of short novels, Iyer mercilessly stages the farcical life that breaks through the threadbare remains of literature; as my next chapter shows, this aesthetic program has clear affinities with the late work of J.M. Coetzee. If *Remainder* and *Reality Hunger* testify to the persistence of affect beyond the end of the novel, Iyer and Coetzee give shape to the diminished modes of life that correspond to those affects.

Tom McCarthy and the traumatization of fiction

In the last few years, Tom McCarthy has established himself as a fixture in the British literary scene. The author of three novels—*Remainder* from 2005, *Men in Space* from 2007, and *C* from 2010—McCarthy is also a successful conceptual artist, an accomplished literary theorist (his book *Tintin and the Secret of Literature* from 2006 is both an original exploration of the work of Hergé and a meditation on some of the major figures in the French Theory canon), the founder and General Secretary of the half-serious and semi-fictitious International Necronautical Society, and an almost unavoidable interviewee. McCarthy has consistently used his public appearances to recall the world of contemporary literature to the legacies of artistic and literary modernism, and to dismiss what he calls "liberal" or "sentimental" humanism (qtd. in Rourke), as well as the form that has historically sustained that humanism: the novel. His own fictions attempt to do without the elements that are often assumed to make up a novel: readerly empathy, plot and character, social vision, and psychological depth.

In keeping with McCarthy's ambition to break with "the contemporary cult of the individual, the absolute authentic self who is measured through his or her absolutely authentic feeling" (qtd. in Rourke), his two most recent novels refrain from developing a single privileged psychological perspective, and instead opt for a decentered network of characters (in *Men in Space*) or for a main character whose subjectivity constitutes only a moment of crystallization in a network of transmissions (in *C*). Both of these novels can be understood as efforts to map the paradoxical remainder of the novel form after everything novelistic has been subtracted from it. In *Remainder*, this subtraction is not yet achieved: the excision of psychology, which the later works take for granted, is what the book aims to carry out in its bid to critique the humanist tradition of middlebrow fiction. It challenges this tradition's reliance on psychological depth and significant feeling by taking on what it identifies as the most recent instance of that tradition: *Remainder* is an attempt to debunk the customary pieties of trauma fiction. The book borrows the "grammar" of post-trauma, which thrives on "repetition and reenactment" (qtd. in Orwell 1), while it remains conspicuously indifferent to the ethical dimensions of artistic engagements with the extreme violence and the psychological suffering that characterize trauma.[2]

Yet in spite of this studied indifference, a careful reading of *Remainder* shows that its attempt to elide sentiment and psychology does not lead to a neutral and affectless text; instead, McCarthy's project ends up replacing the strong feelings and identifications it finds in the retrograde humanism of middlebrow fiction with what can be analyzed as intractable and asignifying affects. The novel generates non-subjective affects in the very place where middlebrow fiction has taught readers to expect emotionally significant encounters with fleshed-out characters. This is, of course, the very emotive scenario that this study traces through contemporary fiction and that delivers a more tentative and muted kind of innovation than the one McCarthy's public pronouncements seem to promise. By focusing on this scenario, and by tracing the novel's move from psychological depth to an asignifying affective remainder, we can appreciate how it contributes to our understanding of the literature of trauma in at least two ways. First, by departing from the habituated routines of trauma fiction, it shows that much trauma fiction remains in thrall to the conventions of psychological realism, and to the belief that formal features can represent psychological events. Second, the novel's shift from subjective depth to non-subjective affect renders the structure of traumatization in a way that escapes the mimetic constraints of psychological realism. *Remainder* shows that the novel is less a form that represents the after-effects of trauma than a form that transmits the "after-affects" that the traumatized subject leaves in its wake.

From its very first paragraph, *Remainder* presents itself as a challenge to trauma fiction: the sudden event that triggers the novel's plot is described as "involv[ing] something falling from the sky. Technology. Parts, Bits" (5). *Remainder* does not pause to assess the psychological damage the accident inflicts on its nameless narrator, nor does it qualify its representation of the traumatized mind by registering its awareness of the ethical stakes involved in the rendering of others' injury and pain.[3] The narrator notes that he "can say very little" about "the accident itself": "It's not that I'm being shy. It's just that—well, for one, I don't even remember the event. It's a blank: a white slate, a black hole" (5). Instead, the novel is made up of the depthless, a-psychological registration of the narrator's meticulously plotted and elaborately designed reenactments of particular scenes from his life, and later on from other people's lives. These reenactments are financed by "the Settlement," a vast sum of money the narrator receives from an anonymous party in compensation for the accident, and which, the narrator notes, "was held up to [him] as a future strong enough to counterbalance [his] no-past, a moment that would make [him] better, whole, complete" (6). Predictably, this chimeral completeness is never restored, and the novel unfolds as the deliberately repetitive account of the failure of such restoration. Trauma, far from registering as a psychologically significant event, is merely mobilized as a device that triggers and structures the plot: it furnishes a lack that the novel's development can (impossibly) attempt to fill, and through the settlement that follows from it, it provides its protagonist with the funds he needs to finance his elaborate reenactments; trauma, in other words, by indirectly funding the events that make up the novel's plot, provides the novel with the narrative capital it needs to keep going for some 280 pages.

Roger Luckhurst has remarked that, even if trauma is routinely theorized as an event "that exceeds the possibility of narrative knowledge" (*Trauma Question* 81), its refusal to make immediate sense has, in the last few decades, paradoxically made it a fertile literary resource. Contemporary culture, Luckhurst notes, "is saturated with stories that see trauma not as a blockage but a positive spur to narrative" (83). From its very first pages, *Remainder* makes this productive role of trauma explicit. What qualifies the novel as a provocation to conventional trauma fictions is that it never stops to register the tension between the productivity of trauma and the equally prevalent notion that trauma should, on ethical or therapeutic grounds, be acknowledged as something that resists integration, development, and understanding. McCarthy's studied depthlessness serves as a deliberate affront to the customary pieties of trauma fiction.[4]

Remainder's critical afterlife has focused less on its disparaging of trauma than on its critique of the middlebrow novel. This afterlife was inaugurated by a widely noted review essay by Zadie Smith in the *New York Review of Books*. Pairing *Remainder* with Joseph O'Neill's rather conventional post-9/11 novel *Netherland* from 2008, Smith hails *Remainder* as "the strong refusal" of the tradition that O'Neill's novel (albeit anxiously) perpetuates. She calls this tradition "lyrical realism": a realism that invests in "the transcendent importance of form, the incantatory power of language to reveal truth, [and] the essential fullness and continuity of the self." While lyrical realism is committed to the illusion of psychological depth, *Remainder* "empties out interiority entirely." And while the realist tradition allows no part of reality to escape from an "adjectival mania" that relentlessly converts the stuff of life into significant realities, McCarthy's novel is marked by "a rigorous attention to the damaged and the partial"—by a materialism that "let[s] matter *matter*." It offers us the world "as a series of physical events, rather than emotional symbols" that find their real significance in an illusory elsewhere (Smith).

It is remarkable how faithfully McCarthy's increasingly frequent public declarations of his artistic intent have echoed Smith's account, which in its turn borrows heavily from the publications of McCarthy's International Necronautical Society. He consistently identifies his target as the "liberal-humanist sensibility [that] has always held the literary work to be a form of self-expression, a meticulous sculpting of the thoughts and feelings of an isolated individual who has mastered his or her poetic craft" ("Technology"). In its stead, he persistently promotes an "anti-naturalist, anti-humanist" aesthetic in which "we're being given access not to a fully rounded, self-sufficient character's intimate thoughts and feelings as he travels through a naturalistic world, emoting, developing and so on—but rather to an encounter with structure" ("Stabbing"). In a review of the work of the Belgian novelist Jean-Philippe Toussaint, from which this last salvo is taken, the renewed interest in human relationships that characterizes Toussaint's most recent novels is immediately suspected of being "a crypto-reactionary step backwards towards humanism, sentimentalism, positivism and the whole gamut of bad isms that the vanguard 20th-century novel expended so much effort overcoming" ("Stabbing").

The heightened tenor of these pronouncements is decidedly uncommon in contemporary literary criticism and arguably even more so in a British context. The simultaneous co-optation and policing of Toussaint as an avant-garde writer who annoyingly fails to remain sufficiently anti-humanist points to the momentous scale of the arena in which McCarthy wants his fiction to operate. This arena is nothing less than the place where the historical fate of the English novel is being decided. If the literary mainstream comes to this battle using "a kind of humanistic, idealist" "operational manual" that incapacitates it as "a branch of the entertainment industry" (qtd. in Hart and Jaffe 677), McCarthy's position is backed up by an impeccable French pedigree. What makes *Remainder*, in Smith's assessment, "one of the great English novels of the past ten years" is that it refuses the middlebrow and instead updates a countertradition whose postwar life begins with Alain Robbe-Grillet's *nouveau roman*, and which peaks "in that radical deconstructive doubt which questions the capacity of language itself to describe the world with accuracy" (Smith). The future that *Remainder* scripts for the English novel, in other words, is French; among postwar English novelists, only J.G. Ballard makes the cut.

The momentous stakes of McCarthy's novelistic project are relevant for an understanding of *Remainder*, if only because they intimate that the novel can hardly live up to these grave claims and that, as I argue, its real interest lies in the specific ways in which it fails to deliver the related deaths of humanism and the novel—the ways, that is, in which its imperfect displacement of subjectivity clears space for subjectless affects.[5] At the same time, McCarthy's programmatic overstatements foreground certain assumptions that the study of trauma fiction generally takes for granted. Smith and McCarthy jointly characterize *Remainder*'s intervention in the history of the English novel as an attempt to break with three crucial features of realist fiction: first, it performs a "brutal excision of psychology" (Smith); second, it fearlessly confronts a reality that refuses to fit available social or existential templates; and third, instead of giving us thematic or psychological depth, "it works by accumulation and repetition" and the superimposition of surfaces (Smith). McCarthy's project, in other words, aims to disrupt our ideas of psychological integrity and the customary ways in which the self relates to society—ideas that, as we have seen in the introduction to this book, he is not alone in associating with the novel form. At the same time, the resolute terms in which this "post-novelistic" program is articulated cannot but recall the notion of trauma. McCarthy's project in *Remainder* makes visible the proximity between the end of the novel and the structure of trauma; it suggests that literary responses to trauma—to events that, like McCarthy's work, disrupt "previous ideas of an individual's sense of self and the standards by which one evaluates society" (Balaev 150)—must also problematize the status of the novel as an adequate vehicle for representing the effects of trauma.

In order to appreciate McCarthy's point, we can consider to what extent trauma fictions, for all their emphasis on fragmentation, repetition, and temporal dislocation, often continue to rely on the psychological realism of (especially) the modernist novel; indeed, the formal features of such fictions are routinely understood as the reflection of a traumatized psyche. Some of the most sophisticated accounts of trauma literature remark that "recurring literary techniques and devices" are ways "to mirror at a formal level the effects of trauma" (Whitehead 84); that another author's "multiperspectival, fragmented narratives provide a formal correlative to the unintegrated details that haunt her testimony" (Rothberg, *Traumatic Realism* 144–45); or that "authors create complex/symbolic structures that mirror the complexities of thought and memory accompanying trauma" (Vickroy 116). The often unquestioned persistence of time-honored figures of mirroring and reflection in such formulations makes clear that customary approaches to trauma literature continue to adhere to what my introduction identified as the novel's unique epistemic power to render characters' interiority. Traumatic realism, in other words, is psychological realism by (not really) other means,[6] and it does not fatally disturb the novel's alleged capacities to represent even extreme psychological states.[7] McCarthy's project shows that such novelistic mediations of trauma obscure trauma's status as something that can precisely *not* be contained within the psyche—its status, that is, as an experience that "violently opens passageways between systems that were once discrete, making unforeseen connections that distress or confound" (Luckhurst, *Trauma Question* 3).

By denaturalizing the connection between the novel and trauma, McCarthy's work indirectly qualifies the way we often conceive of the relations between literature and trauma as essentially *novelistic*. It asks to what extent this understanding perpetuates the novel's traditional investment in the ideal of a self-governing individual that constitutes itself by negotiating its relations to the social reality sustaining it, and that the reader is invited to empathize with (Armstrong, *How Novels Think* 6). His challenge amounts to the charge that trauma fiction has failed to question this generic investment in psychological depth, social accommodation, and empathy; it raises the question of whether the uninvestigated attachment of trauma to individual subjectivity has not obscured the radical transitivity and mobility of trauma. *Remainder* presents a different linkage between literature and trauma—a connection that does not depend on the mimesis of a traumatized psyche, but rather on the unleashing of non-subjective affects that confront the reader with an evacuated subjectivity that, precisely because it does *not* offer a position to identify with, cannot leave the reader unaffected.[8] The reader confronts the elision of codified emotions and of the fullness and integrity of an unharmed psyche, yet this perception of an erased emotion in its turn brings forth non-subjective affects. In this way, the novel dramatizes trauma as a frustrated expectation of emotional fullness and centered subjectivity that materializes as an affective remainder unable to disappear.

Affect and superimposition in *Remainder*

Remainder's anti-sentimental and anti-humanist thrust not only asserts itself in its deliberate denigration of the pieties of trauma narratives, but also in its outright reduction of psychology to the bare distinction between feeling "neutral" and feeling "not-neutral." The latter generally presents itself as "a tingling," a bodily sensation that intermittently besets the narrator and that is often "both intense and serene at the same time" (10). Yet in spite of its official investment in neutrality and affectlessness, and perhaps against its author's intentions, the novel allows a diminished mode of feeling to persist, most conspicuously so in a number of scenes in which it explicity stages that neutrality. In one of these scenes, which I will spend some time unpacking, the narrator is discussing with two friends what he will do with the eight and a half million pounds he has just come into. While one (male) friend suggests he uses it to open an account with a coke dealer, the other (female—the stereotypical gendering of the passage is part of its point) friend suggests a resource fund for development projects in Africa. The narrator tries hard to "feel some connection with these Africans," but this attempt ultimately falters:

> I felt a kind of vertigo. I knew what I meant but I couldn't say it right. I wanted to feel some connection with these Africans. I tried to picture them putting up houses from her housing kits, or sitting around in schools, or generally doing African things, like maybe riding bicycles or singing [...] I tried to visualize a grid around the earth, a kind of ribbed wire cage like on the champagne bottle, with lines of latitude and longitude that ran all over, linking one place to another, weaving the whole terrain into one smooth, articulated network, but I lost this image among disjoined escalator parts [...] I wanted to feel

genuinely warm towards these Africans, but I couldn't. Not that I felt cold or hostile. I just felt neutral. (36–37)

The disparaging of emotion and empathy in this passage seems a clear example of McCarthy's programmatic anti-psychologism. The narrator's incongruent move from an imagining of African life to the visualization of grids and networks "around the earth" is one of the many instances of McCarthy's manifest intent to replace "plot, depth, or content" with "angles, arcs, and intervals" ("Stabbing").

Still, it makes a difference that the narrator's statement of dispassionate neutrality does not appear in a manifesto but as part of a novel. Occurring in a novel, it is inevitably part of an affective interaction between text and reader, which complicates any hope of programmatic purity. The passage conjures the feelings that plans for humanitarian aid can be expected to elicit—compassion, connectedness, sadness, and so on; it goes on to denigrate those feelings and expectations by its deliberately provocative phrasing ("African things"); it prolongs this sense of inappropriateness by failing to remark on the phrasing's offensiveness and by opting for a dissonant imagining of nonhuman lines and vectors instead; and it then asserts the narrator's supposed indifference to the inappropriateness of his thoughts by underlining that the whole scene left him feeling "just" neutral. Even if the passage does not convey a strong emotion that readers can share—that is, *feel*—it does not avoid raising an expectation of such an emotion, only to go on to frustrate it; the passage even emphasizes this sense of frustrated expectation when it begins by referring to the feeling of "a kind of vertigo." In this way, it cannot but transmit a failure to feel, an "unfelt" feeling that, while it is not the kind of empathetic emotional experience that McCarthy associates with middlebrow fiction, is also not neutral. The passage raises ethical and affective issues about which readers cannot *not* care without feeling something; this means that a failure to care makes itself felt as an uncomfortable and dysphoric affect. Sianne Ngai has described such a second-order feeling, which I already discussed in my introduction, as "a feeling which is perceived rather than felt and whose very *nonfeltness* is perceived" (76). Far from leaving the reader neutral, such a "perception of an unfelt feeling produces a secondary, dysphoric emotion" (83). While it is impossible to determine the quality of this secondary feeling, it is decidedly weak and dysphoric, as it is inevitably shadowed by the frustrated expectation of a stronger emotion.[9]

Other scenes in the novel confirm that the strong emotions that we tend to associate with the human subject—and, therefore, with the literary form that has historically sustained that subject—make way in McCarthy's text for diffuse and non-subjective affects. As I noted in my introduction, the vocabulary dealing with feelings and passions is notoriously unstable, yet recent affect theory has begun to deploy a consistent distinction between emotions and affects. While emotions have a semantic and cognitive dimension, affects are intractable intensities that escape narrative sequencing and conceptual capture. Affects cannot be codified as expressions of an individual's interiority; they are, in the words of Brian Massumi, "inseparable from but unassimilable to any *particular*, functionally anchored perspective" (Massumi 35). Affects disturb the customary link between feeling and centered subjectivity. In her book *Feeling in Theory*, Rei Terada argues that sovereign subjectivity would in fact immunize human life from being affected; feeling requires the absence or the elision of subjectivity (8). *Remainder*, by repeatedly staging expectations of strong subjectivity and emotion only to empty them out, makes it possible to perceive a lack of emotion and to perceive vanished subjectivity as the site of the emergence of non-subjective and dysphoric affects.

In another scene, the narrator is watching a group of homeless people from the window of a coffee shop. He decides to go up to one of them and invites the man to share a meal. At one point during their meal, the narrative breaks down:

> the waiter leant across me as he took the tablecloth away. She took the table away too. There wasn't any table. The truth is, I've been making all this up—the stuff about the homeless person. He existed all right, sitting camouflaged against the shop fronts and the dustbins—but I didn't go across to him. (56)

What is remarkable about this passage is not the metatextual twist—which is conventional enough since postmodern fiction—so much as the fact that the novel does *not* offer a psychological motivation for the narrator's act of fabulation (or, for that matter, for the waiter's sudden transformation into a "she"), nor for his sudden retraction of this fabulation. In an emotive scenario that is reminiscent of the one discussed before, the novel presents readers with an ethically and affectively charged situation—the clash between privilege and poverty, the privilege of narrative power—only to leave a blank failure of response instead of the elaboration that they are led to expect. The novel bluntly refrains from offering a strong emotion, yet it makes a perception of that non-feeling inescapable—a perception that in its turn materializes as second-order dysphoric affect.

McCarthy's critique of the traditional novel officially wants to do away with feeling and subjectivity, but what it fails to banish is affect. Indeed, this affective force emerges precisely through *Remainder*'s paradoxical intent to bury the novel form in what ultimately remains a novel. The engagement between text and reader is framed by particular expectations—by what Lauren Berlant calls a "loose affectual contract" ("Intuitionists" 847) that binds them together; in the case of the novel, that contract promises significant emotions and an occasion for empathy. *Remainder* cannot avoid being bound by the terms of that contract; even if it tries to overwrite those terms by an affectless neutrality, the superimposition of both cannot avoid generating a perception that the initial contract remains unfulfilled, just as it cannot avoid that that perception of non-feeling provokes affect.[10]

The novel repeatedly dramatizes this movement in which the superimposition of two things does not lead to the cancellation of one of them, but rather to the paradoxical production of an affective remainder. The minimal affects that afflict the narrator-protagonist are often the result of the superimposition of two different images or experiences. A discussion with Naz, the main facilitator whom the narrator engages to take care of the logistics of his reenactments, brings on "a clearly defined picture" of the building to be reconstructed, until "Naz's office superimposed itself over that"; when this second image "started fading" in the narrator's mind, he does not experience a return to the clarity of the first image, but rather a "sudden surge of fear [...] through the right side of my body," which only disappears when the first image finally "eclipsed the image of the office" (85). Later on, when the protagonist finds himself in the street, this experience is superimposed with the imagining of an overhead view of the city that allows him to take in "the pattern" of his team of facilitators walking around (91); this superimposition brings on the feeling of "a light breeze moving round [his] face," and of "a tingling creeping up the right side of [his] body" (92). Once the building is ready and the narrator is contemplating it, he "trie[s] to X-ray through the door," and the attempt to project things again leads to a "tingling [...] from the top of [his] legs" (102).

This dynamic, in which the displacement of one thing by another is bound to leave a remainder, and in which every attempt to erase something results in a messy superimposition, is at the heart of McCarthy's enterprise. *Remainder* avoids the evocation of psychological depth, and instead offers what McCarthy has called, in a different context, "a non-humanist type of depth" that emerges through the superimposition of different two-dimensional surfaces (qtd. in Hart and Jaffe 670–71). After his accident, *Remainder*'s narrator feels "self-conscious, embarrassed" (15). His reenactments are attempts to overcome the sense of inauthenticity that marks his condition and to return to an illusory condition of pre-reflexive, "un-marked" authenticity and spontaneity.[11] Time and again, the reenactments confront him with the disappointing realization that "[e]verything must leave some kind of mark" (11). Instead of offering a saving transubstantiation, the ending of the novel presents a narrator who initially seems to have left earthly matter behind as he has taken flight in an airplane, only to be confronted with a damningly material cloud that is "gritty, like spilled earth or dust flakes on a stairwell" (284). So much for escape, so much for transcendence.[12] The novel's last words are "turning, heading back, again" (284). The stain of materiality cannot be overcome, and the attempt to defeat it cannot avoid generating friction—in the same way that *Remainder* cannot write the affectual contract between novel and reader out of existence.

Throughout the novel, the friction between reality and the attempt to sublate it through reenactments consistently transforms reality into a site of affect. At the beginning of his first elaborate reenactment, the narrator moves across the landing and down the staircase he has walked over "a hundred times before"; whereas it had earlier been "just a floor," "now it was fired up, silently zinging with significance," seeming "to emit a kind of charge, as invisible as natural radiation—and just as potent" (133). This intensity returns during the novel's last reenactment when the narrator and his team stage a bank heist: the "markings of the surface of the road—perfect reproductions of the ones outside my warehouse, lines whose pigmentation, texture and layout I knew so well—seemed infused with the same level of significance" (260–61). Such intense sensations that can neither be measured nor controlled are the only yield of the narrator's effort to stop feeling "fake" and "second-hand," and to become "real," "perfect," and "authentic" instead (15, 23, 24, 62–63). This dynamic also elevates forensic procedure into an artistic practice, as the work of retracing an original event engenders frictions between two (inevitably dissimilar) events. In a description that reads like an allegory of the novel's own reduction of psychology, the narrator explains that the diagrams used to plan the reenactments, "with all their outlines, arrows and shaded blocks" may "look like abstract paintings," but are in fact "not abstract at all": "Each line, each figure, every angle—the ink itself vibrates with an almost intolerable violence, darkly screaming from the silence of the white paper: something has happened here, someone has died" (173). The ink on the white page transmits the remainders of the subjects whose disappearance it records. The super-imposition of schemas and structures over the density of actual lives generates the affects released by a missing emotion.

This movement of superimposition is not only at work in *Remainder*'s shift from codified emotion to trackless affect, but also in its replacement of the conventions of realism with more direct evocations of materiality. Traditionally, the reality that a novel decides to shape is elevated from the status of mere matter into what Zadie Smith calls an "emotional symbol," into a part of the significant world that the novel writes into existence. *Remainder* instead locates the narrator in a setting that has become radically meaningless for him; instead of writing it back into significance through the narrator's recovery, and, for instance, a restored correspondence between personal experience and social world, *Remainder* offers us the record of his numerous failed attempts to sublimate matter into meaning through meticulous reenactments. Still, the residue of these efforts is not nothing. Reality is produced as that which remains after—and thus resists—the attempt at transubstantiation, in the same way that the novel produces affects as the residue of a subject that is unable to disappear. Reality is endowed with an intangible intensity that cannot be converted into a particular meaning for any subject and that in fact derives its force from its refusal of such a reduction.

The novel's final reenactment scene consists in a simulated bank heist that the narrator and his crew have meticulously rehearsed in a warehouse. This "fake hold up" may very well refer to one of the key texts that theorize the ways in which contemporary reality has been infiltrated by images and simulacra that no longer simply complement but rather drastically distort that reality. In his classic essay "Simulacra and Simulations," Jean Baudrillard illustrates the postmodern inability to distinguish between reality and simulation in any meaningful way by coining the idea of "a simulated hold up" (180). According to Baudrillard, a simulated hold up cannot avoid leaking into reality, as there can be no verifiable difference between a real and a simulated hold up: "the web of artificial signs will be inextricably mixed up with real elements (a police officer will really shoot on sight; a bank customer will faint and die of a heart attack [...])" (181). *Remainder* presents a telling variation on Baudrillard's possible scenarios (De Boever 133–37): the simulation does not fail when it is confronted with reality, or even with the resistance of something tangible, but rather when the friction between the "real" simulation and the earlier rehearsals for—that is, simulations of—this "real" simulation produce a material remainder.

During the rehearsals, one of the reenactors always trips on a "kink in the carpet"; in the "real" reenactment of these rehearsals, there is no such kink, and as the "half-trip" has become "instinctive, second nature" for the actor, he falls over when he *fails* to encounter the kink he had anticipated (267). The actor falls against another actor, and the clash sets off the latter's gun, which kills a third actor. Instead of the tension between reality and simulation, *Remainder* explores the strain between different superimposed simulations. This is another instance of the novel's signature dynamic, in which a remainder emerges from an impossible attempt to cancel one reality by the imposition of another. This residue has an undeniable reality; even if the friction between the rehearsals and the actual reenactment is nothing tangible (such as a real, physical kink in a real carpet), it produces real-world effects: "[t]hanks to the ghost kink, mainly—the kink the other kink left when we took it away" (273). Here as elsewhere, "[e]verything must leave some kind of mark" (11).

The novel condenses the movement in which frustrated expectation makes room for intractable affects in a series of two scenes that uncharacteristically display (or at least name) emotions. Visiting a garage, the narrator asks the boys in charge to refill his car's empty windshield washer reservoir. After the boys have filled up the reservoir, the liquid somehow seems to have disappeared. The narrator feels "wonderful" (159), even "elated and inspired" (160): it is as if "matter—these two litres of liquid—becom[es] un-matter—not surplus matter, mess or clutter, but pure, bodiless blueness" (159). On starting the car, the blue liquid, far from having disappeared, gushes all over him. His disappointment when "the scene of a triumphant launch" turns into "the scene of a disaster" (162) is perceived as "something very sad—not in the normal sense but on a grander scale" (161). Predictably, the narrator goes on to attempt to overcome this sadness through another reenactment that will, or so he hopes, allow him to master the traumatic inevitability of matter. The reenactment confirms the idea that trauma takes shape as the engendering of affect in the place of an evacuated subjectivity. Not only does the narrator himself not participate in the reenactment—he watches it from an especially constructed "raised viewing platform"—the reenactor shows a blank where we expect to see his face: "he wore a white ice-hockey goaltender's mask, so as not to overrun my personality with his—or, more precisely, so as not to impose any personality at all" (164). The (subjectless) reenactment generates "a mixed sensation" (165); it does not cancel the traumatic disappointment, but only translates it into the register of affect.

There is a final twist to the tensions between McCarthy's programmatic dismissal of psychological realism and the execution of that program in *Remainder*. As the novel progresses, the superimposition of psychological realism and its attempted erasure is no longer confined to particular moments but comes to define the *tone* of the whole novel, if by "tone" we mean the work's "global or organizing affect, its general disposition or orientation toward its audience and the world" (Ngai 28). If *Remainder* officially wants to convey a tone of sturdy and affectless imperturbability in order to debunk the pieties of trauma fiction, this program is progressively complicated as the narrator gets caught up in obsessively detailed reenactments of seemingly random scenes. This deployment of the narrative grammar of compulsive repetition *without* the motivation of a psychological trauma—the moments that are reenacted are decidedly non-traumatic, and the whole reenactment campaign is triggered by a seemingly insignificant moment of *déjà vu* at a party—is an obvious part of the novel's campaign against the psychological and ethical registers in which trauma is customarily presented. Yet in spite of this decoupling of the grammar of repetition and the psychology of trauma, the novel does not sustain its foreclosure of psychology until the end. In the last third of the novel, the deliberate schematism and formalism of the reenactment plans begin to make way for the narrator's increasingly monomaniacal obsession with them, which completely alienates him from his social surroundings. The disjunction between the narrator's delusions and the normative social world is marked most clearly by repeated visits from a doctor; the narrator initially refuses the doctor's help (180–81), but soon finds himself "drifting into and out of trances" (203) while under observation by the same doctor, who diagnoses him with "the autonomic symptoms of trauma" (204).

Here, it becomes hard to resist reading the novel's narrator as (also) a pretty conventional modernist unreliable narrator and to classify the novel as (also) a modernist novel of consciousness. The studied flatness and neutrality of the narrative voice can retroactively be understood as an expression of post-traumatic numbing rather than as a radical affront to the novelistic evocation of psychological depth. Even if such a psychological reading only really emerges as a possibility in last third of the book, it alters our interpretation of its sustained affectless and irreverent tone, as it raises the possibility of reattaching the text to an individual perspective and of reading it as the mimesis of a traumatized mind, and thus of reducing it to what McCarthy's official novelistic project would categorize as one more trauma fiction. When the narrator begins to "drift into and out of trances" (203), the novel also begins to take the liberty of abandoning the rigorous pace that accompanied the narrator's reenactments step-by-step before this moment in the story, and begins to use more ellipses. Here again, it is perfectly possible to read these ellipses as a mimesis of an intermittently unconscious mind. The routines of psychological realism, it seems, are harder to shake off than McCarthy's programmatic declarations seem to promise. The insistent possibility of a return to (traumatic) realism forces the reader to continuously perceive the novel's overt attempt to escape such realism—to perceive an elision of feeling that, in a movement that I have traced throughout the novel, gives off dysphoric and non-subjective affects. These affects are the material remainders of McCarthy's dismissal of psychological realism; far from being a radical alternative to such realism, *Remainder* is a compromised effort to move beyond realism that confronts readers with the absence of emotional fullness and centered subjectivity only to deliver affects when it makes this confrontation with non-feeling inescapable.[13]

In an essay exploring the interface between the modern novel and technology that was published in *The Guardian* just before the publication of his third novel, *C*, McCarthy notes that the modern novel's concern with the link between melancholia and technologies of transmission is firmly grounded in modern history. He recalls that the nineteenth-century emergence of phonographs and gramophones inspired a fad for recording children's voices, which, when these children happened to die a premature death (a common enough occurrence), made the plate or roll where their voices survived into "a kind of tomb" ("Technology"). The rise of communication technology, that is, inaugurated "a cult of mourning." McCarthy remarks that Laurence Rickels, on whose book *Aberrations of Mourning* he is drawing here, "even suggests replacing the word 'mourning' with the phrase 'the audio and video broadcasts of improper burial.'" For McCarthy, the literature that emerges in the wake of this cult of mourning—the modernism with which he has tirelessly affiliated himself—is "this cult's expression, its record, its holy script." Following this logic, we can see that in *Remainder*, McCarthy performs the deliberately "improper burial" of the novel—a form unable to disappear and surviving itself in the transmission of affects that no longer belong to a proper subject, and that tracklessly resonate in the lifeless crypt where the traditional novel has taught us to look for fleshed-out individuals. In a typically contrarian statement in a 2007 interview, McCarthy remarks that "mainstream middle-brow fiction [...] pretends you can just go ahead and write without addressing the whole issue of impossibility and failure, and so, paradoxically, produces genuinely dead novels" (qtd. in Kuitenbrouwer). Where mainstream fiction inadvertently produces dead novels while anxiously trying to keep the form alive, McCarthy's own programmatic attempt to hasten the death of the novel paradoxically inaugurates the afterlife of an undead and improperly buried form that cannot help but continue to transmit disparate and discordant affects. The end of the novel, as I explained that phrase in my introduction, plays an enabling role in *Remainder*'s unleashing of affect: the mainstream novel serves as the corpse to which McCarthy's project anchors itself in order to morph into a process of perpetual burying, rather than the definitive burial it wishes to be.

Improper burials: affects of the real in David Shields' *Reality Hunger*

A burial of the novel that gets entangled in the complexities of its burial rites: this is also the story that David Shields' *Reality Hunger* ends up telling. *Reality Hunger* does not take the form that one expects from a manifesto, which is how the text advertises itself. It consists of 618 numbered sections, loosely collected under 26 thematic subheadings, one for each letter of the alphabet. More than half of these sections are (often silently edited) unattributed quotations, while the rest are mostly confessional in nature (which is not to say that none of the quotations are confessional). This peculiar combination points to the text's ambition to frame a personal sense of *ennui* with the inherited forms of the novel as a diagnosis of a broader cultural malaise; at the same time, it exemplifies Shields' proposed cure for that condition: an intense confrontation of the self with "'raw' material, seemingly unprocessed, unfiltered, uncensored, and unprofessional" that hopes to achieve "a blurring (to the point of invisibility) of any distinction between fiction and nonfiction" (5). *Reality Hunger*'s message is not hard to discover, if only because its length and its fragmentary make-up, together with its declaratory intent, invite a rhetoric of repetition that it does little to resist. Yet these repetitions not only serve the book's programmatic ambitions: in this section, I argue that they reflect the text's need to sustain the confrontation between the form it dismisses and the new poetics it does not quite manage to articulate *without* this confrontation. Ultimately, the repetitive and almost obsessive rhythm that shapes this encounter between the old and the new comes closer to the sense of reality for which the text officially hungers than its explicit message.

Even if Shields made his name as a writer of novels, he chooses to register his dissatisfaction with the novel *as a reader*. Appropriating E.M. Cioran, he notes that "[t]here's only one thing worse than boredom—the fear of boredom—and it's this fear I experience every time I open a novel" (203). This fear reflects a personal change: "something has happened to my imagination, which can no longer yield to the earnest embrace of novelistic form" (199). Yet there is a more general—that is, not merely personal—ground for this impasse: fiction "has never seemed less central to the culture's sense of itself" (177), a statement that recalls Eliot's dictum that the novel "will no longer serve." For Shields, as for Eliot, this means that the novel form can now safely be dismissed: "Forms serve the culture; when they die, they die for a good reason: they're no longer embodying what it's like to be alive" (111). The comparison to Eliot is instructive, as it points up a disabling difficulty for Shields' intervention: while Eliot could point to Lewis's *Tarr* and Joyce's *Portrait* as "more formless" novels in which dissatisfaction with the form was publicly on display, and thus immediately elevated from a deeply personal to a broader cultural phenomenon, Shields locates his impatience in his own readerly sensibility. This not only accounts for the book's indulgence in repeated confessional passages, but it also explains why, as I will argue, *Reality Hunger* itself comes to stand in for the "more formless" novels of Lewis and Joyce that Eliot could present as exhibits in his case for a new poetics.

Shields' chief complaint is that the novel fails to capture the intensity and complexity of twenty-first-century life, and that it therefore needs to be replaced by more adequate literary forms. One half of his argumentative strategy consists in presenting a rather monolithic picture of the traditional novel—a critique that, like McCarthy's, leans rather heavily on Robbe-Grillet (16–17, 19, 21)—the other in promoting "more technologically sophisticated and more visceral narrative forms" (78). The novel, we read, presents life as "a coherent, fathomable whole" (113), and it "tends to impose the image of a stable, coherent, continuous, unequivocal, entirely decipherable universe" (17); as contemporary life lacks such coherence and significance, the novel increasingly "goes hand in hand with a straitjacketing of the material's expressive potential" (23). Other literary forms achieve a better fit with contemporary reality. There is the "short-short-story," whose excision of "downtime" manages to "gain access to contemporary feeling states more effectively than the conventional story does" (126). There is, especially, the lyric essay: Shields quotes extensively from Ben Marcus's essay "The Genre Artist," which promotes this genre that, unlike fiction, does not carry the "burden of unreality," but can afford to start out "with something real" (26). The lyric essay combines a direct grasp of reality—"it leaves pieces of experience undigested"—with an authentic sense of intimacy: it "emerge[s] from the sensation of the self" (131). This brings the lyric essay close to Shields' third privileged literary genre, the memoir, which, as Shields does not fail to remind the reader, "rightly belongs to the imaginative world" (133). For Shields, the privilege of literature itself never really comes into question.

Significant literary work "matches the complexity of life with an equally rich arrangement in language" (200); it is "equal to the complexity of experience, memory, and thought" (54); it delivers "the real world, with all its hard edges, but the real world fully imagined and fully written, not merely reported" (69). In light of Shields' professed impatience with the novel, his unconditional insistence on the task of capturing and conveying experience is remarkably novelistic. Indeed, Shields' belief that literature should respond "to life itself" rather than "to the history of [its] art so far" (27) has a venerable pedigree in the canon of novel theory. It recalls, for instance, Ian Watt's claim for the novelty of the novel as a form whose "primary criterion was truth to individual experience" (*Rise of the Novel* 13), which informed its unprecedented use of "non-traditional plots" (15); at the same time, it echoes Henry James's equally canonical preference for novels' authentic rendering of experience—for "the more or less close connection of the subject [...] with some sincere experience" (45). Shields' expulsion of the novel, in other words, is powered by a realist ethos that almost defines the modern novel. What makes the lyric essay, the memoir, and the short-short-story privileged forms, it seems, is that they are more novelistic than the novel.[14]

Nor is this the only way in which *Reality Hunger* remains in thrall to the novel. Shields' commitment is to lived experience, that is, to a reality that the stale conventions of novelistic realism tend to obscure. Shields is sufficiently sophisticated to know that reality can never be accessed in an unmediated way, as he does not cease to point out: "Anything processed by memory is fiction" (57); "Everything is always already invented" (68); real life is "always fiction in the first place" (85).[15] Still, this knowledge does not cancel his hunger for reality. In a characteristic move, this hunger is generalized into a cultural condition: "Living as we perforce do in a manufactured and artificial world, we yearn for the 'real,' semblances of the real" (239). As the quotation marks around the "real" and its apposition to "semblances of the real" make clear, the main conceptual problem *Reality Hunger* faces is how to understand this reality that can neither be conflated with the unmediated world *out there*, nor with the outcome of the novel's formulaic deformations of that world. How to conceive, then, of a sense of reality that is neither naive nor conventional?

Reality Hunger does not answer this question—nor could it, as one half of its program (the pursuit of the real) is deeply implicated in the history and theory of the very thing (the novel form) that its second half wants to eliminate. Still, if this sense of reality cannot be conceptualized, I argue that it is paradoxically generated in the 200-odd pages long textual process through which *Reality Hunger* aims to formulate it—an attempt that constantly draws it to renewed confrontations with a novel form it cannot conclusively leave behind. The fact that the book begins with an "Overture" that confidently summarizes its new program and (almost) ends with a "Manifesto" that presents 30 more sections to finally bury the genre that keeps haunting it, testifies to this halted progress, and to its structural entwinement with the form it aims to abandon. *Reality Hunger* is a prolonged, and ultimately inconclusive, attempt to work through its disavowed reliance on the novel form; indeed, with the teasing sentimentality of its title, its novel-like (and very non-manifesto-like) length, and the overt presence of a continuous consciousness that guides the reader from the very first page, it can hardly avoid being read as (also) a novel.

An attempt to get over the novel that takes shape as a novel: this is the very dynamic of superimposition and of imperfect cancellation that is also at work in McCarthy's *Remainder*. And just as this dynamic generated intractable affects and a paradoxical sense of reality in *Remainder*, *Reality Hunger* only escapes the conventionality of the novel form and the equally deadening predictability of the book's own public message through the continuous friction between the two. The text's deeply contradictory performance transforms its different sections into moments and passages that demand to be read both as declarations of the end of the novel and as novelistic passages; the result of this radical undecidability is that the "loose affectual contract" (to return to Lauren Berlant's phrase) that obtains in the case of a manifesto and the one that holds in the case of a novel interfere and overlap in unpredictable ways. Instead of codified emotions, the reader confronts awkward and discordant affects. These affects are the only elements in *Reality Hunger* that escape the conventionality and predictability that it officially decries. On its own terms, they are the only things that count as real.

Many of *Reality Hunger*'s formulations confirm its investment in the imperfect transgression of established formal conventions. Already on the very first pages, we read that art should "smuggle more of what the artist thinks is reality into the work of art" (3), and that artists are "breaking larger and larger chunks of 'reality' into their work" (3). As we can now see, and as the quotation marks and the lexical hedging make clear, the sense of reality at stake here is not that of the material that is being "smuggled" or "broken" into the work; it exists, rather, in the sense of transgression and rupture conveyed by the verbs "smuggle" and "break"—activities that momentarily provide the thrill of breaking with the conventions that, the book believes, otherwise make reality unavailable. Such a sense of reality emerges when "[p]lot, like erected scaffolding, is torn down" (49), when we "break[...] through the clutter" and this break generates "autobiographical frissons" (81). Interesting literature is "happening on the fringes of several forms" (199), on the "generic edge" (191), "between the interstices of fiction and non-" (177). At stake is "the startling fragment, left over from the manufactured process" (36). When Shields writes that he wants "[a] deliberate unartiness: 'raw' material" (5), the quotation marks around "raw" signal that this sense of rawness is not an unmediated reality *out there*, but can only be achieved by "un-cooking" a (necessarily) "cooked" (that is, mediated) reality. All these processes require the novel as an inevitable reference point; it is the corpse that *Reality Hunger* insistently declares dead but does not manage to bury once and for all, because it is only by intermittently rubbing against it that it can generate a glimmer of the more-than-unreal. As I noted before, this radical dependence on the novel is another reason for *Reality Hunger*'s repetitiveness: instead of making a point about reality, it generates a sense of reality in the protracted (and ultimately unsuccessful) process of formulating that point.[16]

The affects that texts like *Remainder* and *Reality Hunger* produce are non-subjective; they do not simply belong to one individual. This is no problem for McCarthy's assault on liberal humanism, but it does not sit easily with Shields' much more compromised position. *Reality Hunger* cultivates the reader's uncertainty about the provenance of the book's 618 different sections; borrowings are not attributed in the text, but only in an appendix. In an interview, Shields notes that "[t]he very essence of the book is to argue for the excitement of doubt regarding genre, provenance, quotations, citation, and appropriation" (qtd. in Albanese 31). The decision to include documentation at the end is not Shields', but, as he underlines, that of Random House lawyers who want to avoid copyright issues (209). For a manifesto that is proudly indifferent to issues of appropriation and plagiarism, Shields' insistence on the authorship of the documentation (it's the lawyers', not his) is strange; it signals an unwillingness to let the contingencies that the text officially welcomes detract from his authorial sovereignty. This inconsistency is a constant feature of the book: Shields holds on to the certainties of authorial control—the book mentions his "intent" on its very first and its very last pages. Add to this the text's intermittent recourse to the supposedly firm distinction between "the life lived and the novel written" (167), and it becomes all the more tempting to read the text as a continuous confession. Such a reading is at the expense of the radicality of the unattributed borrowings, which are then naturalized as parts of the text's sustaining confessional voice.[17] On this reading, the shifts between the different fragments—which are always sizeable and syntactically complete chunks of meaningful text, never challenges to intelligibility—merely reflect the doubts, loose threads, and associations of an inquisitive mind. This is psychological realism, and not the reality *beyond* realism that *Reality Hunger* hungers for—a reality that it only intimates through the sustained tension between its critical program and the stubborn persistence of the form that this program wants to erase.

Lars Iyer: toward farcical life

A careful reading of McCarthy and Shields makes clear that their works deliver an affective dynamic that cuts across the borders of the individuals they present, and that exceeds their works' official messages. A third prominent intervention in contemporary debates over the end of the novel, Lars Iyer's 2011 essay "Nude in Your Hot Tub, Facing the Abyss," is more clear-eyed about the power of affect to undo the alliance of feeling and the individual, as well as about the importance of that force for the question of the (im)possibility of the novel today. As the text's self-deprecatory subtitle ("A Literary Manifesto after the End of Literature and Manifestos") indicates, this sobriety reflects the fact that Iyer is interested neither in *épater le bourgeois* nor in announcing a new departure for literature. For Iyer, these are struggles belonging to a past when "Literature" was still alive. Today, it is not only the novel that has ended, but the whole literary regime in which a radical break with the novel, such as that performed by Eliot, still made sense. Literature today no longer has a hold on the lives of individuals: "The *dream* has faded, our *faith* and *awe* have fled, our *belief* in Literature has collapsed." Iyer's essay lucidly registers that the ambition to bury the middlebrow novel is a belated attempt to reanimate that dream—to affirm the continued relevance of literature while declaring the death of its most popular

form. Such illusory ruptures today mean no more than "play[ing] pup-
pet with the corpse"; staged attempts to bury the novel are covert
ways of re-sacralizing with one hand what one wishes to profane with
the other. Instead of writing the next chapter in literary history, "the
only subject left to write about is the *epilogue* of Literature." For Iyer,
"Literature is a corpse and cold at that," and taking that lesson seriously
means that one does not even bother to bury that corpse.

Iyer's "literature which comes after Literature" does not feel the
need to concern itself with the perpetuation of its own existence. The
paradoxical strength of this position is that it thereby liberates writing
to attend to other needs—to those aspects of contemporary life that
cannot be captured by a continued concern with sovereign selfhood.
It frees literature to attend to the pathetic remainders of life that can
no longer be heroically transformed or redeemed. In the next chapter,
I show how J.M. Coetzee's late work gives shape to this awkwardly persistent life that "faces its own demise and survives." For Coetzee, this
materializes as a species of "creatural life"; Iyer, for his part, refers to it
as "gloomy, farcical life": it is a life "whose vast sadness is that it is less
than tragic," or indeed less than novelistic, and for which the loss of
tragedy makes itself felt as farce.

Iyer ends the essay with "a few pointers" about what a post-Literary
literature should look like. Remarkably, many of these elements correspond closely to the "key components" of Shields' new poetics (5).
Iyer's insistence on "unliterary *plainness*" resembles Shields' "deliberate unartiness"; his injunction to "[w]rite about this world" resonates
with Shields' emphasis on reality; and his imperative to "[r]esist closed
forms" echoes Shields' investment in "[r]andomness, openness to
accident and serendipity." The difference is that Iyer's openness is
a willingness to engage "the draft of real life—gloomy, farcical life,"
while Shields' is a readiness to render individual experience in confessional form. Iyer notes that "[t]he author must give up on aping genius.
Rather show the author as ape, the author as idiot." For Iyer, the author
is implicated in the farcical life to which his writing must respond,
not its sovereign observer—an insight that Coetzee, as we will see,
embodies in the persona of Elizabeth Costello. Liberated from the obligation to either debunk or promote sovereign selfhood, Iyer's position
opens up a broad range of affects: farcical life is "sickly and cannibalis-
tic, preposterous and desperate, but it is also, paradoxically, joyous and
rings with truth."

Iyer's own trilogy of novels (*Spurious*, *Dogma*, and *Exodus*, published
between 2011 and 2013) has drawn comparisons to the work of Thomas

Bernhard and Samuel Beckett. The books narrate the uneventful friendship and inconsequential conversations of Lars and W., two British academics and intellectuals surviving in the ruins of the contemporary university. The books consist of sections that are only one or a few paragraphs long; their very loose sense of order or development, and their elaboration of a limited set of motifs (Judaism, Hinduism, German idealism, Kafka, the university, alcohol, ...) betrays the novels' origin in a series of blogposts that Iyer published in the years leading up to the publication of the novel. Even if the provenance of these chunks of texts is more straightforward than in *Reality Hunger*, Iyer's novels more successfully manage to escape the monological mode that overtakes Shields' book. They do this by almost never allowing their first-person narrator, Lars, to speak for himself; instead, Lars mainly renders W.'s verbal abuse of him, mostly in free indirect discourse (in which Lars is referred to as "I"), sometimes directly (in which he appears as "you"). Most first-person pronouns are in the plural—Lars himself is little more than an empty shell, and his "I" mainly appears in W.'s (that is, "double-u's/double-you's") discourse. Iyer's decision to lend his first name to his narrator reflects his awareness that authors are affected by the degradation and discomfort that their writing occasions. Both *Spurious* and *Dogma* open with Lars repeatedly being called "stupid" on their first pages. Still, in the domain of the farcical, the two characters are riveted to each other precisely *because* it is the realm of farcical life, and not of individual subjectivity: "You can exorcise a ghost. But how can you rid yourself of an idiot?" (*Dogma* 31).

Most of the novels are taken up with inconsequential, rambling, and often highly intellectual conversations, which regularly deal with German philosophy and literature. There is a pervasive sense of bathos, as this high-minded talk is embedded in the pedestrian triviality of the actions of and the relationship between Lars and W., whose only way of connecting is by verbally abusing Lars and denigrating his (stalled) intellectual achievements. The dialogue is propelled by intellectual clichés: "long periods of warehouse work and unemployment" bring you "into contact with *the essence of capitalism*" (*Dogma* 12); "The Anglo-Saxon mentality is opposed to abstraction and metaphysics [...] It is completely opposed to German profundity" (*Dogma* 81); Kafka's *The Castle* "was literature itself!" (*Spurious* 19). These remainders of literary life float through the novels without informing transformations or provoking reactions—they are just part of the infertile cultural landscape in which the two characters live out their tragicomedy of contemporary intellectual and academic life. Their lateness offers no consolations: "What did we expect? Some Kant-like resurgence, late in life? Some late awakening from our dogmatic slumbers?" (*Dogma* 47). W. and Lars are literary characters who have come too late for literature. They are "*landfill philosophers*" (*Dogma* 55), living "each day as though it were the day *after* the last" (214). Even though the novels (especially *Spurious*) evoke ideas of apocalypse and of the messianic, their sad fate is that their lateness will not end: "It's time to die, says W. But death does not come" (*Dogma* 223). Human life no longer has a purpose and a meaning that literature can give a significant shape, and yet it persists. Lars's and W.'s gloomy, farcical lives are suspended between lofty insights they do not comprehend and the basest animality—it is divided "between the highest thought and the basest idiocy" (207). Lars and W. "felt things, great things" (212), but they cannot ascribe meaning to the intimations of significance to which they are remorselessly exposed: "Like great, dumb animals, we were only feeling [...] What could we understand of what we had been called to do?" (208). For Iyer, the contemporary novel exposes a form of life that is protected neither from insights it cannot comprehend nor from its proximity to animal life; it is no longer a human possession that can be clearly separated from the realms of animal and supernatural being. In the next chapter, I theorize this precarious mode of persistence as "creatural life," and I track J.M. Coetzee's literary figurations of it. Iyer and Coetzee share an awareness that the form of life to which the contemporary novel responds can neither be shaken off (as McCarthy wants to believe) nor valorized as significant individual experience (as in Shields): instead, it is a farcical and creatural life to which the remainder of the novel finds itself attuned.

2
Abandoned Creatures
(J.M. Coetzee)

Fact, affect, fiction

In an often-quoted interview from 1990, J.M. Coetzee describes the relation between his literary work and his personal life in unexpectedly direct terms:

> Let me add [...] that I, as a person, as a personality, am overwhelmed, that my thinking is thrown into confusion and helplessness, by the fact of suffering in the world, and not only human suffering. These fictional constructions of mine are paltry, ludicrous defenses against that being-overwhelmed, and, to me, transparently so. (*Doubling* 4)

Such a plain statement was all the more surprising coming from a writer whose work was, at the time of the interview, routinely categorized as "metafiction." Coetzee's occupation with issues such as the reciprocal imbrication of discourse and violence and the ineluctable role of texts in our access to reality and history were often disparaged as deliberate evasions, if not obfuscations, of the pressing realities of apartheid South Africa. Even if Coetzee's "turn toward textuality" need not automatically entail "a turning away from history" (Attwell, *J.M. Coetzee* 17), the metafictional complexities in his work were routinely opposed to the overtly topical and realist thrust of the work of a writer like Nadine Gordimer. It is remarkable that this Coetzee confesses that he is deeply affected by the very thing his fictional work, on an ungenerous reading, seemed unable to confront directly: "the fact of suffering in the world." Coetzee's statement explicitly connects this affective experience to his writings, which are not to be taken as an avoidance of the affect generated by the fact of worldly suffering, but rather as so many "defenses" against it; his fictions serve as strategies to contain the "overwhelm[ing]" intensity of affect. Yet if they manage to mitigate this intensity, they do not neutralize it completely: the defenses constructed by fiction are "paltry, ludicrous."

Coetzee's remark not only offers us a glimpse into the affective econ-omy propelling his fiction, it also obliquely registers a limitation of his early work; in this way, it anticipates several of the trajectories that his work would go on to explore after 1990. Coetzee describes his ambition to convey an affective response to suffering, yet he also subtly signals an awareness that his work has failed to do so effectively when he notes that the status of his fiction as "paltry, ludicrous defenses" is a fact, and "to me [Coetzee], transparently so." This phrasing indicates that such an understanding of his fiction is less transparent to people other than the author, as the reception of his early work seems to confirm. There are at least two suggestions embedded in this dense passage, both of which are instructive for an understanding of Coetzee's trajectory since the 1990s: first, it announces Coetzee's testing of different modes of writing that more successfully communicate the affect of suffering, and second, it indicates that two of the notions that will have to be renegoti-ated in such a writing practice are "authorship" and "authority."

Coetzee's fiction in the last two decades has returned time and again to these two closely interlinked projects. The reconsideration of author-ship and authority was already central in *The Master of Petersburg*, the first novel he published after the interview, and it directly implicated the person of Coetzee himself in his three peculiar autobiographical fic-tions (*Boyhood, Youth*, and *Summertime*). And as David Attwell has noted, in *Elizabeth Costello, Slow Man*, and *Diary of a Bad Year*, "the practice of authorship itself" has become "[t]he overriding subject" ("Mastering" 217); the same can be said about his Nobel Lecture, "He and His Man." As for the attempt to convey a more direct affective response to suffer-ing, the publication of *Disgrace* in 1999 seemed to announce a shift to a markedly more topical and realist register in its merciless depiction of the life of a white man in a post-apartheid South Africa that has drasti-cally redefined the terms of the social contract that used to pertain. The outspoken reactions to the novel's depictions of new race relationships, lingering xenophobia, and sexual abuse seemed to signal that Coetzee, without abandoning his signature self-reflexivity, had finally managed to convey and provoke an affective response to the reality of suffering to which his work is committed.

It is somewhat surprising, then, that Coetzee's twenty-first-century novels have not continued in this more realist vein. Indeed, novels like

Slow Man (2005) and *Diary of a Bad Year* (2007), on which I focus in this chapter, are infused with a certain abstractness, and a definite disinterest in conveying the lived experience of Australia, Coetzee's new home since he left South Africa. Even if both these novels are set in Australia, the setting is never made more specific than the perfunctory mention of a few geographical signifiers and, in the case of *Diary*, references to a recognizably Australian cultural and political context that, however, hardly informs the characters' everyday lives. The "language of minimalist denotation" (Boehmer 9) in the novels references an Australian context, but they are uninterested in using these references to play the literary game of bringing contemporary Australia to life through the lives of their characters, and in doing what novels are traditionally supposed to do: trace the reciprocal relations between subjective interiority and social space.

Through a reading of *Slow Man* and *Diary*, and of Coetzee's rewriting of Hugo von Hofmannsthal's *Chandos Letter* in the postscript to *Elizabeth Costello*, this chapter interrogates this weary abstractness of Coetzee's late fiction—a periodizing term whose appropriateness will become clear along the way. It shows how this mode of writing contributes to what I take to be the key theme of Coetzee's late fiction (which is not to say that it was missing from his earlier work): its examination of a particular mode of suffering that is produced by the revelation of the fragility and contingency of time-honored forms of life, and by an exposure to what I call, following Eric Santner, the twitchings and fluctuations of creatural life—a form of life that is inextricably linked up with, while not reducible to, animal life. The late fiction stages this condition by presenting us with characters who can no longer depend on the conventions and certainties of the form that has historically sustained and implemented modern notions of subjectivity and community: the novel. Coetzee's protagonists are abandoned creatures: bereft of the social, moral, and political values that were reflected and inculcated by the modern novel, they inhabit the carefully constructed post-novelistic space that McCarthy, Shields, and Iyer, in their different ways, encountered in the first chapter of this book. For Coetzee, this space allows for the tentative testing and elaboration of new forms of life and the unleashing of intractable "after-affects." To return to the passage with which we began, his late novels convey a sense of creatural suffering that is produced when the "paltry, ludicrous defenses" that literary and social fictions have constructed have been rendered inoperative; they take on the inability of fiction to defend against the overwhelming intensity of suffering as a vital concern of the contemporary novel, and as an occasion to explore new modes of being and feeling. In this way, they constitute a crucial chapter in the story of the end of the novel in contemporary fiction.

After *Disgrace*: desire and the end of the novel

Paul Rayment and JC,[1] the protagonists of *Slow Man* and *Diary of a Bad Year*, are both emotionally needy and physically frail old bachelors; they both hire professional help, and they all too predictably fall in love with the young, attractive female foreigners whom they pay to provide that help. Yet as their frailty—old age in the case of JC, an amputated leg and old age in the case of Paul—makes them less than attractive to the objects of their love, their stories do not develop into anything resembling a traditional love plot, and instead offer the sad spectacle of unactualized desires in all their impotent barrenness. Paul and JC inhabit bodies that do not allow them to exercise what David Lurie, the protagonist of *Disgrace*, grandiosely calls "the rights of desire" (89). The halted narratives of *Slow Man* and *Diary* decline to use desire as an organizing principle; in that way, they surrender what, as I discussed in my introduction, is often considered the key element in narrative interactions. As Peter Brooks has influentially argued, "[n]arratives both tell of desire—typically present some story of desire—and arouse and make use of desire as dynamic of signification" (37). Desire, in other words, organizes traditional novel plots, while it at the same time implicates readers in the development of that plot. Coetzee's late novels radically preempt the operations of desire, and thus of narrative, by presenting a world in which the desires of the protagonists have become strictly irrelevant. Such irrelevance is something entirely different from a dynamic in which the satisfaction of desire is postponed or suspended, a procedure that would precisely serve as a way to propel the narrative forward, and to keep the reader in thrall. By dispensing with this device, these novels fail to yield the rich emotive end empathetic experiences novels are expected to deliver.

After he has been visited by the novelist Elizabeth Costello, *Slow Man*'s Paul Rayment muses that she, as a novelist, engages in what amounts to a "biologico-literary experiment" (114). I argue that *Slow Man* and *Diary* are "biologico-literary experiments" that test and explore the forms of life that are produced when the elements that traditionally make up the world of the novel have ceased to function.[2] As I have explained in my introduction, over a century of theoretical reflection on the novel has understood it as a cultural form that has inaugurated and sustained modern forms of individuality and community; it has done so, moreover, by mobilizing two vital kinds of emotive engagement with the world: desire and empathy. Even if such a monolithic account of the novel is a critical fiction rather than a literary historical fact, as Coetzee knows (if only because two of his most overt influences, Kafka and Beckett, constitute drastic exceptions to it), he enlists it in his late fiction only to trace what lies in its wake. Coetzee's late fiction, that is, renders desire and empathy inoperative in order to make room for the investigation of different affects and modes of life.[3]

Looking back over the trajectory of Coetzee's career, we can see that *Slow Man* and *Diary* radicalize an investigation already begun in *Disgrace*. This novel begins in an urban setting as a rather conventional campus novel in which David Lurie, a middle-aged bachelor and intellectual, lives by the rules of desire, as a self-professed "servant of Eros" (52), who takes the liberty to scan the female student population for potential sexual partners with what the novel calls his "desiring gaze" (12). The first few chapters tell the story of Lurie's disgrace, as his sexual contacts with one of his students prove incompatible with the post-apartheid dispensation. The rest of the novel finds Lurie in partly self-imposed exile in the countryside, in an environment where his customary ratiocinations about his actions mean nothing. The novel's main indices of this mismatch are, first, the ubiquitous dogs, who, as his daughter Lucy assures him, "won't ask and they won't care" about his motives (77), and second, his daughter's black neighbor Petrus, whose behavior is inscrutable to Lurie, and who drives home the lesson that the social and racial relations that he had come to take for granted, and that underwrote his life of desire, no longer apply. *Disgrace*, in other words, demonstrates the clash between the rights of desire and the new South African reality (in its first few chapters), and explores the gradual and halting shift from desire to care (in the rest of the novel), as Lurie increasingly devotes his time to caring for the animals on Lucy's farm, and for the corpses of the dogs that the animal clinic, in one of the novel's key phrases, "takes care of."

Coetzee's "biologico-literary experiments" in *Slow Man* and *Diary* simply dispense with the careful narration of this move from a world governed by action, reason, and desire to a world of dependence and care, and drop their protagonists in a position of dependence from the very beginning. Already in the first paragraph of *Slow Man*, Paul is caught by a "blow [...] sharp and surprising and painful, like a bolt of electricity, lifting him up off the bicycle," which lands him in a hospital bed on the third page, and with(out) an amputated leg on page six (1–6). From the very start, Paul's "rights of desire" are forcefully denied, and he is abandoned to a world where there is "no cure, just care" (63); "just nursing, just care" (33).[4] *Slow Man* condenses the movement that takes up two-hundred odd pages in *Disgrace* into the story's very premise. Right at the beginning of the much more sketchy story of *Diary*, JC, the aging (ex-) novelist whose series of short essays we read at the top of the page and whose story is told at the bottom and in the middle part of every page, is struck by the appearance of Anya: she is described as a "quite startling young woman," only to have JC realize that he himself must strike her as "a crumpled old fellow in a corner who at first glance might have been a tramp off the street" (3–4). Acting on his desire for Anya is never an option—what we get is the painful spectacle of a needy and naive old man who is powerless to prevent being robbed by Alan, Anya's partner; in the end, it is Anya's goodwill that saves JC from Alan's scheme. No longer organized by desire, and therefore also unable to solicit readerly empathy in any straightforward way, Coetzee's late fictions are novels from which almost all novelistic elements have been subtracted. These books abandon their characters in a zone where the routines of desire and other novelistic ploys can no longer guide them. At the same time, they expose these characters to the gaze of readers who are equally disoriented; they invite the reader "to be wary of generic labels and, more particularly, of the habits of reading, feeling, and thinking that the novel has helped to naturalize" (McDonald 494). Returning to Lauren Berlant's definition of genre as a "a loose affectual contract that predicts the form that an aesthetic transaction will take" ("Intuitionists" 847), we can say that Coetzee's unsettling of generic conventions overwrites the terms of this contract and opens readers' encounters with the novels to a range of affects that are less strictly codified.

The frequent intertextual references to iconic moments in the history of the modern novel (Beckett, Defoe, Cervantes, and Flaubert in *Slow Man*, Dostoevsky and Tolstoy in *Diary*) signal that these books very self-consciously negotiate their relation to the novel tradition and to the social forms that it used to reinforce.[5] Coetzee's late novels inhabit a space where that tradition fails to exercise its hold on the novels' characters, and this conveys a sense that these social and cultural forms have exhausted their usefulness in the early twenty-first century. Mark Sanders has remarked that, in Coetzee's recent work, we are dealing with fictions in which "aging characters weave, with increasing revulsion and repulsion, in and out of the social text of their, which is also our, time" (644). Even if a revulsion to the body has been a staple of Coetzee's writing from the beginning, his recent work is marked by a particularly intense attention to bodily processes and unanswered emotional needs, even "a studied vulgarity" (Sanders 644), or what Timothy Bewes has called "a level of personal and historical detail that is almost as scandalous as was the earlier reticence" (*Event of Postcolonial Shame* 150). This vulgarity and this specificity do not serve to situate these characters in a densely imagined social world; instead, they are the barren remainders that are left when the social texts that used to undergird such a stable world have become fragile and unstable. They do not help the reader fill in ready-made emotional templates, but they go hand in hand with an eery sense of abstraction. Instead of inaugurating "a new order of directness," these fictions deliver, as Bewes writes, "a new opacity" (151)—a form of resistance to the terms we tend to use to make life more transparent. They embody the insufficiency and obsolescence of the social textures that used to shape our ideas of subjectivity and community, and they do so as novels that empty themselves of all the elements—plot, characters, empathy, desire, setting, and so on—that allowed the form to implement and undergird these social forms in the first place.

A work that has arguably done more than any other to consolidate our understanding of the culturally formative role of the novel is Ian Watt's *The Rise of the Novel* (1957)—a text with which Coetzee engages directly (Hayes 121). Watt connects the rise of the form in the eighteenth century to the development of "a culture which, in the last few centuries, has set an unprecedented value on originality" (13). This "individualist and innovating reorientation," far from issuing in an unconditional affirmation of individual freedom, requires a cultural form to regulate the interactions between the individual and the collective and to prevent the one from overwhelming the other (13, 17–18). On account of this, the novel is first and foremost a technology for regulating these interactions; Nancy Armstrong has defined the novel as an "*ubiquitous cultural narrative* that not only measures individual growth in terms of an individual's ability to locate him- or herself productively within the aggregate but also and simultaneously measures the aggregate in terms of its ability to accommodate the increasing heterogeneity of individuals" (*How Novels Think* 51). The modern novel, in other words, helps society in "maintaining, upgrading, and perpetuating its most basic categories" in the face of historical changes that threaten to unsettle the relations between the individual and the group (83).

What makes Armstrong's and Watt's reflections particularly pertinent is that they both uphold Daniel Defoe's *Robinson Crusoe* (1719) as a landmark in the development of the socially formative role of the novel. As is familiar enough, Coetzee's 1986 novel *Foe* interrogated the violence and exclusions besetting the forms of individuality and sociality that Defoe's novel helped to institute. Paul's statement in *Slow Man* that he is "not Robinson Crusoe" testifies to Coetzee's intention to continue that critique in his later work, but in a different form (14). Where *Foe* pointed to the ethical and political limitations of dominant forms of individual and collective subjectivity, his late fiction responds to a sense that the hegemony of these forms has been revealed as tenuous and contingent. At the beginning of the twenty-first century, being a self-reliant, enterprising Crusoe is no longer an option, not even for a metropolitan white male like Paul. The late novels undermine the illusion of an achieved subjectivity in order to make room to mine the afterlife of the novel for intimations of what I will call "creatural life."

Creatural abandon

Coetzee's late fictions address the tension between the "overwhelming" intensity of suffering and fiction's "paltry, ludicrous defenses" by making the flimsy status of his works unmistakable. By staging characters who fail to find a footing in the social world, their lives "overwhelm" the forms that aim to contain them. Facing a world that is not organized by novelistic conventions and readers who are not bound by the terms of a generic contract, these characters are, if anything, *exposed*. An emblem of this excessive exposure is Paul's decision, at the beginning of *Slow Man*, to refuse a prosthesis for his amputated leg. Declining the consolations of artificial wholeness, Paul exposes himself to "the pitiless gaze of the young," to "the gaze of an outsider" (13, 38, 96)—to a gaze, in other words, that is no longer, as was the case at the beginning of *Disgrace*, automatically linked to desire.[6] This gaze squarely focuses on the abject reality of the "zone of humiliation" (13, 61) created in the gap where novelistic devices have ceased to function. Through this movement of subtraction, the missing leg takes on an uncanny reality. As Zoë Wicomb has noted, what enters the narrative as "[t]he absence of a leg" becomes "the real presence of a stump that the reader encounters in all its raw physicality" (229). The stump is a fleshy, physical excess generated by the palpable inability of novelistic devices to cover it up.

   In the case of *Diary*, this zone of exposure is created through the particular layout of the reading page, which deprives JC of any control over his narrative. Almost all pages are divided into three parts—exceptions to this rule are almost always significant, as I will explain. At the top, we read the short essays that JC is writing for a German publication entitled *Strong Opinions*. At the bottom, we initially read JC's diary, in which he tells us of his encounter with Anya; this section is pushed up to the middle of the page as Anya herself begins to take up the bottom part when we are 25 pages into the novel, and we effectively get three different layers on (almost) every page. The frictions between these different genres—the essay, two diaries, and later also a long letter by Anya to JC taking over the space of JC's diary—serve to expose the sadness of JC's plight to the reader who, unlike JC himself, can read how Anya and Alan initially think about him as a naive, needy, and slightly pathetic old man. In particular, Alan, a cynical arch-neoliberal, ruthlessly shatters any illusions the aging novelist might have about his relevance for the contemporary world. The latter is exposed as a survivor from an age when the literary imagination was still connected to the real world in a meaningful sense—a remnant, that is, from the age of the novel. Alan declares this age to be decidedly over: "in the English-speaking world, the world of hard heads and common sense, a book of pronouncements on the real world won't get much traction, coming from a man whose sole achievement lies in the sphere of the fanciful" (206). Again, Coetzee evokes the end of the novel form and stages the suffering that survives it.

So how are we to understand this form of suffering that emerges when novelistic devices fail? It is interesting that Coetzee, in the quote with which we began this chapter, carefully qualifies his concern with suffering "in the world" to include "not only human suffering." In retrospect, it is tempting to see that Coetzee is here already announcing his increasingly intense occupation with the lives of animals in his later work. Still, his twenty-first-century work makes clear that this passage might also indicate a suffering that gains visibility after the dissolution of the conventions that used to define what counted as fully fledged "human" (heroic, tragic, cathartic, redemptive) suffering. As noted, the plight of Paul and JC is crucially tied to the fact that the time-honored social textures that used to organize modern life have become fragile and contingent. This does not mean that they somehow cease being human and become animal; it is a crucial aspect of their condition that they remain riveted to cultural forms that can no longer defend them from their vulnerability. This is less a form of biological or animal vulnerability than what Eric Santner has called a "creaturely" vulnerability. I will refer to this condition as "crea-tur*al*" life, if only to signal that my understanding of it slightly departs from Santner's, as will become clear when I turn to Erich Auerbach's work in the next section. Santner defines this creatural dimension as follows:

> It signifies a mode of *exposure* that distinguishes human beings from other kinds of life: not exposure simply to the elements or to the

fragility and precariousness of our mortal, finite lives, but rather to an ultimate lack of foundation for the historical forms of life that distinguish human community [...] We could say that the precariousness, the fragility—the "nudity"—of biological life becomes potentiated, amplified, by way of exposure to the radical contingency of the forms of life that constitute the space of meaning within which human life unfolds, and that it is only through such "potentiation" that we take on the flesh of creaturely life. Creatureliness is thus a dimension not so much of biological as of *ontological vulnerability*, a vulnerability that permeates human being as that being whose essence it is to exist in forms of life that are, in turn, contingent, fragile, susceptible to breakdown. (*Royal Remains* 5–6)

The novel is one such "form of life" whose felt and perceived precariousness exposes human beings to the insistence of creatural life and suffering. Coetzee's late works of fiction are "biologico-literary experiments" that provoke a crisis in the novel form in order to explore the lives of creatures like Paul and JC.

As I noted, Coetzee's protagonists do not immediately invite readerly empathy: they hardly act or develop, and they consistently fail to meet the standards of a life worth telling. Yet their helpless exposure to the gaze of their world and their readers invites an affective response all the same, even if it is only one of disappointment, frustration, impatience, or bafflement (Dancygier 245, Walton 282–83). In the novels, both JC and Paul ultimately become the objects of somewhat unrealistic minimal acts of care and generosity. Such a weaker, less grandiose affective attentiveness is one way of responding to creatural suffering in the absence of more codified forms of empathy and identification—an absence that generates creatural suffering in the first place. Santner refers to the mode of attentiveness that emerges after the breakdown of these outmoded protocols as "a new, yet still inarticulate, mode of *Einfühlung*, as a thinking responsive to the 'twitchings' of creatural life, a thinking that attempts to inhabit the 'neighbourhood' of its always singular appearances" (*Royal Remains* 178). Interestingly, Santner makes this point in relation to the German writer Hugo von Hofmannsthal's famous *Chandos Letter* from 1902, a key document in the modernist experience of the breakdown of a time-worn universe of meaning. Coetzee takes on the same text in the postscript to *Elizabeth Costello*.[7] A brief consideration of Coetzee's postscript reveals that he is crucially concerned with probing the affective charge and the ethical challenge of the loss of seemingly self-evident social and cultural forms—something that my reading of *Slow Man* and *Diary* confirms. Just as Hofmannsthal is interested in grasping the advent of modernism, Coetzee probes the aftermath of models of subjectivity and community underwritten by the novel form.

Like Hofmannsthal's text, Coetzee's short postscript takes the form of a fictional letter to the sixteenth- and seventeenth-century philosopher Francis Bacon. But unlike Hofmannsthal's original, Coetzee's letter is not written by Lord Chandos as an apology for "his complete abandonment of literary activity" (Hofmannsthal 69), but rather by his wife, "Elizabeth, Lady Chandos." That the imaginary Lady Chandos shares the name of the aging novelist at the center of *Elizabeth Costello* is an open invitation to read this postscript as a coded meditation on the fate of the contemporary novel. Lady Chandos's letter deals with her husband's letter, which, she explains, has accidently come to her notice, and about which she wants to reassure Bacon that it was not, as she suspects he might suspect, written "in a fit of madness" (227). The status of Lady Chandos's letter is significant: it comes to the aid of a (seemingly) mad person, the person who, in Hofmannsthal's original, had been overcome by the sudden intensity of creatural life; it is an oblique response to a letter (her husband's) that was not even addressed to her. In this way, Coetzee's letter *embodies* the mode of attentiveness and responsiveness to suffering that Santner and others have located in Hofmannsthal's letter. In the "many months" she has known of her husband's affliction, Lady Chandos writes, she has "suffered with him" (227).[8]

The letter makes clear that this mode of responsiveness surfaces after the forms of desire, communication, and identification commonly associated with the novel form have been intensified to breaking point:

> There was a time, I remember, before this time of affliction, when he would gaze like one bewitched at paintings of sirens and dryads, craving to enter their naked, glistening bodies. But where in Wiltshire will we find a siren or a dryad for him to try? Perforce I became his dryad: it was I whom he entered when he sought to enter her, I who felt his tears on my shoulder when again he could not find her in me. (227)

The form of life in which such intense forms of desire and identification—what Reingard Nethersole calls "the libidinal surge to merge with the desired object of beauty" (258)—made sense has become obsolete; now Lord and Lady Chandos live in a zone "where words give way beneath your feet like rotting boards" (*Elizabeth* 228). Instead of inhabiting familiar cultural forms that mediate their relation to the world, Lord and Lady Chandos, and the characters in Coetzee's late fiction more generally, are exposed to their creatural condition, in which they are no longer shielded from the intimate proximity of their fellow creatures (what Santner calls "the 'neighbourhood' of [creaturely life's] always singular appearance"), nor from the insistent attraction of transcendent powers. Now that the borders cordoning off the realm of human life from other forms of being have disappeared, Lady Chandos has to live "with rats and dogs and beetles crawling through [her] day and night, drowning and gasping"; at the same time, she is afflicted with the uncontrollable proliferation of intimations of higher meaning: "Each creature is key to all other creatures. A dog sitting in a patch of sun licking itself [...] is at one moment a dog and at the next a vessel of revelation" (229). When the established hierarchy between the divine, the human, and the animal realm has been rendered inoperative, these different orders of being find themselves in creatural proximity.[9]

Lady Chandos describes this oscillation between the divine and the bestial as a condition in which "[a]ll is allegory" (*Elizabeth* 229). And while "allegory" is a notoriously slippery term, Hofmannsthal's original text clearly locates it in the crisis it is describing, which is the very crisis that the postscript to *Elizabeth Costello* transfers to Coetzee's late fiction. For Hofmannsthal's Chandos, "allegory" names the loss of the power to conceive of "the whole of existence as one great unit" in which "the spiritual and physical worlds seemed to form no contrast" (71–72). When he is reduced to creatural suffering, "everything disintegrated into parts, those parts again into parts; no longer would anything let itself be encompassed by one idea" (74). Not only the real world, but also the spiritual realm that used to infuse this world with significance has become meaningless, and this establishes the link between creatural life and allegory: "the mysteries of faith have been condensed into a lofty allegory which arches itself over the fields of my life like a radiant rainbow, ever remote, ever prepared to recede should it occur to me to rush toward it and wrap myself into the folds of its mantle" (72). "All is allegory," in other words, as the creature finds itself simultaneously in uncomfortable proximity to its fellow creatures and ruthlessly exposed to a transcendent order it cannot comprehend. The spiritual and the physical no longer constitute a harmonious unity. Yet what does this oscillation between the twitchings of creatural life and intimations of higher things have to do with Coetzee's attempt to interrogate the legacy of the novel form? How, that is, can we understand the relations between allegory, creatures, and the novel?

The rise of the novel and the domestication of creatural life

In order to probe the relations between allegory, creatures, and the novel, this section traces the vagaries of the notion of "allegory" in Ian Watt's account of the rise of the novel, an account that Coetzee has explicitly endorsed (Hayes 121), and in one of Watt's source texts, Erich Auerbach's *Mimesis*. While Watt rather unproblematically positions the novel form as a clear alternative to allegory, Auerbach shows how the rise of the novel domesticates an intensification of creatural life in the wake of the demise of a harmonious, unified world—a moment that resembles nothing so much as the condition in which "all is allegory." I will further develop the affinities between creatural life, allegory, war, and the anthropocene in my coda; for now, I emphasize that Auerbach's attention to the tensions between the novel form and creatural life can help us understand Coetzee's turn to creatural life as a strategy for exploring new forms of life after the end of the novel.

In *The Rise of the Novel*, Watt supports his decision to position Defoe and Richardson as the originators of the novel form by noting that they "are the first great writers in our literature who did not take their plots from mythology, history, legend or previous literature" (14). In the novel, the plot is acted out "by particular people in particular circumstances," rather than "by general types against a background primarily determined by the appropriate literary convention" (15). The defining innovation of the novel, in other words, is that ordinary life is treated with proper seriousness:

> The novel's serious concern with the daily lives of ordinary people seems to depend upon two important general conditions: the society must value every individual highly enough to consider him the proper subject of its serious literature; and there must be enough variety of belief and action among ordinary people for a detailed account of them to be of interest to other ordinary people, the readers of novels. (60)

The novel's serious treatment of ordinary life is, according to Watt, unprecedented in Western literary history. It was simply not available to classical literature, where genre theory prescribed a strict *Stiltrennung* (separation of styles): "tragedy described the heroic vicissitudes of people better than ourselves in appropriately elevated language, whereas the domain of everyday reality belonged to comedy which was supposed to portray people 'inferior to ourselves' in an appropriately 'low' style" (79). The emergence of the novel neutralizes this distinction and makes it possible to treat every individual with the seriousness that was earlier only accorded to the heroes of myth and tragedy. The opposition between comedy and tragedy is, in other words, overcome by the novel's invention of what Watt calls "formal realism." The seriousness accorded to earthly life also means that the latter no longer requires transcendent sanction. This is why Defoe rather than Bunyan is considered the first novelist: in works like *Pilgrim's Progress*, "the significance of the characters and their actions largely depends upon a transcendental scheme of things: to say that the persons are allegorical is to say that their earthly reality is not the main object of the writer" (80). Thanks to its unprecedented power to wed the tragic and the comic, the novel, for Watt, is an inherently anti-allegorical form.

This seductively neat picture of the relation between allegory and the novel becomes less straightforward when we look at one of Watt's barely acknowledged intertexts (its author and title are mentioned only once in *The Rise of the Novel*): Erich Auerbach's *Mimesis*, his study of the representation of reality in Western literature, which was translated into English in 1954, three years before the publication of Watt's book.[10] Watt duly attributes the idea of the importance of the mixture of styles to Auerbach, but he also silently borrows Auerbach's conception of realism as "representations of everyday life in which that life is treated seriously, in terms of its human and social problems or even in its tragic complications" (*Mimesis* 342). For Auerbach, whose historical and geographical scope is much broader than Watt's, this realist literature develops out of a "figural" (or typological) tradition, which he directly opposes to allegorical forms of textuality and interpretation. On the basis of his unique knowledge of the history of Christian literature, Auerbach concludes that, while allegory abstracts historical particulars into ahistorical meaning, and thus fails to treat everyday life with full seriousness, figural interpretation connects two distinct moments in a historical continuity: "The two poles of the figure are separate in time, but both, being real events or figures, are within time, within the stream of historical life" ("Figura" 53). Figural interpretation preserves "the historicity both of the sign and what it signifies" (54); it assures that historical significance is possible without a transcendent moment, as it assumes that there is a meaningfulness inherent in worldly affairs. It is not hard to see how this figural mode announces the emergence of a style that neutralizes the opposition between the comic and the tragic, and that infuses everyday life with an unprecedented literary dignity.

So far, so anti-allegorical. But while it may seem that for Auerbach, as for Watt, allegory does not feature in the genealogy of novelistic realism, it does make an all-important cameo appearance in it. In *Mimesis's* central chapter, Auerbach explains how realism comes into its own in Dante's *Commedia*. In Auerbach's reading, the *Commedia* sets out to affirm the dignity of human life within a Christian framework, only to discover that the vitality and variety of earthly life possesses a power that operates quite independently from the Christian scheme that first granted it its dignity. Dante, for Auerbach, "created a world of earthly beings and passions so powerful that it breaks bounds and proclaims its independence" (200), as life acquires a seriousness that no longer depends on transcendent sanction. Dante discovers that human life is intrinsically worthy of attention and narration, and no longer requires validation in an eschatological scheme. Instead of awaiting divine judgment, self-fulfillment in Dante "comprises the individual's entire past [...] involves ontogenetic history, the history of an individual's personal growth [...] we are given to see, in the realm of timeless being, the history of man's inner life and unfolding" (202). It is this pattern of earthly self-actualization that Watt will claim as the unique territory of the novel; in the novel, the primacy of "the pattern of the autobiographical memoir" over the plot constitutes a "defiant [...] assertion of the primacy of individual experience" (Watt, *The Rise of the Novel* 15).

In Watt's account, Auerbach's description of the emergence of earthly vitality is transcribed as the story of individual development, which Watt sees as the proper subject of the novel. Still, when we read Auerbach carefully, we note that something gets lost in this transcription. In Auerbach's history of Western literature, earthly life emerges at a threshold moment: the moment of the demise of a harmonious and all-encompassing framework that sets free the intensities and energies that the discredited framework used to organize and contain. In fact, Auerbach's earthly life comes close to the creatural excess whose eruption Hofmannsthal and Coetzee also locate in moments when self-evident social textures become fragile:

> The result [of Dante's realism] is a direct experience of life which *overwhelms* everything else [*einer alles anderen überwältigenden, unmittelbaren Erfahrung des Lebens*], a comprehension of human realities which spreads as widely and variously as it goes profoundly to the very roots of our emotions, an illumination of man's impulses and passions which leads us to share in them without restraint and indeed to admire their variety and their greatness. (201–202, my italics; 196)

Auerbach's sketch of creatural life deploys the very term ("overwhelming" [*überwaltigend*]) that Coetzee uses to describe the insuffiency of the novel form to capture the fact of worldly suffering. Even while he furnishes the terms in which Watt will influentially celebrate the rise of the novel, Auerbach captures a critical moment in the form's genealogy that undermines Watt's thesis that the novel has decisively moved beyond the split between the tragic and the comic and is a confidently post-allegorical form.[11] In this critical moment, the human is exposed to "impulses and passions" in which it is invited to "share [...] without restraint," while the transcendent framework that used to organize the world has become inoperative. In Auerbach's narrative, these impulses migrate to "the Franco-Burgundian culture of the fifteenth century" (260); in a work that the minor author Antoine de la Sale wrote in old age—Auerbach remarks that "there is something of senile circumstantiality in the style of the work" (243)—Auerbach finds a savoring of "crass effects" and an emphasis on "excess and crude degeneracy" that embodies "man's subjection to suffering and transitoriness" (247–49). This indulgence in the realization that beneath man's "class insignia" "there is nothing but the flesh" (249) is explicity called an "unconcealed creatural realism" [*hüllenloser kreatürlicher Realistik*] (247; 236).[12] This creatural realism will soon enough be recoded as part of "triumphant earthly life" in Rabelais (276) and Montaigne (310), but it emerges in Dante and de la Sale as a mercilessly exposed fleshy excess. This is, on Hofmannsthal's and Coetzee's terms, a creatural condition in which "[a]ll is allegory," where allegory can be understood as "the symbolic mode proper to the experience of irremediable exposure to the violence of history" (Santner, *On Creaturely Life* 20). This condition emerges when old cultural and social forms are breaking down; Coetzee's late work provokes this condition in order to explore modes of affect and life that break through when the end of the novel is enacted.

Paul's plight in *Slow Man* can be understood in terms of the overwhelming return of allegory and of the division between the comic and the tragic. The "blow" that "catches" him and lifts him "up off the bicycle" in the first lines of the novel, and that will lead to a complete turnaround in his life, is a banal accident caused by an inattentive young driver, while it, as Arne De Boever has already remarked (27–28), at the same time resonates with a much more momentous incident in the history of the West: the famous passage, narrated in Acts 9, in which the later St Paul, then still called Saul, is blasted from his horse on the road from Tarsus to Damascus, as part of a divine plan in which he features as Jesus's "chosen vessel" who must bear His name "before the Gentiles, and kings, and the children of Israel" (Acts 9: 15). The blow that hits Saul not only brings about a radical conversion in his life (he used to persecute Christians), but also in the history of the globalization of Christianity. While the accident that opens *Slow Man* inevitably recalls this moment, the radical diminishment of Paul's life and his failure to extend his love into the world underline his inevitable remove from such a higher meaning. This is precisely the allegorical condition that Coetzee and Hofmannsthal are describing.

Paul captures his own uncertainty about the bearing of the accident in the genre theoretical terms that Watt imported into the definition of the novel. In conversation with a friend, Paul explains that he does not intend to sue the young man who drove into him, as that leaves "[t]oo many openings for comedy" (15). Later on, he explains to Elizabeth Costello that his life story is not fit for fiction: "Losing a leg does not qualify one for a dramatic role. Losing is leg is neither tragic nor comic, just unfortunate" (117). The option of converting his life story into a novel—which, after all, could potentially neutralize the distinction between tragedy and comedy—is no longer available to Paul. The literary form that could accord "the unfortunate" the seriousness due to earthly events is no longer operative: "as regards his condition in general, considering what can and does happen to the human body when it is hit by a car going at speed, he can congratulate himself that it is *not serious*. In fact, it is so much the reverse of serious that he can count himself lucky, fortunate, blessed" (6). Lacking a cultural form that can render his misfortune with all due seriousness, Paul is led to conclude that what happened to him is "the reverse of serious"—that, in fact, he has even been fortunate. Such are the oscillations besetting creatural life when there is no novel form to house it. In the rest of this chapter, I will trace how *Slow Man* and *Diary* intimate modes of responsiveness and attentiveness that are appropriate to this creatural abandonment.

The author as creature: *Slow Man*

Slow Man's intent to map the affinities between creatural life and the demobilization of the novel form is especially apparent in its revision of the traditional relations between author and character, or between creator and creature. In the book's thirteenth chapter, Paul's indolence is interrupted by a visit from the novelist Elizabeth Costello, a character who is familiar from Coetzee's eponymous 2003 novel, and as Coetzee's *porte-parole* in several of the public lectures he has delivered since the mid-1990s. Her introduction immediately upsets the novel's discursive situation when she begins to recite the opening sentences of the novel and turns out to know all about Paul's life (81). Paul's suspicion that he is merely a character in one of Elizabeth's novels is only strengthened when he discovers notes about his life in her notebook. The result is an overwhelming sense of betrayal, because what he had assumed to be his private life turns out to have been part of a "biologico-literary experiment," and to have been meticulously recorded by a hidden agent: "All the time he thought he was his own master he has been in a cage like a rat, darting this way and that, yammering to himself, with the infernal woman standing over him, observing, listening, taking notes, recording his progress" (122).

It is important to note what this passage describing the relation between author and character is *not* saying. For one thing, it does not present the spectacle of a manipulative master and a passive victim, as "the infernal woman" (the author), in this passage, is not interfering, only observing and recording. Whatever authority she has is in any case no omnipotence, and is the result of careful observation and meticulous recording, not of the sovereign operation of the imagination. If there is any spontaneous action in this passage, it is on the side of the rat (the character). This confirms a suspicion that Elizabeth's visit almost automatically raises, and that the rest of the novel supports: traditional authors do not visit their characters, and Costello's doing so reveals that she depends as much on Paul as the other way round. It demonstrates that the relation between author and character, far from being a matter of unidirectional domination, is in fact a relation of *reciprocal dependence*.

Elizabeth and Paul are condemned to each other, and his failure to live an active, desiring life, a life "that may be *worth* putting in a book" (229), is also a problem for her, as her life is also tied up with the continued existence of books—of the zones, that is, in which creatures are exposed to the disintegration of the form that used to sustain them. As long as Paul does not "choose to act" (136) and to initiate a veritable plot, Elizabeth "ha[s] to put up with" him and his immobile, indolent life, and she "cannot go back to [her] own life, which is a great deal more comfortable" (136). Paul's descent from subject to creature also drags the author away from her site of sovereignty to "the zone of humiliation" that is Paul's "new home" (61). The option of a return to comfort and self-sufficiency has become obsolete, as Elizabeth realizes: "When I am with you I am at home; when I am not with you I am homeless. That is how the dice have fallen" (159). Elizabeth reminds Paul that their reciprocal dependence also means that his refusal to accept her as part of his life entails a diminishment for himself: "Bringing me to life may not be important to you, but it has the drawback of not bringing you to life either" (159). After Elizabeth has arranged an awkward sexual encounter between Paul and a blind woman he spotted earlier in the novel, he wonders whether "the Costello woman [might] be writing two stories at once, stories about characters who suffer a loss [...] which they must learn to live with" (118). *Slow Man* tells the story of two people who must learn to cope with the loss of the social and cultural forms on which they used to depend for making sense of loss, and in the absence of which they have to improvise a new mode of existence in and through their relation to each other.

The result is a work without credible psychological development, a significant setting, or a compelling plot; instead, we get seemingly unchoreographed changes in the character's proximity to and repulsion from each other and in the degree of vitality of the two aging characters, which intermittently sinks to a depressing low. The only thing that seems to keep Paul from suicide is that "he does not *want* death because he does not *want* anything" (26). Unable to act, his life is "cast over with a grey monotone" (139) and becomes "repetitive and circumscribed and duller by the day" (229). At one point, Elizabeth confesses: "I can't begin to tell you how tired I am [...] The tiredness I refer to has become part of my being. It is like a dye that has begun to seep into everything I do, everything I say" (160). This waning of vitality is explicitly linked to the crisis of the form that used to support their notions of a life worth living when Paul searches out one of Elizabeth's novels only to stop reading because "[h]e is not going to expose himself to any more of the colourless, odourless, inert, and depressive gas given off by its pages" (120). Not much difference, then, between the remains of the novel and the creatural remainder of life.

If Coetzee's late fiction declares the time when the novel form could authoritatively shape lives to be over, the expectations of what constitutes a life worth describing (or novelizing) have not ceased to make themselves felt. Elizabeth's and Paul's dejection are tied to the fact that these expectations continue to address them even when the conditions of their realization are no longer in place. Paul's self-beratement when he realizes that he is "not a hero" (117), when he cannot muster the "gross desires" that he yet knows are "expected of him" (14), when he fails to exercise the "passion that makes the world go round" (228), is the result of expectations that continue to haunt him at a time when their actualization has become impossible. This is why theirs is a creatural, and not an animal, form of suffering: not just the physical pains of biological life, but also a sense of vulnerability and precariousness that comes from the fragility of the forms that used to provide human life with meaning.

In order to recast the relation between author and character as a form of reciprocal creatural exposure, *Slow Man* needs to dismantle the logic of sovereignty, which Santner identifies as a historical strategy used "to organize, manage, and administer" the creatural fluctuations to which human life is subject (*Royal Remains* xx). The logic of sovereignty has of course also informed notions of authorship, and the novel's revision of such notions is not only apparent in Elizabeth's development, but also in that of Paul. The first pages of the novel subtly link his demotion from independence to disability to a gradual erasure of the power of authorial intention. In the very first paragraph, Paul reacts to the blow that hits him by a double act of (self-)narration: "*Relax* he tells himself as he flies through the air [...] and indeed he can feel his limbs go obediently slack. *Like a cat* he tells himself" (1). These acts of telling are credited with the power to contain the impact of the accident, and with an undiminished effectiveness ("and indeed"). Only a few lines later, this linguistic power is beginning to abandon him, and the novel's short first chapter ends thus: "He wants to ask what has become of his bicycle, whether it is being taken care of, since, as is well known, a bicycle can disappear in a flash: but before those words will come he is gone again" (2). The intention to speak cannot be actualized; it is first overtaken (and de-individualized) by the *idée reçue* that "a bicycle can disappear in a flash," and the unwelcome silence that follows the intention to speak finds the vanishing speaker at the mercy of words that won't come—a situation that cancels his selfhood: "he is gone again." The rest of the novel explores new forms of life in the gap left by the vanishing of sovereign selfhood; as Paul writes in a letter to Marijana, the nurse he falls in love with, following another incident later in the story: "I am just using the opening created by this unpleasant incident to let my pen run and my heart speak" (225).

The second chapter, in which Paul finds himself tied to a hospital bed, not only chronicles his physical decay, but also his loss of control over his speech. Even if he intends to speak, he faces the problem that "if he utters the words he will lose control, he will start shouting" (8), and he unsuccessfully "tries to create an interrogative" "[o]ut of the muddle in his head" (4). The self-evident effectiveness from the first paragraph, signaled by the "and indeed," has migrated to the impersonal hospital: somebody says that the doctor will come, "[a]nd indeed before a minute has passed" he comes (4). Paul has not only lost the power of articulation—he feels as if in "a cocoon of dead air," "as if he were encased in concrete" (3)—the accident has also afflicted his relation to his own body: the pain in his leg does not register directly, but instead "[h]e hears his own gasp, and then the thudding of blood in his ears" (5). The noise he does manage to make is not intentionally produced, but "wells up and bursts from his throat," coming "from the cavern within" (3).

In Paul's development in the novel, the assumption of self-reliance makes room for a halting recognition of his exposure to his fellow creatures, a relentless exposure produced by the fragility of the social textures from which his accident has torn him away. One of the novel's key terms for capturing this exposure is "flesh." In a conversation with Elizabeth, Paul describes himself as an immaterial node adequately suspended in a network of signifiers: he is a "a kind of ventriloquist's dummy"; it is not he "who speak[s] the language, it is the language that is spoken through me" (198). He considers himself "*hollow at the core*," yet Elizabeth promptly reminds him that his accident has put paid to such fantasies of "ethereal being": having come "crashing down to earth," he is "nothing but a lump of all too solid flesh" (198). Paul has become a material "residue," a "sediment" of the social order (63, 51). No longer able to "perform what man is brought into the world to perform," he is now "[a] man not wholly a man [...] a half-man, an after-man, like an after-image" (33–34). The instantaneous "flash" of the accident has produces the "flesh" that Paul must learn to inhabit: "Flash. A flash of lightning. Flesh is what we are made of, flesh and bone" (54).[13]

The notion of "flesh" plays a key role in Santner's analysis of creatural life. The flesh is the excess of life that cannot be organized in a body; it names, more precisely, a dimension of somatic life that is animated by our exposure to fellow creatures when that exposure is no longer contained within a (social) body. According to Santner, the body is transformed into "a bundle of excitable flesh" when we are faced with the "inability to inhabit and to feel *libidinally implicated* in the space of representations" (*Royal Remains* xiv)—the very space that the novel used to organize by its choreographing of desire, and which Paul finds himself expelled from at the beginning of the book. The flesh is "the virtual yet unnervingly visceral substance of the fantasies that both constrain and amplify the lives of modern subjects" (xxii), which Paul must learn to assume as part of his life. Paul's stump serves no particular function in his biological life, and his refusal of a prosthesis makes sure that it will not be enlisted for the smooth functioning of his body in the future. In this way, it crystallizes the "fleshy" dimension of his life that stands out and remains exposed to the gaze of others.

A crucial step in Paul's gradual acceptance of the reality of the flesh and the disarticulation of the body is the encounter, orchestrated by Elizabeth, with a blind woman he earlier spotted in the hospital. The woman's blindness ensures that Paul does not feel her gaze, yet the requirement that he also cover his own eyes denies him the comfort of confronting her as an integral body: "groping his way," he feels "heavy breasts and spreading, unnaturally soft buttocks," yet "he cannot make the parts cohere"; indeed, "[h]ow can he even be sure they belong to the same woman?" (108). Even if the flesh is here confronted while the gaze is suspended, the scene is tinged with the suspicion that they are being watched by Elizabeth, the person who initiated the encounter, and, of course, by the reader, to whose gaze Paul's helpless groping is mercilessly exposed. In this way, the scene is also a step toward Paul's acceptance of his own exposure to the gaze and the care of others. As he notes, "[w]e are on stage, in a certain sense, even if we are not being watched" (103).

Paul's reluctant acceptance of the flesh and the gaze, and thus of the creatural dimension of his life, is postponed by several setbacks. At first, Paul simply denies his creatural condition: not only does he refuse his prosthesis, he also resists professional help; his aim remains to "recover himself," to remain "his old self," and to "take care of [him]self," as if the forms that subtended his former self were still in place (4, 6, 10). Only later does he realize that his particular plight consists in having to live with the disintegration of those forms, without the possibility of realigning them: "[n]ever is he going to be his old self again," yet for all that "[h]e is trapped with the same old self as before, only greyer and drearier" (53, 54). Paul is condemned to live the afterlife of a life that may once have been worth living or novelizing; his loss can no longer be integrated into a narrative of desire and recovery—he will from now on be "the one who aches" (26). Yet the claims of desire prove hard to shake off: evacuated from the realm where his sexual desire can be actualized, and entirely reliant on professional care, Paul transforms care, and the provider of this care—his nurse Marijana—into objects of desire. Not only does he fall in love with Marijana, he also wants to support her family financially so that their son Drago can afford to attend an expensive college. His desire for care has all the intensity of sexual passion: "he will give anything to be father to these excellent, beautiful children and husband to Marijana [...] He wants to take care of them, all of them, protect them and save them" (72).

Marijana and her family have come to Australia from Croatia by way of Germany. *Slow Man* weaves this fact into the novel's affective geography in a way that again underscores its intent to explore life after the collapse of social spaces supported by the novel form. Paul, who was himself born in France, perpetuates the cliché of the Balkan as Europe's interior exotic other. Hearing the name of Marijana's son, he muses "Drago Jokić: a name from folk-epic. *The Ballad of Drago Jokić*" (69). In a letter to Marijana, he writes that she "come[s] from an older and in some respects better world" (225). Croatia appears as a more harmonious and less complicated place—as either a "worker's paradise" or "an immemorial world of donkeys and goats and chickens and water-buckets sheeted in ice in the morning" (64).

The association between simpler and more harmonious life forms and the genre of the epic is not fortuitous. It is one of the organizing conceits of Georg Lukács's classic work *The Theory of the Novel* (1914–15). As I will discuss in much more detail in my fourth chapter, what defines the novel as a quintessentially modern genre for Lukács is its endemic nostalgia for an epic world. In the words of Timothy Bewes, for Lukács, the novel "is a genre defined by its failure: by the yearning for a world of completeness, a completeness that [Lukács] ascribes to the world of the epic, and that the novel is constitutively removed from" (*Event of Postcolonial Shame* 44). The novel "emerges in a world in which the 'natural unity of the metaphysical spheres,' a unity expressed in the pure, sensuous immediacy of the epic, has disappeared forever" (86). Whereas the ethos of a complete world for which the novel impotently yearns was adequately captured by the epic, the modern world in which the spiritual and the material no longer add up to a well-rounded whole can no longer be convincingly rendered by literary form. The novel is unable to restore the unity of life and form, even if it is defined by the persistent desire to do so: for Lukács, "[t]he novel is the epic of an age in which the extensive totality of life is no longer directly given, in which the immanence of meaning in life has become a problem, yet which still thinks in terms of totality" (Lukács, *Theory* 56).[14]

Paul's impossible desire for a Marijana who is linked to the Balkan and to epic form is, in other words, essentially a *novelistic* desire. It is also, as the Balkan's status as Europe's internal exotic other makes clear, a decidedly *European* desire—a desire for an "extensive totality of life" that is impossible to satisfy in Paul's Australian exile. Marijana and her husband learn this with a vengeance. She holds a degree in restoration, and while there was still a living to be made by restoring the master-works of the past in Dubrovnik, she is reduced to doing nursing jobs in Australia, where such a desire for the grandeur and completeness of the past has made way for more pedestrian requirements (86). Miroslav, her husband, even more dramatically embodies the obsolescence of the novelistic illusion of a restored fullness of life. Educated as a specialist "in antique technology," he won his 15 minutes of fame back home by reassembling "a mechanical duck that had lain in parts in the basement [...] for two hundred years," and which he managed to make quack and waddle again (86). In Australia, this feat of rearticulating disparate mechanical parts into the semblance of a functioning and living body has no use, and he ends up working in a car plant.

In his encounter with his creatural and fleshy being, Paul must abandon the novelistic nostalgia for wholeness. He codes his refusal of a prosthesis as a refusal of the reanimation work in which Miroslav engages: "If I had screws I would be a mechanical man. Which I am not" (56). This refusal replaces the dream of wholeness with an acceptance of physical exposure and the concomitant imperative to persist even in the absence of consoling fictions: countering Elizabeth's accusation that he feels aversion to the physical, Paul notes that "[i]t is a testament to my faith in the physical that I have not done away with myself, that I am still here" (234–35). Paul refuses what Lukács refers to as the novel's reluctant replacement of sensation with reflection by returning from the realm of reflection to the raw persistence of creatural life, even if there is no hope of infusing that life with spiritual meaning. While Elizabeth affirms that "the whole of writing [is] a matter of second thoughts," "second thoughts to the power of n," Paul breaks with this hypertrophy of reflection by making it a matter of revulsion: "I used to have lots of second thoughts, I had second thoughts all the time, but now I abhor them" (225). His acknowledgment of an affect of abhorrence introduces a dimension of physicality that cannot simply be reduced to the sensuality and immediacy the novel, on Lukács's account, desires (Bewes, *Event of Postcolonial Shame* 86–87), and that is much closer to the twitchings of creatural life.[15]

In its last few scenes, *Slow Man* offers us a glimpse of a mode of attentiveness that is adequate to creatural life. In a somewhat dreamlike scene, Paul and Elizabeth find themselves as guests in the house of Marijana's family. The family surprises Paul with a recumbent bicycle— a bike that Paul "dislikes [...] instinctively, as he dislikes prostheses, as he dislikes all fakes" (255). Yet this dislike does not seem to matter anymore, as he is now willing to simply go through the motions. Paul has fully accepted his exposure to the gaze of his fellow creatures: "He can feel a blush creeping over him, a blush of shame, starting at his ears and creeping forward over his face. He has no wish to stop it" (254). The image of a "blush creeping" underlines that this response is not the expression of a conscious emotion, but rather the involuntary effect of his exposure to the gaze of others. Gone, also, is the nostalgia for the novelistic capacity to neutralize the tensions between the tragic and the comic: "he should give up his solemn air and become what he rightly is, a figure of fun [...]" (256).

In the conversation with Elizabeth that concludes the novel, Paul seems to finally have accepted a distinction that Elizabeth has time and again reminded him of: the difference between care and love. For Elizabeth, "[c]are is not love. Care is a service that any nurse worth her salt can provide, as long as we don't ask her for more" (154). Paul's relation to Marijana is troubled by his insistent demand "for more," and by the difficulty he has in accepting that "caring should not be assumed to have anything to do with the heart" (165). In his relation to Marijana, Paul confuses the novelistic realm of desire with the properly post-novelistic domain of care; he consistently makes a category mistake, sending her "words of love from an object of mere nursing, mere care" (172). At the end of the novel, Elizabeth surprisingly abandons the firm distinction on which she has insisted when she all at once wants "[l]oving care" (261). Paul's response to her question whether they have "found love at last" is answered by an acknowledgment of loss and is located in a situation of relentless fleshy exposure:

> Half an hour ago he was with Marijana. But Marijana is behind them now, and he is left with Elizabeth Costello. He puts on his glasses again, turns, takes a good look at her. In the clear late-afternoon light he can see every detail, every hair, every vein. He examines her, then he examines his heart. "No," he says at last, "this is not love. This is something else. Something less." (263)

The confrontation with Elizabeth's flesh makes Paul acknowledge that love will henceforth be a thing of the past, that it is "behind them now," and accept a diminished mode of attentiveness ("something less") as the proper attitude toward fellow creatures.

In the reconciliation scene with Marijana's family that immediately precedes this passage, Paul also confesses that he has "misjudged and wronged" her son, Drago (257). Having earlier allowed Drago to stay in his office, Paul has discovered that Drago has stolen one of the valuable nineteenth-century photographs that he collects. *Slow Man* presents photography as a medium whose claims to authenticity have become somewhat antiquated in the age of digital reproduction; in this way, these reflections on photography are also a thinly veiled exploration of the fate of the novel form in the twenty-first century. Paul has a hard time convincing Marijana of the seriousness of the offense: Drago has duly replaced the "original" picture with a copy, and the difference between an original copy and a fake copy seems insubstantial when dealing with a medium to which reproduction is endemic, and in which the notion of "the original" is specious at best; for Paul, it is only "the added thickness that first gives the forgery away" (218). Paul has to accept that the medium of photography is no longer what it used to be, and that questions of "being first" are now "of no account" (212)—in the same way that the completeness of epic life is exposed as a mere illusion once the novelistic desire to return to it has been abandoned. Seeing the results of Drago's tinkering with the picture, Paul wryly notes that "[h]e could never have achieved so convincing a montage in an old-fashioned darkroom" (218).

Earlier in the novel, we have learned that Paul's "first real job was as a darkroom technician"; he then marveled at the camera's "power of taking in light and turning it into substance," at the moment when "the ghostly image emerged beneath the surface of the liquid, as veins of darkness on the paper began to knit together and grow visible" (65). Whereas this "metaphysical" work of transformation then seemed like the very "day of creation," photography has now entered an age in which only the "added thickness" of the paper vouches for the tenuous distinction between real and fake copies. This imagery suggests that, while photography— and the novel—used to have the power to produce something substantial, they nowadays merely produce a "thickness," a fleshy mass that is not shaped by the social and cultural forms that used to guide their operation. If we read this as an oblique comment on the residual powers of fiction, this diminished mode adequately captures the central concern of Coetzee's late fiction: the exploration of creatural life, and of the kind of attentiveness that is adequate to it, after the disintegration of the cultural form that used to give that life a human shape.

Somewhere in the middle of the novel, Elizabeth takes stock of Paul's situation, noting that he has managed to alienate Marijana, her husband, Drago, and Elizabeth herself. She likens the situation to that of "[f]our people in four corners, moping, like tramps in Beckett" (141). This is a clear reminder that the dejection and inaction that mark Paul's life throughout most of the novel have clear affinities to Beckett's universe. In his book *J.M. Coetzee and the Novel*, Patrick Hayes has not only shown how the whole of Coetzee's project is deeply indebted to Beckett's work, but has also accurately pinpointed Coetzee's difference from Beckett. For Hayes, Coetzee refuses the solipsism and sterility that Beckett's writing at times fails to resist, and instead opts for an outright confrontation with embodied alterity. Hayes writes that Coetzee has had "the 'imaginative courage' to move [Beckett's approach] beyond solipsism, and reinterpret it in terms of the dynamics of embodied life: the life that has to confront not only the otherness of the self, but the otherness of the beings that one lives alongside" (36). This trajectory from utter dejection to a recognition of co-creatureliness is apparent in the development of *Slow Man*. This concern with a form of matter that emerges when social textures fail to contain it is also apparent in one of the novel's more enigmatic statements: Paul's question why we admire "the fragmentary image of a woman," and not "the image of a fragmentary body, no matter how neatly sewn up the stumps" (59). This hints at a distinction between, on the one hand, a poetics that revels in fragmentation and experimentation but that keeps the desire for bodily wholeness in place (and it is hard not to think of Lukács's account of the relation between novel and epic here), and, on the other, a more chaste and concrete mode of writing attending to the twitchings and excitations of creatural life that can no longer be composed in an integrated and desirable body. The latter option is not the worst description of Coetzee's exploration of the afterlife of the novel—in *Slow Man* and, as I will go on to demonstrate, also in *Diary of a Bad Year*.

Exposure time: *Diary of a Bad Year*

Before readers can begin to engage with the themes and developments of *Diary of a Bad Year*, they first have to come to terms with its idiosyncratic page layout. This layout immediately conveys Coetzee's ambition to interrogate the habits of feeling and thinking that the novel form has helped to inculcate (McDonald 494), and it challenges readers to find a strategy to navigate the relations between, on the one hand, the (non-narrative) short essays at the top of every page, and the (very schematic) story rendered in the middle and bottom parts on the other. While it may be tempting to understand the exceedingly thin story of the triangular relation between JC, Anya, and her partner, Alan, as a deflationary reminder of the contingency of "the public performance of reason" confidently on display in the top sections (Attwell, "Mastering" 214), there are at least two reasons to resist such a reading. First, seeing the private story as a corrective to the pretensions of high-sounding reason reflects a much less subtle account of the relations between the personal and the ideational than the one embodied in Coetzee's other fictions, or indeed his essayistic work; and second, such a reading misleadingly suggests that the minimal narrative merely complements the essayistic sections, while it is in fact the part of the book that provides a sense of continuity and temporal extension that is missing from the seemingly unordered string of essays. Indeed, even in as ostensibly hybrid a literary construction as *Diary*, the narrative sections are inevitably dominant in the reader's temporal encounter with the text (Abbott 188). The narrative parts choreograph the rhythms and fluctuations of readers' engagement with the book, while the essays are "self-contained and without [...] any particular temporal locations on the narrative time-line" (190). If it is tempting to read the personal story as an antidote to the pretensions of disembodied reason, it is more accurate to invert the relation between the two parts of the novel and to see the short essays as reminders of the persistent inclination to occasionally transcend mundane life.

H. Porter Abbott has argued that reading *Diary* provides a "page-by-page experience of cognitive re-orientation" that makes readers feel the difference between "being in time" and "being out of time" (192). Of course, the relation between "being in time" and "being out of time" is not symmetrical: the intermittent escapes out of time provided by the essays are particularly charged and condensed moments *within* the temporal experience of reading the novel. JC confronts the question of his essays' temporal status when he ponders the possible German translations for what he calls his "little excursions."[16] The publisher is wavering between *Meinungen* or *Ansichten*; the former are "opinions [...] but opinions subject to fluctuations of mood"; so "[t]he *Meinungen* I held yesterday are not necessarily the *Meinungen* I hold today. *Ansichten*, by contrast, are firmer, more thought out" (127–29). The status of the short essays oscillates between (mostly) being subjected to and (occasionally) escaping from the moods and fluctuations of life; even if they intermittently manage to crystallize as self-contained emanations of reason, they are embedded in a narrative flow that time and again ties them back to the rhythms of creatural life. As I already showed when I traced the affinities between creatural life and allegory, such fitful interruptions are constitutive of creatural life, which is shot through by fluctuations, drives, and intensities that are animated by the intermittent temptation of a life outside of time and that are no longer organized by social and cultural forms that mitigate life's exposure to these forces. *Diary*'s layout, in other words, figures this experience of life and transforms the novel into a zone where creatural life can be observed. The tensions between the short essays and the two interwoven narrative flows produce a scene of exposure, in which life is caught between the comforts of novelistic convention and the temptation of a definitive escape from life into death or the afterlife (not coincidentally two of the essays' main topics).

Diary, like *Slow Man*, inhabits the uncharted territory left in the wake of the novel—a space that would not exist without the modern history of the form, but that is now marked by the almost total subtraction of everything that used to characterize that form. As in *Slow Man*, we hardly find psychological depth, significant setting, characters we can empathize with, or a compelling plot; the relations that exist between people in the novel "are tenuous and formed on the basis of whim rather than necessity" (Harvey 28). David Attwell has noted that there "is something slightly perfunctory" about "the narrative itself in which the opinions are embedded," "as if the text were assuming that the assertion of the presence of fictionality were enough to give one the experience of fiction" ("Mastering" 218). This assertion of fictionality signals that the reader is indeed entering the space that used to be furnished by novelistic moves and conventions, but that has now been abandoned together with the forms of subjectivity and agency that used to populate that space. Instead, the narrative stages an aging (ex-)novelist exposed to the gaze of the attractive young woman he engages, of her partner, and also of the readers, who, unlike JC himself, are given access to the thoughts of these other characters, and thus know that he is perceived as an embarrassing and hopelessly naive relic of the past. Here, the time-worn empathy-enhancing novelistic practice of granting the reader access to the thoughts of the characters is turned against the novel's protagonist.

This condition of exposure is reflected in some of the essays' major themes: aging, the obsolescence of cultural forms, death, and the afterlife. These themes are connected by a similar peculiar temporality: they all deal with forms—genres, bodies, lives, moral templates—that have, in a sense, survived themselves: they linger on after the institutions and conditions that sustained them have disappeared, and they are paradoxically animated by this condition of weakened survival. This temporality is voiced most explicitly at the center of the book, right before its second part, at the moment when the essays become more personal. Here we find the only short essay that does not have to share the page with the diaries of JC or Anya. This formal decision reflects the fact that the essay, entitled "On the Afterlife," deals with the last gasps of the illusion of a sovereign self—the illusion whose afterlife *Diary* aims to track. The essay wonders at the surprising persistence of "the notion of an individual afterlife" even in "intellectually respectable versions of Christianity." The notion that the soul "continues to exist as itself after the body dies" reveals, according to JC, "an incapacity to think of a world from which the thinker is absent" (153–54). Such a denegation of death is one possible response to the loss of seemingly self-evident notions of individuality and existential meaning, and one that Coetzee's late novels categorically dismiss: against the wishful perpetuation of a self-reliant self, they outline new and diminished forms of life that respond to the realities of creatureliness rather than to the demands of outmoded fictions of individuality. Coetzee's late fictions imagine survival differently. As Chris Danta has suggested, they are less interested in the afterlife than in "afterdeath" ("Melancholy Ape" 129): the aftermath of a loss that has shattered the very terms in which we would normally seek to articulate our response to loss, and that forces us to make do with weaker, more minimal, and improvised forms of coping.

The end of this short essay notes what abandoning the notion of an individual afterlife entails: "The persistence of the soul in an unrecognizable form, unknown to itself, without memory, without identity, is another question entirely" (154). The novel's second half immediately begins to answer this question in a section entitled "A Dream," which imagines the interval between death and the total disappearance of life, but does so without indulging in the illusion of continued individuality. In the interval between his death and his leaving the world, the dreamer is taken care of by "a woman, one of the living," who does her best "to soften the impact of death" (157). This section imagines the interval as the total erasure of sovereignty, which leaves the remainder of the self totally exposed and dependent on the care of others: "at the moment of death we lose all power to elect our companions. We are whirled away to our allotted fate; by whose side we get to pass eternity is not for us to decide" (159). Clearly, this liminal interval resembles nothing so much as the very space between the traditional novel and the total disappearance of fiction to which Coetzee's late characters are abandoned.

As in the section "On the Afterlife," the layout of the page that carries "A Dream" underwrites the message it contains (and such correspondences are rare enough in *Diary*): the awareness of radical exposure to others is brought home by the elision of the text between the two bars in the middle of the page, where we expect to read JC's voice. In the ten pages that follow, Anya's voice at the bottom of the page is not counterpointed by JC's diary, the space for which remains unoccupied. This means that the development of the reader's image of JC is totally dependent on Anya's account. Anya tells the story of how she and her partner are invited to JC's flat to celebrate his finishing the manuscript;

while they expect "a crowd," the whole of "literary Sydney," they discover that they are the only guests for what turns out to be a rather dismal and awkward affair (157–67). This extremely embarrassing passage exposes JC as a pitiful, sad old man in need of the care that, as the dream recounted at the top of the page suggests, is the unavoidable fate of those who find themselves in the interval of exposure. The novel's page layout and its bipartite division—one part is entitled "Strong Opinions," the other "Second Diary"—reflect the attempt, announced in the essays at the top of the page, to break with the notion of an individual afterlife and to imagine a weaker yet more responsive and companionable form of life. The short essays in the novel's second half turn to more personal reflections in response to Anya's suggestion that JC should address less lofty themes; and just as the layout increasingly makes room for Anya's perspective, JC begins to acknowledge his radical dependence on creatural care after the demise of the illusion of a sovereign self. By making room for such a more attentive attitude, the novel's second half functions as the interval after sovereignty and before the end in which creatural dependence and proximity can assert themselves.

Other sections of the novel explicitly connect this interval to the afterlife of the contemporary novel, and of cultural forms more generally. In a long section "On Music," JC notes that so-called "classical music" is today "no longer cultural currency." According to a logic that echoes Hegel's dictum that art has become a thing of the past, this is taken to mean that music no longer maintains a significant relation to the affective life of the culture in which it exists. The decay of music, that is, also testifies to an affective shift:

> Music expresses feeling [...] gives shape and habitation to feeling, not in space but in time. To the extent that music has a history that is more than a history of its formal evolution, our feelings must have a history too. Perhaps certain qualities of feeling that found expression in music in the past [...] have become so remote that we can no longer inhabit them as feelings. (130)

Classical music has lost its claim on contemporary culture as the feelings that informed that music and that it helped circulate no longer resonate with the moods and dispositions that sustain life today. Still, the fact that "[t]he animating principles of that music are dead and cannot be revived" (134) does not mean that it has become totally powerless: "there are some of us around to whom the inner life of nineteenth-century man is not quite dead, not yet" (130). The phrase "not quite dead, not yet" accurately captures the mode of persistence that pertains in the interval between fully inhabited forms of life and the complete erasure of life—the interval that classical music, the novel, and Coetzee's late characters, unable to disappear completely and surrender to the comforts of lifelessness, all inhabit.

Diary explicitly extends this temporality, in which cultural forms suffer their afterlives rather than just disappear, to the novel genre. Several of the essays deal with Tolstoy and Dostoevsky, and several more can be read as thinly veiled comments by Coetzee on his own late fiction. JC remarks that parts of Dostoevsky's *The Brothers Karamazov* can still bring him to tears (223), while recent fiction can no longer "truly touch" him; that "deep touch" is only conveyed by the classics, by works that can no longer be produced in the post-novelistic present (189), and whose paradoxical power somehow *depends* on their obsolescence. In the same essay, JC—who is here probably closer to Coetzee than anywhere else in the book—notes that he is discovering that he himself is not, in fact, a real novelist, and that this realization is becoming increasingly inescapable late in his life: in response to critics who write that "[a]t heart he is not a novelist after all," he begins to wonder "whether they are not right—whether, all the time [he] thought [he] was going about in disguise, [he] was in fact naked" (191). This nakedness, which used to be covered by novelistic conventions, is revealed for what it always already was when older writers dispense with the effort of furnishing a credible fictional world, and when their "prose becomes thinner, their treatment of character and action more schematic" (193). "Of late," he writes, "sketching stories seems to have become a substitute for writing them" (185).

So how do we relate this sketch of JC's and Coetzee's late fiction to the claim for the particular potency of novels that have survived from the times when novels still shaped the affective life of a culture? Novels that truly engaged the heart of a culture are a thing of the past, yet they somehow "still retain [their] power to move us" (135), even if that paradoxical power can no longer be transferred to contemporary fiction. What contemporary novels—such as *Slow Man* or *Diary*—can do is stage and extend the afterlife of the novel form, and prolong the aftermath of the time when it still mattered; instead of dispensing with the novel form altogether, or of writing novels as if its cultural and social currency had not diminished, Coetzee's late novels assert the persistence of a zone in which the former powers of the form, and of the selves and communities that it used to imagine, can be recalled and confronted.

Even if the achievements of a Tolstoy and a Dostoevsky cannot be repeated, the novel today can consciously decide to inhabit their after-life and enlist them as part of its imagining of a more minimal, more mournful form of responsiveness that is attuned to the realities of crea-tural life. As Ankhi Mukherjee has noted, Coetzee "write[s] innovative metafictions of the loss of the novel's ability to represent" (535), and these fictions stage that breakdown in order to furnish the evacuated space with new forms of care and attentiveness that can respond to the forms of life surfacing amid the form's ruins. Coetzee opens the decrepit house of fiction to what *Diary* calls "the mute appeal of the unwanted," of "ugly pieces of furniture that have stubbornly stayed alive" (188).

Ultimately, the slight development of the novel recalls the move-ment that we could also observe in *Slow Man*: JC's life develops his exposure to manipulation and to the trials of old age into an increas-ingly caring proximity to others. The second part of the novel offers more personal and intimate reflections, whose content and tone no longer exist in tension with the personal narrative on the same pages, but instead underscore and reinforce the narrative's affective claims. Already after 25 pages, JC concedes the bottom part of the page to the voice of Anya, while he himself ascends to the middle part, which is later given over to a letter from Anya to JC, at which point JC's voice is completely silent (191). Near the end of the book, we find brief sec-tions: "On the Birds of the Air" and "On Compassion." In the former, JC imagines the life of a magpie that he observes in "a public park for two-legged animals," and that he always accords "the full respect, the full attention he demands" (209). The latter section is devoted to one of his neighbors, Mrs Saunders, who provides water for little frogs during a heatwave. This inspires JC's observation that human beings are part of the same "ecological process" that connects the frogs and the heatwave, and that "our compassion for the wee beasties" is a crucial element of this ecology (211). These two scenes are subtly brought together in the imagining of creatural care on which the novel ends. In the last sec-tion of Anya's story, she tells the reader about how she has contacted Mrs Saunders and asked her to phone her in case "something happens to the Señor" so she can come down, not in order to help—"I am not a nurse," she notes (222)—but because she doesn't "like to think of him all alone, facing, you know, the end" (222). She wants to do that, she tells us, because she "was always a little more" than a neighbor to him, being "the one he was in love with, in his old man's way." As for this "old man's way," she imagines him "crooning his love song up the lift shaft. Him and the magpie" (225).

Anya's promise of care is intricately connected to the two earlier scenes of creatural concern. It suggests one strategy for coping with the undead subject's exposure to the powers and intensities of creatural life. Yet, like the scene at the end of *Slow Man* in which Paul is reconciled with the Jokić family, Anya's concluding musings are strangely disconnected from the rest of the narrative; lacking clear causal connections to the rest of the story, they display the kind of wish fulfillment normally only encountered in dreams. The suggestion that we are indeed dealing with a dream or a projected wish fulfillment is obviously strengthened by the fact that the scene ends with an imagined apostrophe of a dying JC (226–27), and by the fact that the novel's second part, as we saw, opened with a dream about a young woman who takes care of JC in the interval in which he "had died but had not left the world yet" (157). That the mode of care that the novel formulates is hedged by such dissociation and derealization is entirely appropriate in a literary project situating itself in the wake of a form that used to solidify the connections between subjects, and between subjects and their social worlds. It will be left to Teju Cole's *Open City*, the novel I discuss in my next chapter, to sustain the dissociation that marks Coetzee's endings from the beginning to the end of the narrative. If *Remainder* and *Reality Hunger* discovered the awkward persistence of the novel beyond its end, and if *Slow Man* and *Diary* populated this aftermath with abandoned creatures, *Open City*'s restless mobility tests whether this undomesticated life can be enlisted for the cultivation of a cosmopolitan ethos.

3
Cosmopolitan Dissociation
(Teju Cole)

> *5—The White Savior Industrial Complex is not about justice. It is about having a big emotional experience that validates privilege.*
>
> —@tejucole

In the first two chapters of this book, I have traced the ways in which works by Tom McCarthy, Lars Iyer, David Shields, and J.M. Coetzee dramatize the end of the novel in order to probe the aftermath of the forms of agency and subjectivity that they, together with a long theoretical and critical tradition, associate with that form. Together, these texts exemplify the paradoxical productivity of the deliberate dismantling of the novel form for the exploration of non-emotional affects and forms of life that can no longer be characterized as simply modern or human. While it may be tempting to assume that the significant echoes and overlaps between these writers' projects validate the central thesis of my book, we must note that they also point to the risk of a disabling insularity. Indeed, not only are the authors I have discussed so far all white, metropolitan, and male, they are all (or have been) university professors. Nor are their intellectual backgrounds very different: all are deeply influenced by poststructuralism and/or French theory, which are not coincidentally domains in which the critique of modern subjectivity has been a primary concern for decades.

In order to argue, then, that the end of the novel is not merely a provincial issue, the rest of *Contemporary Literature and the End of the Novel* highlights decidedly more worldly contexts. After all, if the death of the novel is a routine reference point in the theoretical currents that Coetzee, McCarthy, and others tap into, a more encompassing assessment of contemporary literary culture cannot miss the persistent vitality of the novel form in, most notably, discussions of cosmopolitanism, transnationalism, and human rights discourses. In interrogations of the complexities and affordances of intercultural relatedness and international justice, the novel form continues to be solicited for its critical and/or connective potential. It is my contention in the rest of this book that a number of contemporary fictions have attempted to stage the limits of the conceptions of the novel that underlie such solicitations in order to intuit different forms of affect and life. Ultimately, these fictions argue, cosmopolitan and transnational mobilizations of the novel tend to simply perpetuate the form's traditional investments in the human and the individual. In my next chapter, I show how novels by Dana Spiotta and Hari Kunzru sidestep the expectation that post-9/11 fictions adopt a less domestic and more global perspective in order to renegotiate the very powers of fiction to access the world. In James Meek's *We Are Now Beginning Our Descent*, which I discuss in my coda, the irruption of geological time scales explodes fantasies of intercultural connectedness. I begin my exploration of more worldly ends of the novel in this chapter by looking at Teju Cole's debut novel *Open City* (2011). While *Open City* seems to invite celebration as a commendable cosmopolitan novel, it ends up staging a more sinister form of life that extant cosmopolitan discourses cannot contain, and that brings it in line with the works discussed in my first two chapters.

Flights of memory

If the many accolades it has received are any indication, Teju Cole's *Open City* managed to hit a nerve in contemporary literature culture.[1] *Open City* is the first novel that Cole, a Nigerian-American writer, photographer, and historian, published outside of Africa, and it stands out for its rather grandiose literary ambitions. The novel rigorously ties itself to the perspective of Julius, a young psychiatrist with Nigerian and German roots. It combines an investment in cultural difference with a markedly melancholic tenor that is inescapably reminiscent of the work of W.G. Sebald, one of Cole's avowed influences. And if this were not enough, the novel unapologetically inhabits a high-cultural frame of reference—there are discussions of Jan Van Eyck, Paul Claudel, Diego Velázquez, Gustav Mahler, and many others. These multiple concerns are strung together by the novel's two main organizing devices: first, Julius's compulsive habit of walking the streets and traveling the public transport systems of New York and Brussels, which generates a number of intense aesthetic experiences as well as a series of encounters with a whole catalogue of storytellers; and second, Julius's memories, which connect the narrative present and the stories of Julius's interlocutors to his and his family's Nigerian and German pasts. The critical reception of the book has unfailingly focused on the peculiar narrative perspective that ties the novel's disparate stories and concerns together. In the eyes of many critics, Julius's wanderings and ruminations constitute a perspective that is both intimate and detached, engaged as well as estranged. Even if Julius is sometimes strangely uninvolved in the stories and experiences he collects, critics underline that this distantiation yields an epistemic advantage; it produces, as James Wood writes in a review in the *New Yorker*, "a productive alienation"; because Julius enjoys "a cosmopolite's detachment from his American experience" (Messud), the novel can approach multifarious realities, stories, and memories in a way that allows multiple resonances and interconnections to emerge.

Open City's successful mix of metropolitanism, aestheticism, and intercultural curiosity clearly connects it to a cosmopolitan tradition, and it is no surprise that it is customarily read as an exemplary cosmopolitan performance. From its title onwards, *Open City* seems to embody the cosmopolitan conviction that the cultivation of curiosity and attentiveness is an appropriate tool for fostering connections beyond ethnic, cultural, or national borders. In this respect also, it appears as a very timely achievement indeed: the study of literature in the last two decades has increasingly invoked "cosmopolitanism" as a label for literature's—and, by implication, literary studies'—claims to continued relevance in a globalized world. Julius's perspective, simultaneously alienated and engaged, can be recognized as an example of the signature cosmopolitan dynamic of "(re)attachment, multiple attachment, or attachment at a distance" (Robbins, "Actually Existing" 3). *Open City* can easily be read as a magisterial display of literature's enabling role in fostering cosmopolitan feeling and understanding.

This investment in a "productive alienation" resonates in another notion that recurs throughout the novel's reception: the criticism of the book time and again identifies Julius as an early twenty-first-century update of the figure of the *flâneur* (Foden, Messud, Wood). Famously theorized by Charles Baudelaire and Walter Benjamin, the *flâneur* has become "a key figure in the critical literature of modernity and urbanization" (Wilson 93). The nineteenth-century *flâneur* was a leisurely wanderer who was acutely attentive to the spectacle provided by the processes of commodification and urbanization that surrounded him.

An aesthete who uniquely manages to engage with the realities of the modern city without fully surrendering to them, the *flâneur* can be— and has been—condemned as a fatally bourgeois figure attempting to reprivatize public space (Buck-Morss). Still, he emerges from Baudelaire's and Benjamin's work as a dialectical figure "who presented himself as open to everything but who actually saved himself from the chaos of randomness through his pretensions to epistemological control" (Rabinovitz 7). In this way, the *flâneur* anticipates a cosmopolitan ethos that thrives on intercultural curiosity and the virtues of the aesthetic.

In this chapter, I argue that *Open City* interrogates rather than celebrates such a literary cosmopolitanism. Even if the novel is thoroughly occupied with the question as to how aesthetic form can contribute to the furthering of cosmopolitan understanding, it ends up as a catalogue of failed attempts to forge intercultural connections by artistic means. The novel strings together numerous accounts of human rights abuses and testimonies of culturally very diverse experiences, yet these fail to register in even a minimally transformative way in the narrator's fatefully dissociated mind. When read carefully, we can see that Julius's posture as a cosmopolitan *flâneur* is shadowed by the contours of a more sinister, and mostly forgotten, nineteenth-century figure of restless mobility: the *fugueur*. *Fugueurs* emerged in urban areas in France at the end of the nineteenth century; they were "mad travelers" who unaccountably walked away from their lives and, when found, were unable to remember what had happened on these trips, let alone what had motivated them to set out on them in the first place. Ian Hacking, who has devoted a monograph to the late nineteenth-century fugue epidemic, notes that fugues need to be understood as a parody of the mass tourism that was then emerging (48), and even as the pathological flip side of the *flâneur* (27–28).

Open City subtly evokes this dark counterpart of the cosmopolitan *flâneur* in order to indicate the limits of the cosmopolitan imagination, and to remind contemporary novel criticism of the need to supplement current discourses of cosmopolitanism with other, less tractable forms of ethical and political engagement. The novel carefully constructs a panorama of cultural and historical difference, yet filters this through a perspective that remains strangely unaffected by it; it collects all the gestures that define the cosmopolitan novel, only to show that they do not add up to a significant ethical or political achievement. If McCarthy's and Coetzee's novels, as we have seen, operate through a movement of *subtraction*, Cole's novel displays a dynamic of *disarticulation*; instead of removing all novelistic elements, it collects them without assembling them into a functioning novel world. *Open City* dramatizes the end of the novel by locating its cosmopolitan commitment in a future that is beyond the reach of the formal features through which the cosmopolitan imagination is expected to materialize. Instead, these formal features point to their own insufficiency. *Open City* responds to—and agrees with—the prevalent critique that cosmopolitanism is unable to effect change beyond the domain of culture by highlighting how another much-criticized aspect of literary cosmopolitanism—its reliance on a rarified repertoire of aesthetic postures, gestures, and styles—paradoxically provides it with the tools that allow it to make the "culturalist" limitations of literary cosmopolitanism visible. Instead of crediting literature's ability to create "sympathy and empathy through identification" (Fojas 21), *Open City* insistently denies its readers the illusion that imaginative transports can stand in for real global change. It forcefully reminds its readers that empathy and intercultural understanding *alone* cannot achieve the changes to which cosmopolitanism is committed, and that they can only point readers to the world outside— to a global landscape riven by injustice and inequality. Ultimately, *Open City* suggests that approaching these realities requires affects and scales that strain the limits of the human, as well as those of the novel form.

/

Cosmopolitanism, human rights, and the novel: Kant to the present

In the past two decades, the terms "cosmopolitan" and "cosmopolitanism" have become a staple of defenses of literature in an age when its virtues seem more contentious than ever.[2] In contrast to the term "international," cosmopolitanism signifies a commitment to a community beyond rather than between nation states (Spencer 6); compared to "multiculturalism," it underlines the values of reciprocal translatability and common norms (Robbins, "Actually Existing" 12–13); and unlike discourses of empire and globalization, it is increasingly rooted in a commitment to human rights (Benhabib 16–17). "Cosmopolitanism," in other words, is an intrinsically normative term, and its frequent mobilization in literary criticism by itself signals a desire to argue for the relevance of literature. Yet the strategic linkage of the literary and the cosmopolitan does more than that: it situates contemporary literary studies in an intellectual tradition that has always depended on the contribution of culture to supplement its mainly political, philosophical, and legal ambitions.

Already in the work of Immanuel Kant, which is routinely assumed to have inaugurated modern cosmopolitanism, culture in general and the novel genre in particular are assigned a crucial role in promoting a sense of belonging to humanity (Juengel 62, Siskind 337). While world trade, for Kant, serves as the indispensable historical basis of cosmopolitanism, the latter is only achieved when the conceptual universality of reason is actualized in concrete cosmopolitan institutions (Siskind 336). As this transition from the fact of global connectedness to desirable economic, legal, and political institutions that embrace the whole of humanity is far from self-evident, it requires the cultivation of a particular ethos, of "a sense of belonging to humanity" (Cheah, *Inhuman Conditions* 22). Already in Kant, the ultimately political and philosophical ambitions of cosmopolitan discourse are wedded to a particularly elevated conception of the role of culture in promoting such a sense of belonging. And culture, more often than not, means the novel: in an offhand suggestion near the end of his essay on the "Idea for a Universal History with a Cosmopolitan Purpose," Kant notes that "only a *novel*"—like cosmopolitanism, an eighteenth-century invention—can "narrate a *history* according to an idea of how the course of the world would have to progress" toward a more cosmopolitan dispensation (Kant 14–15). Because novels, unlike philosophy, are not tied to the universal but can artfully articulate the particular and the general, they are an indispensable companion in the worldly realization of cosmopolitanism, as they have the power to perform "the imaginative work of tracing the natural sociality of the coming cosmopolitanism" (Juengel 62). Even if *conceptualizing* the process of globalization is the proper province of the philosopher, "the challenge of *imagining* the world as a reconciled bourgeois totality of freedom could fall on the novel" (Siskind 337). Novels can make "the process of globalization available so that reading audiences can work through the transformations they are experiencing at home" (337).[3]

In a very comparable way, the novel genre has assisted the development of human rights discourse since the eighteenth century. Allowing readers to identify with the suffering of people whose lives were remote from theirs, eighteenth-century novels served as training grounds for sensibilities that facilitated the spread of the idea of universal human rights (Hunt 35–69); novels were a crucial aide in helping cosmopolitan attitudes and human rights gain acceptance in the larger culture (Slaughter 25). When contemporary criticism flaunts literature's cosmopolitan credentials, then, it does not just state that literature circulates in transcultural networks—for this, notions such as "global literature" and "world literature" will do; more than that, it invokes literature's prestigious pedigree as a vital part of efforts to promote political and legal institutions beyond ethnic, cultural, and national borders.

Broadly speaking, literary cosmopolitanism has given rise to two (closely related) critiques: first, that it privileges cultural over material change, and begs the question of how the former can meaningfully shape the latter; and second, that it is not merely *culturalist*, but outright *aestheticist* in its preference for a rarified set of (far from universal) styles and attitudes. Kant's invocation of the novel already prefigures the slippage from universalism to cultural pluralism that makes possible these critiques. While Kant envisions a community that embraces the whole of humanity and that is cast as the actualization of the universality of reason, its reliance on a genre that is distinguished by its ability to embody concrete lived experience announces an oscillation in cosmopolitan discourse between, on the one hand, a principled universalism, and, on the other, an awareness that the implementation of supranational solidarity might more realistically proceed by fostering multiple attachments rather than principled detachment.[4] To put this differently, Kant makes it possible to see that the novel can promote a cosmopolitan ethos in two (not mutually exclusive) ways: by "imagining the world as one community [and] capturing it inside the vision of a single narrative" (Schoene, *"Tour du Monde"* 43),[5] or, more modestly and much more commonly, by inviting readers to confront different modes of life that make them aware of the contingency of their own ways of life. In the latter scenario, cosmopolitanism is no longer necessarily oriented toward humanity as a whole, but is rather defined by a more minimal willingness to recognize pluralism and diversity, which does not necessarily require the globalized subject to abandon its own locality. In Kwane Appiah's "rooted" cosmopolitanism, which has received a lot of airplay in literary criticism, for instance, novels do not so much convey "a commonly understood common nature," but they rather extend "an invitation to respond in imagination to narratively constructed situations" (Appiah 257). This position can serve as a strong legitimation for disciplines such as postcolonial studies, world literature, and comparative literature, and it is not surprising that Domna Stanton mobilizes it in her 2005 address as President of the Modern Language Association, entitled "On Rooted Cosmopolitanism." For Stanton, the profession of literature "explemf[ies] and promote[s] a cosmopolitan education"; it initiates "an encounter with people who are markedly different [...] a complex encounter made in a sympathetic effort to see the world as they see it and, as a consequence, to denaturalize our own views" (629).[6]

This dedication to intercultural connectivity invites the criticism that cosmopolitanism is all too *culturalist*, and that an excessive focus on the virtues of literature has unmoored literary cosmopolitanism from the broader ambition to effect change in the global economic, political, and legal spheres. From this perspective, self-congratulatory celebrations of literature's power to connect readers to "the customs, culture, and beliefs of places other than their own" (D. Stanton 629) substitute cultural and aesthetic pseudo-solutions for worldly engagement. Conceived as goals in themselves, the intercultural encounters that literature affords can easily be dismissed as forms of intellectual tourism. Novels then come to serve as mere repositories of the exotic that may satisfy sophisticated metropolitan tastes, but that leave the real power divisions and inequalities that inflect the experiences of global subjects unaddressed (Huggan). Indeed, even if cosmopolitanism has increasingly engaged with a broad variety of often unprivileged transnational experiences, it has generally continued to capture these experiences in cultural terms. While it has tracked different new cosmopolitan practices, it has insufficiently located these "within the force field of uneven globalization" (Cheah, "Cosmopolitanism" 495). Timothy Brennan, one of the most trenchant critics of the culturalism besetting cosmopolitan discourses, has argued that it "falls prey to cultural fascination with new diasporic communities at the expense of questioning the market" (674). Disconnected from the material conditions and the globalized market forces affecting contemporary life, cosmopolitanism is, for Brennan, marred by a fatal irrelevance: it "is exceedingly narrow in what fascinates it, failing to link the market with imagination, and then failing to link that nexus itself to the non-Western world" (674). As I show, *Open City*'s resistance to its own aesthetic achievements can be seen as a strategy to heed this critique, and to remind readers of the insufficiency of the merely aesthetic pseudo-solutions that the novel on a superficial reading seems to invite.

Cosmopolitan discourse has recently tried to bolster its materialist claims through an increasing emphasis on the linkage to human rights issues—another eighteenth-century invention with which cosmopolitanism, and indeed the novel, share a history.[7] For Daniel Levy and Natan Sznaider, for instance, "[t]he emergence of a Human Rights Regime [...] reflects the political-cultural and institutional embodiment of the new cosmopolitanism through which global experiences and local experiences become enmeshed" ("Human Rights" 195). Still, it is far from self-evident that artistic and literary engagements with human rights abuses have more purchase on international power relations than other cosmopolitan practices. As Andreas Huyssen has noted, literary and artistic works tend to become "vacuous exercise[s]" when they fail to link up with "the political dimensions of rights discourse"

(608, 616). While they can offer a welcome corrective to the tendency of human rights discourse to slip too quickly into ahistorical abstraction, their work of offering concrete cases and of training the imagination amounts to very little if it fails to connect to real-world politics (617). When Levy and Sznaider write that "the main difference between the universalistic origins of human rights and their recent cosmopolitan manifestations is that the latter unfold on the background of a globalized imagination" ("Human Rights" 204), the problem is arguably that this globalized imagination is just that—a work of the imagination. Human rights discourse, far from anchoring cosmopolitanism in the realities of the international division of labor and the legacies of colonialism and anti-imperialism, may itself be complicit in the culturalism that literary cosmopolitanism is often charged with.

Open City participates in this turn toward human rights issues. The panorama of cultural and historical difference that the novel develops is mainly made up of scenes of violence, abuse, and exploitation, almost always tinged by a racist component. The novel recounts the American persecution of its domestic Japanese populations during World War II, the violent suppression of Native Americans by the Dutch settlers in the Americas, the suffering of Ugandan Indians under Idi Amin, the lingering legacies of slavery, the situation in contemporary Iraq, and the suffering of Germans at the hands of the Red Army after World War II. Such memorial atrocity exhibitions—another element that brings the novel into the orbit of the work of Sebald—resonate with recent calls to have cosmopolitan criticism attend to the legacies of the violence besetting colonial encounters.[8] *Open City*'s decision to string together numerous instances of human rights violations may seem to consolidate the alliance between cosmopolitanism and human rights; but again, the failure of these stories to register in any minimally transformative way in the narrator's life is a forceful reminder of the need to supplement the novel's aesthetic performance with a more materially effective program.

In order to make this point, *Open City* takes on a second line of critique routinely leveled at literary cosmopolitanism. This critique holds that cosmopolitanism is not merely *culturalist* (and to that extent anti-materialist), but also unabashedly *aestheticist*; it not only mistakes cultural solutions for worldly action, but it also privileges a rarified set of high-cultural gestures at the expense of a more inclusive approach. As we will see, *Open City* mobilizes the power of such gestures in order to make visible the critique of literary cosmopolitanism's culturalism. The most spirited defense of cosmopolitanism *as* aestheticism is Rebecca

Walkowitz's *Cosmopolitan Style*. Walkowitz argues that the concept of style, understood "as attitude, stance, posture, and consciousness" informs many literary and non-literary cosmopolitan practices. For Walkowitz, modernist writing conveys an awareness "that conditions of national and transnational affiliation depend on narrative patterns of attentiveness, relevance, perception, and recognition" (6); indeed, "there is no critical cosmopolitanism without modernist practices" (18). The critical potency of aesthetic styles and postures is not disqualified by their elite provenance, as "cultural strategies of posture have a significant role in even those cosmopolitan paradigms that involve actors who are not social elites or whose position in the world is not in all ways privileged" (17). Walkowitz's argument echoes Bruce Robbins's contention that, even if cosmopolitanism is often identified with a global elite, this does not automatically render it ineffective. Rather, it shifts the critical issue to the—properly aesthetic—task of finding "a proper tone in which this [elitism] can be acknowledged" and negotiated (Robbins, "Village" 16).

For Robbins, the novel is the "place where such matters of tone are most searchingly experimented and reflected on" (16). Even if Walkowitz and Robbins fail to answer the charge that they provide merely cultural solutions to global challenges, their generous assessment of the self-critical potential of literary style intimates *Open City*'s attempt to make the limits of a merely aesthetic cosmopolitanism visible by literary means. *Open City* experiments with a flat, nearly affectless tone in its depiction of Julius's dissociated mind. It does so *not* in order to find appropriate ways to think "about people whose lives are geographically or culturally unrelated to one's own" (Walkowitz, *Cosmopolitan Style* 79), but rather in order to signal the insufficiency of such merely imaginative exercises. Throughout, the novel is occupied with the challenge of finding an adequate medium or form. The intense evocations of aesthetic experiences test several aesthetic paradigms for this role: the portrait, the symphony, the fugue, the photograph, the cathedral, and so on. From its very first pages, it is clear that the book privileges the contrapuntal principle of composition that is commonly associated with the musical fugue form. According to this contrapuntal principle, particular elements (stories, thoughts, memories, characters, images ...) are offset by very different, even contrasting elements, thereby allowing these elements to resonate with each other, leaving the reader with a virtual web of echoes, contrasts, and connections between and across different domains. Still, the novel consistently resists the aesthetic realization of the fugue form, and the fugue will gradually reveal its second and more obscure meaning: that of a dissociative mental condition that the novel renders through its affectless tone, and that warns readers not to mistake aesthetic transport for a cosmopolitan achievement.

Fugue form and the monotony of noise

For Walkowitz, a cosmopolitan stance is defined by two "principal characteristics": "an aversion to heroic tones of appropriation and progress, and a suspicion of epistemological privilege, views from above or from the center that assume a consistent distinction between who is seeing and what is seen" (*Cosmopolitan Style* 2). Cosmopolitan connectedness requires the suspension of sovereign, self-sufficient forms of subjectivity, and aesthetic form has traditionally been seen as one way to effect such a suspension. Throughout, *Open City* engages in a self-conscious struggle to decenter the single narrative perspective to which it confines itself. From its very first pages, it links up figures of suspended agency with intimations of relatedness. The novel's opening pages tell of Julius's new habit of "aimless wandering"; this follows an earlier habit he "had fallen into" of "watching bird migrations from [his] apartment," during which he used to listen to "Internet stations from Canada, Germany, or the Netherlands" and to read books (translated from "one of the European languages"), activities which often seemingly seamlessly morph into sleep (1–4). All these exemplary observations of migratory life duly trigger Julius's comparative imagination: he wonders whether the bird watching and the wandering "are connected"; he notes "the comparison" between himself, "in [his] sparse apartment, and the radio host in his or her booth"; these "disembodied voices," in their turn, "remain connected [...] with the apparition of migrating geese"; reading aloud, he observes that he "gave voice to another's words" (1–3). The suspension of agency activates a heightened receptivity and, it seems, initiates exemplary cosmopolitan scenarios of detachment and reattachment.

With remarkable consistency, the novel codes these scenarios as aesthetic achievements. The walks, we read, serve as "a counterpoint to [...] busy days at the hospital" (1). While the latter are associated with tight regulation, perfection, and competence, the trope of the "counterpoint" suggests that the complement of the nightly walks helps to compose Julius's life into a harmonious, polyphonic whole. If this were the novel's last word about this, rather than its first page, it would readily deserve the critique that it traffics in aesthetic pseudo-solutions that distract the reader from sociopolitical divisions. Yet the novel immediately challenges this harmonious suspension as it describes the interaction of the radio and Julius's reading voice as a "sonic fugue" composed of a "voice mingling with the murmur" of the radio; this lends his evenings a fateful "monotony"—a word that here acquires its full acoustic sense (3–4). In a deflationary movement that sets the tone for the rest of the novel, the harmonious composition that promises cosmopolitan connectedness turns out to be indistinguishable from a mere monotone that dissolves all difference.

The walks Julius takes not only serve as a "counterpoint" to his working life, but also as an attempt to "break" with the monotony of his evenings at home. But instead of offering release, the street affects him as "an incessant loudness [...] as though someone had shattered the calm of a private chapel with the blare of a TV set" (6–7). At the beginning of the novel's second chapter, street noise again interrupts Julius's splendid isolation: a group of female protesters intrudes as "noises from far off, noises that were hardly audible to begin with," words that "did not resolve into meaning" (22). Initially, this sonic blur is wishfully posited as a "counterpoint" to the voice of Julius's soon-to-be-ex-girlfriend on the telephone from San Francisco (24). Yet far from forging relations, the passage shows the promise of distant attachment unraveling into total disconnection. The street noise inspires an excursus on jazz, which ends in Julius's realization that he lacks "a strong emotional connection" to it. The counterpoint between the unsignifying noise and the girlfriend's voice ends with the former's meaninglessness overtaking the latter's better intentions: while they had promised to make an effort to keep their relationship afloat, Julius ruefully notes that they "had said the words without meaning them" (24).

Already in its first two chapters, *Open City* launches the counterpoint as its privileged principle of composition, only to signal its failure to become a paradigm for distant and multiple connectivity.[9] The novel can be read as a catalogue of failed attempts to live up to the expectation of achieved polyphonic form. Instead of a cosmopolitan connectedness, the novel's main figures of transport—walking, memory, and art—at best provide experiences of shared isolation. This is how the novel's intense first sequence of telescoped experiences ends:

Aboveground I was with thousands of others in their solitude, but in the subway, standing close to strangers, jostling them and being jostled by them for space and breathing room, all of us reenacting unacknowledged traumas, the solitude intensified. (7)

This sentence accurately announces that the novel will to a large extent consist in the patient recording and acknowledging of the personal and inherited traumas of others. This is what Walkowitz, in relation to the work of Sebald, identifies as the operation of a "Horkheimian gaze": the "insistence on comparison and distinction among various acts of international violence" (*Cosmopolitan Style* 158). The distinction between the subway and street in the sentence also indicates that this effort will be actualized as what we can call, again with Walkowitz, an archeological "Benjaminian gaze": an "effort to display the acts of barbarism and exploitation that underwrite monuments of European civilization" (158). One of the novel's signature gestures consists in sudden shifts from the contemplation of a monument of civilization to the imagining of the violated life buried underneath. During a conversation about the Belgian industrialist Édouard Empain, who developed the Egyptian luxury capital of Heliopolis as well as the Paris metro, for instance, Julius's thoughts drift from those "expression[s] of optimism and progress" to "the numberless dead, in forgotten cities, necropoli, catacombs" (93–94). Walking the streets of Brussels, whose grandeur was paid for by the spoils of the Belgian exploitation of the Congo, Julius muses on how these streets were constructed over streams, and how after the reconstruction, the water, which the passage ominously sees "returning [...] in the form of rain," was covered over and "waterside houses suddenly found themselves looking out on traffic" (145–46). When walking through lower Manhattan late in the novel, Julius provides an extensive description of the history of the long-unacknowledged African Burial Ground located there; the memory evokes "the echo across centuries, of slavery in New York" (221).

The sentence above introduces a distinction between experiences "aboveground" and those "in the subway," yet it does so only to underline how immaterial the difference between them is: the former appears as the realm of untraumatized solitude, the latter as the realm where traumas are reenacted rather than acknowledged, which only intensifies the solitude that reigns aboveground.[10] There is only a difference in intensity, not in tone, and the two variations are too close to each other to be organized in a contrapuntal relation. The novel's investment in experiences of relatedness is consistently shadowed by their imminent relapse into numbed disconnection; juxtapositions of different legacies of suffering, of the personal and the collective—as when the description of the African Burial Ground morphs into Julius's memory of the burial of his father—oscillate between their status as felicitous montage and their fate as inconsequentially contiguous bits. In the novel's own terms, this amounts to the maddening indistinguishability of fugal harmony and mere noise; in terms of the novel's critique of literary cosmopolitanism, it means that the novel is no longer mobilized as a tool for aesthetic articulation, but as the site where this indistinguishability is registered, and where the insufficiency of a merely aesthetic cosmopolitanism is signaled. Cosmopolitan connection, that is, can be achieved only beyond the end of the novel.

The contiguity between the aesthetic success of a "fugue of voices" (216) and the actuality of sheer noise is reflected in the novel's texture by the absence of quotation marks. This allows the different conjured voices to dissolve into a continuous discourse in which the lack of distinctions between reported speech, free indirect speech, and interior monologue robs these voices of their dialogic, agonistic, or contrapuntal potential; at the same time, it sabotages the operation of two of the novel form's key devices (free indirect speech and interior monologue) for rendering the realities of psychic life. The decision not to use quotation marks leads to passages in which it is unclear whether we are reading the interior monologue of the narrator, his own speech, or the reported speech of one of his interlocutors.

The most notable example is a particularly demoralizing dialogue between Julius, Farouq (a North African he has met in Brussels), and the latter's friend Khalil. Khalil rehearses uninspired clichés about American foreign policy, Israel, Hamas, and so on. The conversation inevitably drifts to the topic of Al-Qaeda: "Khalil said, True, it was a terrible day, the twin towers. Terrible. What they did was very bad. But I understand why they did it. This man is an extremist, I said, you hear me Farouq?" (120). On first reading, it is unclear whether the last sentence is Julius interrupting Khalil's speech and addressing Farouq, or Khalil reporting his initial reactions on Bin Laden to Farouq at the time of the attacks. The point of the confusion—soon resolved when it becomes clear that it is indeed Julius calling Khalil an extremist—is that the difference is disconcertingly immaterial: Julius realizes they are just playing "a game" in which he "was meant to be an outraged American," and in which Khalil and Farouq pretend to think "how Americans think Arabs think" (120). Typically, the indifference and inconsequentiality of the conversation undercuts the redemptive aesthetics of the counterpoint: suddenly realizing that Farouq's face "was the very image of Robert de Niro," this comparison serves as "a meaningless visual counterpoint to whatever else was going on as we talked and drank" (121). Again, this is a far cry from the cosmopolitan mobility that *Open City* may on a superficial reading seem to deliver.

The aesthetics of the "still legible"

The novel features several meticulously crafted descriptions of Julius's aesthetic experiences. While these may seem to establish the paradigm for successful performances of the cosmopolitan imagination, it is remarkable that they never trigger cosmopolitan connections in Julius's life or mind. Visiting a record store that is about to go out of business, Julius muses that music stores should be "silent spaces," as loud music "spoiled the pleasure of thinking about other music." Yet this time Mahler's *Lied von der Erde* does allow him to "enter the strange hues of its world," "a stronger, surer mood," a "trance." This rapture is carried over to all of Julius's activities in the following days; in a quintessentially modernist valorization of the redemptive intensities of sense-perception, "[t]here was some new intensity in even the most ordinary things [...] as if the precision of the orchestral texture had been transferred to the world of visible things" (16–18). The way these pages string together an excessive mass of familiar aesthetic tropes is inevitably reminiscent of the perfunctory manner in which Khalil, in the passage I discussed just before, amasses familiar sound bites of anti-imperialist critique.

Unsurprisingly, aesthetic experience fails to generate the intercultural associations that literary cosmopolitanism claims it can provide. Julius carries this heightened experience out of the store into an aestheticized version of daily life when he notes that "[i]t simply wasn't possible to enter the music fully, not in that public place" (17). He leaves the store, takes the train, and spends the train ride fully disconnected from "the crowds" filling that train. The chapter ends with a conversation with his next-door neighbor, in which he learns that the latter's wife died five months before, a revelation that makes him realize that he "had noticed neither her absence nor the change [...] in his [neighbor's] spirit." Music, like the novel, offers no guarantees for cosmopolitan contact: "I had known nothing in the weeks when her husband mourned, nothing when I had nodded to him in greeting with headphones in my ears" (21).

In another self-undermining passage, Julius encounters the intense silence that he failed to find in the music store during a visit to the American Folk Art Museum. Contemplating the paintings of the nineteenth-century artist John Brewster, Julius is struck by the "air of hermeticism," "the feeling of quietness," "[t]he stillness of the people depicted." The pictures are "records of a silent transaction between artist and subject," and this instigates a synaesthetic spreading of silence to Brewster's signature "muted colors," and further to the "quiet and calm" of the gallery (37–38). Yet Julius learns that this experience of temporal and aural suspension is not grounded in an aesthetic achievement, but in the brute fact "that John Brewster was profoundly deaf, and the same was true of many of the children he portrayed" (37). Nor does this experience carry over into a scene of humane connection: upon leaving the museum, Julius inadvertently insults his black cab driver by not saying hello to an "African just like [him]" (41). Again, the chapter stops here; again, the novel's commitment to the aesthetic and its investment in cosmopolitan connectedness fail to add up to a viable cosmopolitan aesthetic.

Julius motivates the stand-off between himself and the taxi driver by noting that he "was in no mood for people who tried to lay claims on [him]" (40). The visit to the Folk Art Museum spins off into a closely related scene a week later, when Julius is approached by a dark-skinned young man who remembers him from the museum, explaining that he works as a guard there (53). The man's presumption that their skin color amounts to a significant connection makes Julius uneasy, and leads him to break off the conversation. The point, here as elsewhere, is emphatically not that Julius does not *want* a sense of relatedness: when he first meets the character Farouq in Brussels—who, as if to foreground the trope of global communication, runs a phone shop—he addresses him as "my brother," only to immediately check himself when he wonders "how this aggressive familiarity had struck [Farouq]" (102). The point is, rather, that the novel chronicles Julius's difficulties to manage his distances from and attractions to the lives of others, and that the aesthetic experiences that are explicitly invoked to aid this management of affective and cognitive distance turn out to be of no help. Reading the novel, then, is a protracted experience of the limitations of the cosmopolitan imagination.

This chapter also ends on a note of painful disconnection; recalling the sprawling, multicultural reality that had to make way for the World Trade Center, and tracing this conviviality back to the period before the Dutch settlement of New York, Julius notes:

> Generations rushed through the eye of the needle, and I, one of the still legible crowd, entered the subway. I wanted to find the line that connected me to my own part in these stories. Somewhere close to the water, holding tight to what he knew of life, the boy had, with a sharp clack, again gone aloft. (59)

This dense passage encrypts a reference to Julius's earlier visit to the Brewster exhibition, while it also, as we will see, announces the novel's alternative aesthetic program. The boy going aloft not only evokes the skateboarders Julius has just encountered, but also the "painting of a child holding a bird on a blue thread"—a work generally known as *Francis O. Watts with Bird*—that he contemplated in the museum (38). Julius uses the encounter of Brewster and the young Watts to elaborate on Brewster's family tree leading back to the *Mayflower* and on the "elite Federalist milieu" in which he grew up, as well as on the prominent public career Watts would go on to make as an adult. While these historical connections may seem to underwrite an ethic of cosmopolitan "hyperlinking," they are delivered in an insipid tone that also surfaces elsewhere in the novel and that is inevitably reminiscent of a Wikipedia page.[11] Still, Brewster's art is said to have the effect of "somehow" bracketing the distance separating Julius from this historical expanse, and of immortalizing the moment it captures: "for the moment of the painting, and, therefore, for all time, he is a little boy holding a bird by a blue string" (39). Art's failure to inspire a sense of correspondence in Julius is palpable when, in the passage quoted above, the lifelines that the aesthetic is supposed to weave together come apart "with a sharp clack," that is, with a sound that all by itself discredits an aesthetic, like the one Julius attributes to Brewster, premised on silence. The curious fact that the novel's figural language makes the boy (rather than the bird) fly away when the lifeline breaks further emphasizes that the aesthetic fails to play its role of keeping the boy (and Julius) attached to life.

Escaping from the museum guard's claim on him, Julius runs off to contemplate Ellis Island, the traditional gateway for immigrants into the United States, observing that it hardly serves as a significant node in African-American memory: "it had been built too late for those early Africans [...] and it had been closed too soon to mean anything to the later Africans like [the museum guard], the cabdriver, or me" (55). All they share, it seems, is their dissociation. He walks on to the site of the attacks of 9/11, and again notes how the desire for multiple associations threatens to dissolve particular stories and events into a totalizing natural history of violence: "atrocity is nothing new, not to humans, not to animals" (58). 9/11 "was not the first erasure of the site"—earlier there was, after all, the multicultural diversity that had to make way for the buildings that the 9/11 attacks erased in their turn: "The site was a palimpsest, as was all the city, written, erased, rewritten" (58–59).

In light of the critique of aesthetic cosmopolitanism that it performs, *Open City*'s main aesthetic challenge is the following: how can it do justice to the diversity it encounters without absorbing its constituents in an indistinct blur? Undoing history's violent erasures and restoring lost histories of suffering is one option, but one that has only a limited critical purchase, as the novel time and again conveys its concern that the aesthetic does not have the power to initiate significant, empathetic encounters with the diverse experiences it recounts for its readers. Instead, the passage discussed above subtly suggests a more minimal program for the novel. The figure of the city as a palimpsest where history is "written, erased, rewritten" points to a minimal practice of marking history, of preserving the past as a legible trace, rather than composing it into the raptures of aesthetic experience.

In a passage that I already quoted, Julius calls himself "one of the still legible crowd"—the observer or author who has to make or keep things legible, and also somebody who will himself be read by future readers. This phrase not only underlines the responsibility of novelists to testify to histories of suffering that they, unlike the victims of those histories, can still read and render legible, but they also open up the perspective of a future in which the present will one day be read. Indeed, the image of a "legible crowd" conjures a not-quite-human perspective that observes the movements of human life from a temporal and spatial vantage beyond the scale of the human, and beyond the constraints of the emotional codes that define the novel form. As I show in my readings of Spiotta's *Eat the Document* (in my fourth chapter) and Meek's *We Are Now Beginning Our Descent* (in my coda), such an imagining of a posthumous reader is an important strategy for contemporary fiction in its attempt to figure life and affect after the end of the novel. In *Open City*, as will become clear, the novel's protagonist offers one (radically insufficient) instance of a strangely unaffected and not-quite-human perspective. By means of its intimation (through the idea of future legibility) and staging (through Julius) of such a dissociated perspective, the novel acknowledges the limited critical purchase of contemporary fiction, as well as the need to defer the hope of more significant connectedness to the novel's afterlife.

This more modest and compromised position is also apparent in the novel's subtle gloss on its own title, which makes it hard to read it as a celebration of metropolitanism and cosmopolitanism. The phrase "open city" occurs when Julius notes that Brussels, in spite of the "countless wars fought on the territory" surrounding it, was not firebombed in World War II. If Brussels stands today as a ("legible") monument to historical achievement and destruction, it is because the Belgian government made the (at the very least) morally debatable decision to compromise with the German occupier:

> there had been no firebombing of Bruges, or Ghent, or Brussels. Surrender, of course, played a role in this form of survival, as did negotiation with invading powers. Had Brussels's rulers not opted to declare it an open city and thereby exempt it from bombardment during the Second World War, it might have been reduced to rubble [...] As it was, it had remained a vision of the medieval and baroque periods, a visa interrupted only by the architectural monstrosities erected all over town by Leopold II in the late nineteenth century. (97)

Its compromised past makes the city available—that is, legible—for future uptake. In a closely related way, *Open City* itself renders stories of violence and suffering legible, even if it self-consciously refrains from composing them into an occasion for empathetic recognition.

Another theme in the novel underlines the importance of the minimal program of making things legible through language—the task, that is, of making things apprehensible that would otherwise slip under the perceptual radar. In the novel's second half, Julius is increasingly occupied by bedbugs. These bedbugs are "the unseen enemy," and as such serve as a figure for the altered "terms of transnational conflicts": both in the case of bedbugs and that of global security threats, "the enemies were now vague, and the threat they posed constantly shifting" (173). The bedbugs figure a dimension of global life that resists materialization as a tangible experience that the cosmopolitan imagination can invite us to share; instead, they figure a largely virtual, non-dramatic, non-eventual sense of unease that only the aesthetic or the literary can make apprehensible for the first time: bedbugs fight "a conflict at the margins of modern life, visible only in speech" (173). The work of rendering things visible in speech is the novel's decidedly unheroic operation. This emphasis on visibility and legibility also explains the rather startling tagline of the novel's first half: "Death is a perfection of the eye" (1). Read in tandem with the novel's commitment to keep the traces of the past visible and to render the palimpsests of history resolutely legible, this line associates death, closure, and erasure with an optic that is too intent on perfecting, completing, and purifying whatever comes into its purview. *Open City* instead keeps the bits of life that it collects radically imperfect, incomplete, and therefore—as the tagline suggests—visible and undead.

The *flâneur* and the shadow of the *fugueur*

The tagline to the novel's second half reads "I have searched myself."
It is tempting to marshal a passage near the end of the novel as a con-
firmation that Julius, through all his wanderings, has in the end finally
found himself:

> Each person must, on some level, take himself as the calibration
> point for normalcy, must assume that the room of his own mind
> is not, cannot be, entirely opaque to him. Perhaps this is what we
> mean by sanity: that, whatever our self-admitted eccentricities might
> be, we are not the villains of our own stories. In fact, it is quite the
> contrary: we play, and only play, the hero, and in the swirl of other
> people's stories, insofar as these stories concern us at all, we are never
> less than heroic. (243)

James Wood quotes this passage at the culmination of his discussion of
the book. For Wood, it testifies to a "selfish normality," an "ordinary solipsism" that freely admits "the limits of sympathy," while it is yet the very
possibility condition "enabl[ing] liberal journeys of comprehension."
This reading seems to bring the novel in line with the figure of the *flâneur*,
as well as with forms of cosmopolitanism that do not require a full-scale
detachment so much as a dynamic of reattachments or multiple attachments in which a confidently rooted subject never fatally loses itself.

I have been arguing that the novel does not endorse this program,
and it is unsurprising that the passage is decidedly more complicated
than Wood makes it out to be. The passage is part of the only sequence
in which the novel abandons its signature combination of the casually
chronological flow of the narrative present and the repeated excursions
into Julius's or his interlocutors' narrated pasts—the only sequence,
in other words, that radically ruptures the composure of the *flâneur*
that the rest of the novel seems to sustain. Julius is attending a party
in the spectacular apartment of the boyfriend of Moji, an old Nigerian
acquaintance whom Julius has accidentally run into in New York. Just
before the reflection above, Julius reports how he made his way home
from the party at sunrise, leaving part of the night unaccounted for. In
an unprecedented move, the novel goes on to fill in this lacuna through
a flashback that, for once, ruptures rather than enriches the narrative
present. The novel conveys a conversation between Julius and Moji that,
after Julius's opening question, consists of a monologue by Moji, rendered as free indirect speech, without giving the reader any indication

of Julius's reaction. This lack of response is all the more remarkable given that Moji accuses him of raping her at a party in Nigeria, and of acting like he "knew nothing about it, had even forgotten her, to the point of not recognizing her when [they] met again" (244). Julius's response, when it comes, is startling in its inadequacy. Rather than speaking, he imaginatively converts the river, at which Moji had been staring during her monologue, into an aesthetic spectacle: "the river gleamed like aluminium roofing" (246). At that precise moment, Julius tells us, he thinks of the "double story" of the Roman hero Scaevola and Friedrich Nietzsche. The former, "rather than giving away his accomplices, [...] showed his fearlessness by putting his right hand in a fire and letting it burn"; the latter, when failing to convince his schoolmates of the truth of this story, "plucked a hot coal from the grate, and held it," which led to a scar he carried with him for the rest of his life (246). For Julius, this memory seems to have dissipated the tension between Moji and himself, and the chapter ends abruptly with Julius saying goodbye to some other people at the party, and with the shockingly trivial message to the reader that, as he later discovers, "Nietzsche's contempt for pain had been expressed not with a coal but with several lit matchsticks" (246). The novel does not return to the rape after this, as it did not refer to it before.

On closer inspection, the "double story" that fills in for an adequate response is not entirely arbitrary: the double emphasis on scars and the withholding of speech echoes Moji's assertions that Julius "had been ever-present in her life, like a stain or a scar," and that she had tried "to keep her pain hidden" until now (244–45). These tropes, together with the observation that her voice is "emotional in its total lack of inflection" and that it conveys a "flat affect" (244), qualify Moji as a typical traumatized subject, rendering Julius's inability to connect with her entirely predictable in light of his failure to engage with trauma in the rest of the novel. Julius's double story not only fails to acknowledge Moji's suffering—she repeatedly asks that he "say something"—it also implicitly declares her guilty of a failure to feel the appropriate "contempt for pain"; to add insult to injury, it rationalizes and thus excuses Julius's own failure to speak. The story, in other words, converts the spectacle of traumatic suffering into an assertion of the heroism of inexpressiveness.

This passage, which breaks with the chronological unfolding of the narrative present, leaves little doubt about something the novel's almost affectless tone has continuously been suggesting: that Julius's compulsive walking and remembering are not simply a carefully cultivated case of *flânerie*, but testify to a more sinister condition. Earlier in the novel, Julius has displayed a singular capacity for dispassionate dissociation when his dying friend Professor Saiko asks him to read the newspaper for him: Julius remarks that he "became like one who was no longer there": he reads "fully understanding the printed words but without engaging with them" (171). This foreshadows Julius's later failure to respond to Moji. Yet by exposing Julius's forgetting of the rape, the latter passage links Julius's psychological dissociation to a failure of memory, even to amnesia, while the rest of the novel raises the question of its relations to his incessant walking. As I already noted, the novel's repeated invocations of the fugue form provide a cue for the condition that combines this set of phenomena: the (exceedingly rare) phenomenon of "dissociative fugue."[12] The American Psychiatric Association's *Diagnostic and Statistical Manual* (*DSM*) notes that this condition is characterized by "sudden, unexpected travel away from home or one's customary place of daily activities," and often goes hand in hand with "confusion about personal identity" (523). Ian Hacking, who has devoted a book to the history of this pathology, characterizes it as "impulsive uncontrolled traveling, with confused memories" (77). Julius's amnesia, his compulsive walking, and his dissociation from the stories and memories he encounters all point in the direction of this phenomenon.

The fugue epidemic that swept France between 1887 and 1909 has been relegated to the status of a footnote in psychiatric history; in spite of the popular appeal of the idea of amnesia, one of the fugue's constituent parts, it has "not evolved its own literature" (Hacking 59). *Open City*'s sabotaging of its own aesthetic successes through the use of a *fugueur* narrator may give an indication as to why the fugue resists literary elaboration. It is no coincidence that the *fugueur* differs from the *flâneur* in this respect. Indeed, Hacking makes clear that the *fugueur* can be considered as a dark counterpart to the *flâneur*: while the latter was part of an emerging discourse that exalted mobility and tourism as "exceptional, admired travel, a heightened form of travel," the *fugueur*'s "ambulatory automatism" served as the shadow side of this newly won mobility (52). It was associated with *vagabondage* and the unbearable boredom of modern life. And while *flâneurs* take an acute interest in the world around them in order to enrich the self, *fugueurs*' compulsive escape from their normal lives was "less a voyage of self-discovery than an attempt to eliminate self" (30). The *DSM* notes that cases of dissociative fugue are "usually related to traumatic, stressful, or overwhelming life events" (525). Unlike the urban mobility of the *flâneur*, the unwanted restlessness of the *fugueur* is not an attitude that literary cosmopolitanism can celebrate. By showing how easily the *flâneur* shades into a *fugueur*, and by making the reader experience that fateful proximity through the novel's almost affectless tone, *Open City* resists the complacency of a literary cosmopolitanism that believes that intercultural feeling and understanding equal real-world change. The category of the dissociative fugue is the key to the novel's critique of literary cosmopolitanism.

The novel ends with a final attempt to invest the hope of human connectedness in the powers of art. Julius attends a performance of Mahler's Ninth Symphony, which inspires reflections on Mahler's "genius of prolonged farewells"—his mastery of "the ends of symphonies, the ends of a body of work, and the end of his own life" (250). This "obsession with last things" (252) seems to make Mahler an appropriate guide for ending a novel, as "in the glow of the final movement" the spectacle of a frail old woman beginning to walk up the aisle brings on an ecstatic vision of a final reconciliation of Julius and his estranged grandmother: he notes that it was "as though I was down there with my oma, and the sweep of the music was pushing us gently forward as I escorted her out into the darkness" (253). Yet the situation soon turns into farce: Julius takes the wrong exit, and finds himself alone, locked out of Carnegie Hall, "on a flimsy fire escape," exposed to the rain and the wind (255). The novel's last attempt to affirm the aesthetic cosmopolitanism at which it has insistently hinted is interrupted by a random event that reveals the novel's commitment to another, and more minimal, aesthetic program—to an aesthetic that preserves legible and visible traces rather than promotes virtuous transport. Before Julius manages to climb down to an open door that allows him to return to the music hall, he is surprised to see the stars, as he had not expected to see them "with the light pollution perpetually wreathing the city" (256). The danger that the stars may dissolve in an indifferent blur replays the aesthetic challenge that has occupied the novel throughout: the threat that having stories and memories resonate with each other will not result in a suggestive contrapuntal harmony, but rather in a noisy monotone. Again, the novel refuses to celebrate intercultural feeling and understanding as valuable cosmopolitan achievements in and of themselves; instead, it refashions itself as a humble recording device that renders nonhuman pasts legible in order to preserve them for an uncertain future:

> [the stars'] true nature was their persisting visual echo of something that was already in the past. In the unfathomable ages it took for

light to cross such distances, the light source itself had in some cases long been extinguished, its dark remains stretched away from us at ever greater speed [...] in the dark spaces between the dead, shining stars, were stars I could not see, stars that still existed, and were giving out light that hadn't reached me yet, stars now living and giving out light but present to me only as blank interstices. (256)

Only by faithfully recording the light as well as the darkness can the disasters of the past and the hopes of the future be transmitted. The novel's anticlimactic ending underlines its main insight: that recording the "still legible" world involves a refusal to see the stars as self-sufficient constellations of significant connectedness.

This refusal of harmonious connection recalls the famous opening lines of Georg Lukács's *Theory of the Novel*, to which I turn in my next chapter: "Happy are those ages when the starry sky is the map of all possible paths—ages whose paths are illuminated by the light of the stars" (29). *Open City* offers no such illumination. It turns to the stars to intimate scales that cannot be enlisted for cosmopolitan scenarios of transcultural transport, but that expose the limits of customary human forms of memory and imagination. *Open City* recalls cosmopolitan celebrations of intercultural connection to what Peter Szendy has theorized as an "extraterrestrial" cosmopolitics: an ethics and politics that "would be inscribed neither in a human nature nor in a destiny of humanity" (152), but that manages to acknowledge realities and lives that are not, or not fully, human.[13] Through its evocation of a nonhuman vastness and of a posthumous reader, *Open City* transforms the cosmopolitan novel into a place where the insufficiency of human scales and available emotional templates can be rendered legible.[14] I return to the challenges this nonhuman dimension poses for the contemporary novel in the coda to this book, but not before I have further explored the limitations of transnational worldliness in my next chapter.

4

Epic Failures (Dana Spiotta, Hari Kunzru, Russell Banks)

Lukács's contemporaneity

The central claim of this book is that intimations of the end of the novel animate contemporary fiction and allow it to reconfigure relations between human life, affect, and literary form. This does not mean that apprehensions of the imminent demise of the novel form are somehow unprecedented—indeed, they are constitutive of the form in at least two ways. First, and as I already noted in my introduction and at the beginning of my first chapter, there is the literary historical fact that declarations of the form's exhaustion have a long and venerable pedigree: they are a crucial part of the texture of a literary history premised on innovation and originality. This is a dynamic from which the novel form can, by its very name, not pretend to be exempt.

Underlying this literary historical dynamic, there is a second and more intimate affinity between the novel and the idea of belatedness. This linkage was most famously forged in Georg Lukács's *Theory of the Novel*, a classic work of novel theory that I already invoked in the chapter on Coetzee and near the end of my reading of Cole's *Open City*. Lukács wrote his *Theory* in 1914–15, well before he turned into an uncompromising defender of realism and an arch-opponent of modernism. In 1914–15, these priorities had yet to be decided, and as we will see, such a state of open-ended potentiality left room for fundamental questions of literary (im)possibility. To the extent, then, that these questions still animate contemporary fiction, the *Theory*'s refusal to decide the question of the novel's (im)possibility makes it a privileged resource for an understanding of contemporary writing. The *Theory* casts the novel as a form that is born exhausted: it is marked by a fantasy of formal integrity that it knows to be unavailable in the present yet cannot keep itself from desiring. The name of that illusory wholeness, in Lukács's book, is the epic: while the ancient genre of the epic could still apprehend and express "the natural unity of the metaphysical spheres" in terms of "pure, sensuous immediacy" (*Theory* 36, 62), the novel can only attend to the dissociation between the sensible and the intelligible that besets the modern age—a condition Lukács memorably refers to (with a phrase credited to Fichte) as the age of "absolute sinfulness" [*Zeitalter der vollendeten Sündhaftigkeit*] (*Theory* 152). The novel can only testify to a fateful separation that it cannot undo, as it is thoroughly implicated in this broken world, as much as the epic was immersed in the "extensive immanence" (Aitken 43) of its more fortuitous setting— the novel, in this sense, "is the epic of an age in which the extensive totality of life is no longer directly given [...] yet which still thinks in terms of totality" (*Theory* 56).[1]

While it is tempting to read (and dismiss) the *Theory of the Novel* as a fatally abstract literary historical account of the morphing of the epic into the novel, this last quotation suggests a more interesting reading. It makes clear that the epic does not so much indicate a past episode in literary history as provide a name for the modern desire for imme- diacy and totality. The putative integrity of the epic is, in other words, an expression of the modern tendency to "still think[...] in terms of totality," a tendency that the novel form adopts from the age it inhab- its and emblematizes, as "the problems of the novel form are [...] the mirror-image of a world gone out of joint" (*Theory* 17). Fantasizing a past totality is that world's way of measuring its fateful remove from an integrated world; this condemns the novel, the form in which this remove is reflected, to a protracted leave-taking of an impossible aes- thetic ideal. The novel is always marked by melancholic intimations of its own insufficiency, and by the lingering suspicion that it is merely living out its own afterlife. Read in this light, Lukács's thesis on the novel's paradoxically productive dramatization of its own failure can help us understand why the anti-novelistic polemics of Tom McCarthy and David Shields that I analyzed in the first chapter remain caught in a decidedly *novelistic* dynamic: the *Theory of the Novel* shows that the novel form is constitutively caught up in the question of its own (in)sufficiency, and works like those of McCarthy and Shields that set out to address, in McCarthy's words, "the whole issue of impossibility and failure" (qtd. in Kuitenbrouwer) perpetuate rather than discontinue this enabling sense of crisis.

Lukács's assertion that the novel form is always belated is a welcome addition to merely sociological or cultural approaches to the issue of the end of the novel, for at least two reasons. For one thing, it underlines that the idea of the dissolution of the novel is an animating concern of the novel, and therefore not a mere rumor, even if it is impossible to pinpoint what this phenomenon, process, or event—and the hesitation between these terms reflects the conceptual confusion—amounts to exactly: whether it is tied to the rise of new media, dwindling reader-ships, "the drastic decline of literary fictions' cultural currency," the intensified "intercrossing of the novel's generic and medial bounda-ries" (Tabbi and Wutz 18), or (more often) a combination of a number of these. Lukács's genre-theoretical perspective makes clear that such clusters of concerns merely intensify and update the form's constitu-tive occupation with the prospect of its ever imminent impossibility.[2] Figurations of the end of the novel are, in other words, nothing new; more precisely, contemporary figurations of the end are simultane-ously "new" (they are, after all, contemporary) and part of a persistent movement that blurs clear distinctions between "old" and "new"; after all, contemporary versions of the end are merely "new" instances of concerns that were already "old" even when they were "new." This means that stagings of these concerns in contemporary fiction can fruit-fully be read as instantiations of this more encompassing form-specific dynamic.[3] As Eva Geulen has remarked on the question of the end of art (rather than the novel), the fact that this end has "so far always turned out to be a matter of speech and rhetoric [...] does not mitigate its urgency in any given scenario" (1). This urgency, this contemporaneity, is what *Contemporary Literature and the End of the Novel* wants to capture.

In the first three chapters, we have encountered a set of figures through which contemporary novels simultaneously channel the cultural concerns that energize them and update the novel's endemic concern with its own (im)possibility: a series of negative or minor affects (McCarthy's dysphoric affects, Cole's tonal affectlessness, Iyer's and Coetzee's stagings of farcical or creatural life), a catalogue of fig-ures of diminished consciousness or agency, and a marked concern with the powers of different media (music and painting in the case of Cole, photography in Coetzee, reenactment in McCarthy). While it is easy enough to decode these figures as immediate responses to a read-ily identifiable set of cultural concerns, it is by *simultaneously* reading them as participating in the novel's "sensuous dynamic of possibility, impossibility, and actuality" (Bewes, "Against" 279) that we can grasp the affective and formal work they are doing within these novels and capture their contemporaneity. Giorgio Agamben has noted that "con-temporariness" can only be grasped from a perspective that does not "coincide too well with the epoch" (41). Instead, the contemporary is "a singular relationship with one's own time, which adheres to it and, at the same time, keeps a distance from it" (41). By disjointing contemporary fiction from the present, Lukács's genre-theoretical account provides a perspective from which the novels' figures of the end emerge as crystallizations of these novels' different ways of inhabiting the early twenty-first century. That these novels approach the present through a concern with their own belatedness can be seen as a strategy to become contemporary as, according to Agamben, "contemporariness" "is *that relationship with time that adheres to it by means of being out of sync and anachronistic*" (41). The end of the novel, far from being only a journalistic rumor, activates such an anachronistic perspective and enables contemporary fiction to reimagine its relation to the present without being overwhelmed by it.

Lukács's particular spin on the relation between the epic and the novel is instructive for another reason. By using the term "epic" to name the novel's desire for an illusory integrated form, Lukács codes that desire in genre-theoretical terms. This underlines what I already anticipated when I traced Coetzee's or Cole's testing of the (im)possibilities of other media and forms: novelistic self-reflexivity often manifests itself, both formally and thematically, as a critical interrogation of other forms, genres, and media. Indeed, the epic is only one possible object of the novel's desire; nor is desire, as we will see, the only mode in which the novel relates to its generic, formal, and medial others. Timothy Bewes has shown that contemporary literature often assigns the role that is taken up by the genre of the epic in the *Theory* to cinema.[4] Bewes notes that works such as Salman Rushdie's *Satanic Verses*, E.L. Doctorow's *City of God*, and several of Paul Auster's novels are energized by an attraction to "cinema as having a sensuous, immediate relation to temporality itself" ("Against" 290). In the conception of these writers, cinema is not burdened by "the formal, historical, and ethical melancholy associated, for Lukács, with the novel" (290). Instead, they are "looking to cinema with envy, as to a promise of redemption that will achieve the immanence of the epic" (294). Whether the object of envy is epic, cinema, or another form or medium, Lukács's genre-theoretical perspective is an invitation to read novels' formal and thematic engagements with other genres, forms, and media as strategies through which they negotiate their contemporaneity—that is, their relation to the present.[5]

In this chapter, I capitalize on Lukács's insight to outline one particular strategy through which contemporary fiction disjoints itself from the present in order to interrogate its contemporary viability. The three novels on which I focus—Hari Kunzru's *My Revolutions* (2007), Dana Spiotta's *Eat the Document* (2006), and Russell Banks's *The Darling* (2004)—signal their ambition to escape the present and achieve their contemporaneity through a simple aesthetic decision: even if they were all published in the direct aftermath of 9/11, and even if they all deal directly with crucial aspects of the post-9/11 imaginary—most notably, terrorism and political activism—they all three decline to make the events of 9/11 a central referent in their narratives; indeed, only *The Darling* refers to 9/11, and then only in its very last pages. In the cases of *Eat the Document* and *My Revolutions*, this careful ellipsis indexes their ambition not to foreclose the question of their cultural agency and authority by tying it all too directly to the present—an ambition that is further reflected in their sustained concern with the powers of different media. *The Darling* offers an instructive contrast to these two novels in that it skirts the question of its own agency only to end up discovering its redundancy in a present from which it has failed to dissociate itself.

My exploration of these three novels' experiments in untimeliness is at the same time a study of a particular subgenre of the post-9/11 novel: like, for instance, Susan Choi's *American Woman* (2005), Neil Gordon's *The Company You Keep* (2003), and Christopher Sorrentino's *Trance* (2005), these three novels evoke the memory of political activism and terrorism in the 1960s and early 70s in order to map political and cultural developments in the last few decades.[6] All three novels feature protagonists whose lives have been marked by particularly intense experiences on the thin line between activism and terrorism followed by rather unremarkable and quotidian lives under the radar of public attention. While Banks's self-confident and formally unproblematic historical novel does not use this conceit for a testing of the (im)possibility of the novel, Kunzru and Spiotta intertwine it with an investigation of different media in order to reflect on the form's residual capacity to affect the present. Their novels evoke a brief period of intense but ultimately ineffective activism, which offers at least the temporary illusion of a significant articulation of personal agency and public meaning; after activism spills over into terror, their protagonists need to erase their pasts and slip into anonymous lives. This prevents them from serving as what the later Lukács, for whom the endemic dissatisfaction that defines the novel in the *Theory* has stopped being a critical resource, calls "typical" characters: for Lukács, the type is "a peculiar synthesis which organically binds together the general and the particular" (*Studies* 6).

Typical characters count as representative or even exemplary embodiments of the central forces organizing their world; their literary use depends on an understanding of the world as an articulated totality of which human life is a significant part—a conception that the framework of the *Theory of the Novel*, as we have seen, rigorously proscribes. These novels' decision to refuse typical characters also means that they preempt what I identified in my introduction as the epistemic privilege that is routinely ascribed to the novel form; together with these novels' intense interrogations of different media, this decision sends us back to the *Theory of the Novel* as an intertext for understanding contemporary fiction's persistent occupation with its own (im)possibility. And if it seems that the question of the form's current viability can hardly be formulated without reference to the events of September 11, Spiotta and Kunzru propose a different strategy: they address it by carefully bracketing that context in order to update a more encompassing exploration of the novel form's very possibility.

The revolution will not be novelized: Hari Kunzru's *My Revolutions*

The notion of the type plays a crucial role in Lukács's later renunciation of his position in *Theory of the Novel*. While the *Theory* locates the specificity of the novel form in the unavailability of an articulated totality, the later Lukács opposes "the destruction of the completeness of the human personality and of the objective typicality of men and situations" (*Studies* 6). For Lukács, this completeness is underwritten by the truth of dialectical materialism, which provides "a chart in the labyrinth of our time," and allows realism to serve as "the true, solution-bringing third way" that sublates both the "false objectivity" of naturalism and the equally "false subjectivity" of psychological realism (6). The realism Lukács advocates relies on the "central category and criterion" of the type, an organic articulation of the particular and the general "both in characters and situations" (6). Lukács's criticism moves from a desperate diagnosis of the impossibility of representing the general through the particular to a confident assumption that the type can do just that. Spiotta's and Kunzru's novels dramatize these different positions by constructing their narratives around characters whose trajectory consists of two stages: their early life is marked by an intense bout of political activism, and thus by the momentary conviction of being the vehicles of historical change, and they are then forced to withdraw from public life, which eliminates their powers to serve as representative characters binding together "the general and the particular." The novels' occupation with the inactive afterlife of activism is a gesture of self-limitation through which they make it impossible to stage typical characters, and instead make room to fashion a different mandate for the contemporary novel. As we will see, *My Revolutions*, even if it is concerned with different media throughout, fails to come up with such a new job description, while *Eat the Document* does negotiate the powers of different media in a way that allows it to formulate what I will call, for reasons that will become clear, an *analog* aesthetic.

Like *Eat the Document*, *My Revolutions* spans the period between the late 1960s and the late 90s, while it also narrates the story of a life that has been forced to cancel its public profile. What is impossible, in these novels, is an articulation of private life with public meaning; what is at stake is the relevance of the novel form in a situation in which, in Lukács's words, "[t]he hero and his destiny [...] have no more than personal interest and the work as a whole becomes a private memoir" (*Theory* 137). *My Revolution*'s first-person narrator was born as Chris Carver, but the reader meets him in 1998 as Michael (Mike) Frame, a name that he, like Spiotta's protagonist, borrowed from a dead infant (218). The novel consists of the story of his life as a member of an underground organization (the August 14th group, a fictional collective based on the historical Angry Brigade) whose activities devolve into terrorism, which leads him to spend most of the 70s in exile in Asia, first as a drug addict and then in a monastery, after which he ends up in the suburban comfort that he sees slipping away from him in the course of the novel. His forced escape from his new family, and the monologue we are given to read, are triggered by a visit from his former life in the shape of Miles, an old acquaintance who plans to expose his hidden past in order to smirch a new government minister who shares this activist past, even if she was never personally involved in violent actions. The novel, in other words, catches the narrator at the moment when the public life of his personal past is about to begin again; it is the last moment when his story is his to tell.

The novel cannot completely rely on this external trigger for the return of the past—after all, that would suggest that Mike had made peace with the past, and cancel the tension between Mike's private life and its (lack of) public meaning. That the past had not been dead and buried is demonstrated in a scene narrated at the beginning of the novel, and taking place one year before the narrative present. During a trip in France, Mike catches a glimpse of a woman whom he immediately believes to be Anna Addison, who was one of the leaders of the underground organization with which he was involved. Anna, who is also his former lover, is widely believed to have been killed "in the conference room of the German embassy in Copenhagen in 1975" (16). If this does not make the identification unlikely enough, the novel underlines that it is based on very slim evidence: they cross in the street, "[b]ut she hadn't looked up. And I hadn't been recognized" (16). His willingness to believe that the woman he sees is indeed, impossibly, Anna, testifies that the private afterlife of the past is not dead, its fate not fixed, at the moment when Miles threatens to make it public and terminate its underground existence. From the outset, Mike realizes that "very soon now, days or even hours, my life here will be over"—in fact, it already "no longer exists" (2). The threat of the imminent revelation of his past makes clear that his suburban afterlife has never been a full existence in the first place; it has been a private life that can perpetuate itself only as long as it manages to avoid publicity.

My Revolutions dramatizes the narrative tension that *Eat the Document*, as we will see, also confronts from its very first pages: the (im)possiblity of making a private life matter in public terms, as publicity would seal the end of that private life. Kunzru's narrator only accepts the end of his private life in the novel's very last line, when he decides to identify himself, in a phone call to his wife, by the name he had abandoned decades earlier, and which she has never heard before. This ending allows the reader to imagine that the wife, hearing an unfamiliar name, will not recognize the speaker as the man with whom she has spent almost two decades of her life.[7] Mike only comes to the decision to contact his wife when he has verified that Anna is, indeed, dead. While narrating his story, Mike has traveled to France once more in order to confirm or disprove the impossible encounter with Anna the year before. At the end of the novel, he finally confronts the woman he had wished to be Anna, only to realize that "Anna is dead," and "has been dead all along" (275). Reduced to the status of a "mute," "charred corpse," her memory is finally "fixed in the past like amber" (275), as she is consigned "to a past almost geological in its remoteness from the present" (22). The trip to France resembles nothing so much as the process of "reality-testing" that confirms "that the loved object no longer exists," which Freud famously identifies as a precondition for arresting the destructive force of melancholic grief and for starting a normal process of mourning and healing (Freud 244–45). Having buried the memory of Anna, Mike's private possession by the past is over, and this allows him to accept the end of his private life as such: his life will soon become a public possession. It is significant that this "soon" is a moment that the novel only announces (from its first page) but does not narrate; this reticence underscores that, on the novel's self-imposed terms, it is impossible to make a private fate resonate with public meaning. The device of the aftermath of activism serves to pose the question of the novel form's (im)possiblity by forcing a dissociation between the particular and the general that the type cannot bridge and that calls for a new formal mandate.

How does Kunzru's novel attempt to move beyond the disabling opposition between private life and public meaning? *My Revolutions* tries to undo their rigid incompatibility by consistently endowing fiction with the capacity to soften such rigidity and affirm a more fluid and flexible realm of potentiality. This literary ambition can be glimpsed in one of the novel's mottos. Taken from the Rote Armee Fraktion, a notorious German left-wing terrorist organization, the motto identifies the power of fixation and the impatience with counterfactuals as terroristic forces: "The question of what would have happened if ... is ambiguous, pacifistic, moralistic." The novel associates the inability to sustain uncertainties with terrorism; when life in the activist commune to which Mike belongs is increasingly radicalized, one symptom is the collapse of the distinction between private and public, which makes way for "a policy of absolute openness": everything that is done is done "in the presence, at least potentially, of someone else" (171). In this condition of "totalitarian sharing," it was "as if [they] had no inner life at all" (171). This removal of privacy is linked to the (terrorist) possibility to intervene in the world in a decisive way; the condition of compulsory publicity begins just after they "burned down the first army recruitment office" (172). Terrorism, certainty, effectiveness—these are all things that the novel form in *My Revolutions* is not. Which is not to say that they are things the novel can successfully oppose.

My Revolutions' concern with different media consistently codes a tension between a fixing of time that cancels the viability of the novel, and the novel's own narration that aims to undo the fixating powers of terror and, in terms of the novel's own media ecology, photography and film. Kunzru's novel associates immediacy with violence; through this association, the visual media that are also connected to this immediacy become unavailable as aesthetic models for the novel. As I will show, this is a problem that Kunzru's novel does not manage to overcome. After his return from Asia, Mike Frame lives out his disconnection from a world whose "most pressing issue" is interior design (47) working in a bookshop, the refuge of "educated misfits through the ages" (25). Because of his terrorist past, the account of how he had "actually lost his lost years" (23) is not a story that can have public meaning. This makes his situation paradoxically adequate to an age that, in the words of Miles, the nemesis from his past, has achieved what he considers an enviable inconsequentiality:

> History doesn't care about what you did [...] Ideology's dead now. Everyone pretty much agrees on how to run things [...] You've been able to lead a dull life because there's no real conflict anymore. In a couple of years it'll be another millennium and, with luck, nothing will bloody happen anywhere, nothing at all. (259)

In the novel, these words are spoken three years before 9/11. In reality, they were published six years after it. If we take this double temporality into account, they signal at least three things. First, they indicate the novel's awareness that the conceit of the carefully anonymized afterlife of terror is paradoxically adequate for an age of interior design that considers itself to be posthistorical and postideological. Second, the obvious incongruity between Miles's attitude and the fallout of 9/11 points to a clear awareness that this posthistorical age is over at the time the novel is written—that terrorlessness was a temporary illusion, not an achieved condition. And third, the fact that the novel does not move beyond this impasse points to its ultimate inability to develop a new assignment for the novel form in the wake of 9/11.

So why exactly doesn't *My Revolutions'* media ecology allow it to reimagine the novel's contemporaneity? For one thing, Kunzru consistently understands the powers of fiction as a *counterforce* to the visual media the novel insistently evokes, rather than as a form that is sustained by a desire for the immediacy it associates with these media. For the early Lukács, the novel cannot but desire to *become* epic; *My Revolutions*, in marked contrast, does not even desire to morph into the visual media to which it is in thrall, as it understands itself as a counterforce to the fixating and terrorist powers it ascribes to them. When the young Miles enters the lives of the activists, he initially presents himself as a "revolutionary film-maker," who cuts up "advertising reels and old information films" with "footage of the alienated lives of cleaners and shop-workers" (40). His ostensible goal is to use cinema as a "weapon" to change consciousness, and thus to intervene "in that gray area between the personal and the political" (41). On the face of it, this would seem to make it an enviable model for the novel. Yet *My Revolutions* does not develop this aesthetic option; cinema does not become an object of the novel's desire, and the novel instead unmasks Miles as a police informer; his aesthetic ambitions, then, are merely a cover for an attempt by the security forces to infiltrate and disable the activist underground. Late in the novel, we learn that Mike, just before his escape to Asia, has willingly leaked information to Miles in order to prevent a further escalation of terrorist violence (255). This complicity explains his continued obsession with Anna (as his revelations might somehow have led to her death) and the novel's negative take on visual media. In the novel's narrative present, Miles hires a photographer to take a picture of an encounter that he orchestrates between Mike and the government minister whom he seeks to discredit (206); again, visual media have a real-world power that the novel lacks. Ironically, it is the photographer and film-maker, who is almost by definition a bystander to genuine action, who is able to affect real-world politics. The novel does not fail to underline how the activists themselves rely on the power of audio-visual media when subjecting hostages to a 24-hour display in order to induce "ARC, an acceleration of revolutionary consciousness, to alter their politics with *son et lumière*" (267–68).

Mike's own narration in the novel is presented as a way of virtualizing, softening, and relativizing the fixating power of visual media. It aims to restore the complex personalities of two of his accomplices, whose public image depends on a small number of iconic photos that reduce them to flat and stereotypical figures. One Sean Ward's posthumous image is constructed by pictures that "tend to show him with rock-star accoutrements, dark glasses, his battered biker jacket" (97); Anna, for her part, has "been reduced to the woman in the Copenhagen photo," a "masked figure [that] is as much of a cartoon as Byronic Sean Ward" (107). Mike's narrative aims to restore complexity, nuance, and depth to these clichés, yet this effort is shadowed by the incompatibility of the private and the public that limits the effectiveness of his narration. Even the descriptions of the lives of the activists are thoroughly saturated with references to visual media that convey that these media have a grasp on reality which these novelistic descriptions themselves are lacking. During protest marches, "everything seemed to be happening at a distance, on a screen" (35); the group's fiction of agency can only be sustained as long as they "stay in [their] movie" (101), while the utopian future they project "looked like an advertisement" (42). One vital obstacle in the activists' struggle is the fact that the media refuse to broadcast their actions (184), driving home the message that "nothing takes place, even for the participants, unless it's electronically witnessed and played back [...] Our world became television" (202).

Staring at another picture of Anna in a photobook from the 1960s, Mike realizes that his effort to bring her to narrative life is futile: only photographs have the power to perpetuate life, and therefore "[s]he was alive. She'd been alive all the time" (135). Instead, it is he, the narrator whose image has had no public afterlife, who lacks life: "I was the dead one, the old photograph, frozen in time, my blacks turning brown, my whites yellowing with age" (135). This moment can easily be read as a figure for the novel's lost battle against the visual media it evokes, only to find itself unable to compete with or learn from them. Only those who resist photography end up "frozen in time," deprived of that medium's paradoxical animating powers. Mike identifies his feelings here as "jealousy, a slow, viscous panic seeping out of [his] bones" (135), which is decidedly not the kind of affect that can animate his own narrative. The moment also echoes the wishful encounter with the undead Anna at the beginning of the novel, which can, in retrospect, be read as an index of the novel's medial anxieties and its awareness that the media it wants to present as deadening forces are, in the media ecology it inhabits, in fact the ones that keep the past alive. As I noted, Mike corrects his identification of Anna at the end of the novel, but the anxieties she figures are only laid to rest for the novel to end on a forceful reminder of the disabling dissociation between private and public. Here *My Revolutions* encounters the limits of its medial imagination: visual media are not a desired *model* for the novel's agency, but they are cast as the only possible *medium* for agency, leaving the novel itself, bound as it is to another medium, powerless to imagine its contemporary afterlife. *My Revolutions* successfully brackets the pressures of the present—by sidestepping 9/11—and the Lukácsian logic of the type, and it manages to make room for an interrogation of the (im)possibility of the novel form through a confrontation with other media; still, it is only *Eat the Document* that successfully develops an alternative mode for contemporary fiction to engage reality.

Analog agency: Dana Spiotta's *Eat the Document*

Like Coetzee's *Slow Man*, and like McCarthy's *Remainder*, *Eat the Document* begins with "the undoing of a life" (3); unlike these other novels, it is not fixated on the material or fleshy remainders of lives that (fail to) disappear, but to an exploration of the eery *immateriality* and *insubstantiality* of a life forced to cancel itself and to continue "unnoticed and unobserved" (11). The novel's opening lines immediately evoke this state of suspension, as they introduce the reader to a character named Mary (and later to be renamed Louise) in a Nebraska hotel room:

> It is easy for a life to become unblessed.
>
> Mary, in particular, understood this. Her mistakes—and they were legion—were not lost on her. She knew all about the undoing of a life: take away, first of all, your people. Your family. Your lover. That was the hardest part of it. Then put yourself somewhere unfamiliar, where (how did it go?) you are a complete unknown. Where you possess nothing. Okay, then—this was the strangest part—take away your history, every last bit of it. (3)

The novel opens with a general observation—we catch a faint echo of Tolstoy's *Anna Karenina*—only to go on to instantly ground it in the particular experience of a character that is only temporarily called Mary. A similar urgency animates the narrative voice, which immediately surrenders its overt omniscience to take refuge in the free indirect speech that it will adopt for the rest of the opening chapter. The very nervousness with which these shifts to an experiential perspective are executed announces the novel's abiding occupation with its formal status: what is at stake, here as elsewhere, is the tenuous articulation of the particular and the general, of private life and public meaning; what the novel restlessly explores is its fate as a work of historical fiction in the absence of a protagonist who can meaningfully—that is, *typically*—carry a more-than-individual meaning. Indeed, the simple syntax, the three self-interruptions (one parenthetical and two between dashes), and the "okay" in the quoted passage aim to give these thoughts a vivacity approximating an interior monologue. By almost too emphatically soliciting access to Mary's thoughts and claiming the authority to relay them, this opening passage signals an eminently novelistic ambition to shape a private life into public significance.

Because it is organized around the conceit of a life of action that has been forced into anonymity, *Eat the Document*, like *My Revolutions*, sabotages this ambition from the outset. The novel opens on the moment when Mary's past becomes radically incommunicable: she has just split ways with Bobby, her lover and partner in crime, after a bomb has accidently killed an innocent bystander, and she will spend the next quarter century underground under the name of Louise Barrot—a name she takes, together with a Social Security number, from a dead infant (200). After the story's first section, which focuses on this dramatic moment in Mary's/Louise's life, the novel shifts to the period between 1998 and 2000, where it intertwines the stories of a group of outsiders connected to an alternative Seattle bookstore with excerpts from the journal of Jason, the initially unsuspecting son of Louise. In between the passages set at the end of the century, Louise's free indirect speech fills in the period between 1972 to 1999, when Jason finds her out, in different episodes that take her from a women-only commune to California, and ultimately to her life as a suburban mother at the time the novel catches up with her.

Before we can begin to trace how Spiotta's novel negotiates a new mandate for the contemporary novel through the confrontation with different media, it is important to linger a bit longer on its elaborate effort to bracket more straightforward ways for the novel genre to inhabit the present. The novel's recourse to different narrative perspectives, as well as its palpable nervousness about inhabiting the position of Louise, point to a self-limitation that suspends these habitual protocols: they register an awareness that a character like Louise, who is forced to live under the radar, will not quite do as a vehicle for a novelistic imagining of the social world—in this novel, the United States of the last three decades of the twentieth century, and the slide from political activism to the total commodification of resistance that Spiotta maps onto it. Because Louise must, by necessity, discontinue a life characterized by the illusion of a significant connection between private action and public meaning, her particular perspective does not suffice to articulate the dimensions of the private and the public. In Lukács's terms, *Eat the Document*'s self-limitation brings on the danger that the novel will remain confined to "the fatal, irrelevant and petty character of the merely private" (*Theory* 137); the later Lukács codes this danger, in words he borrows from Engels, as the impossibility for the character to be "simultaneously a type and a particular individual" ("Art" 35).

In order to present a sufficiently general account of the world without recourse to the logic of the typical, and in order to sidestep "the danger of a subjectivity which is not exemplary, which has not become a symbol" (Lukács, *Theory* 137), *Eat the Document* adopts different narrative vantage points. As soon as the reader encounters her in the motel room, Louise's character is reduced to a mere number and a name—the name of a dead infant, moreover, which underscores that she has to reestablish herself as a fully fledged character through the narrative that fills in the facts of her life between 1972 and 1999. The novel remarks that "the fact that she could change her identity so completely changed the very possibility of engagement, or precluded the possibility of real engagement"; her life becomes "both ephemeral and abstract" (224) and not something that can carry a more than private meaning and address an outside reality. Cast out of the public domain, Spiotta's main character cannot hope, like a typical novel character, to depict the "subtlety, richness and inexhaustability of life" by "bringing it dynamically and vividly to life" (Lukács, "Art" 38), because she is prohibited from taking part in that life.

The novel's interrogation of the forms and functions of contemporary fiction does not stop there. In a dialectical twist that we also encounter in *My Revolutions*, the sense of ephemerality and insubstantiality that hollows out Louise's character becomes a paradoxically adequate marker of the period the novel describes. The novel weaves Louise's character into a more encompassing texture of a world of indifference and weightlessness. In its late twentieth-century sections, self-declared leftists and activists have hardly more of a critical vantage on the world than Louise, as they witness the gradual erosion of resistance and the irresistible commodification of the counterculture—the slippage from activism to a fatally reflexive "[a]ntiology, or study of all things anti" (36), which is not an unfair description of the gatherings and workshops that take place at the Seattle bookstore. By generalizing the flimsiness of novelistic character as a more pervasive condition of constrained critical purchase, *Eat the Document* begins to examine (and salvage) its own residual critical potential. The novel suggests that a weightless protagonist is strangely appropriate for an age without substance—a resolutely post-typical age, in which there is no totality left to embody, and in which the novel form has to reconceive its role.

Eat the Document articulates the question of the novel's viability through a patient testing of other media and forms. In one of the many surprising overlaps between *Eat the Document* and *My Revolutions*, the erosion of critical potency is figured by locating the afterlife of activism in an alternative bookstore, stocking "largely fringe texts" (27). This offhand reference to the medium of the book is part of a remarkably consistent affective media ecology that runs through the novel: already in the motel room, Spiotta's protagonist's disconnection from the ways of the world is contrasted to the visual media's saturation of everyday life. She had predicted that she would end up in a room "with only the TV on the broken swivel stand to remind her of the world at large" (11–12), and indeed she finds herself "watching TV shows about regular people" (15). Such an ability to predict the future presupposes a certain grasp of the causal chains that organize the world; this sense of connection is irrevocably interrupted for her on the day of the lethal accident, when the predictable becomes real with a traumatic direct-ness: "Contingencies are never really contingencies but blueprints. Probabilities become certainties [...] And the event, which she could not think about, not yet, the event that she could not even name, she referred to in her thoughts as *then*, or *the thing*, or *it*" (14). The memory of the moment when the possible became actual lingers on as the pure marker of the beginning of a life withdrawn from actuality. Reflecting on the quarter century of her underground life at the end of the novel, she notes that "[m]ost of the time it was just everyday," albeit it that "no experience was ever one hundred percent what it was" (274). The shocking immediacy revealed in the accident condemns Louise to a life of disconnection. At the same time, the association of the "inseparabil-ity of possibility from actuality"—which Lukács situates in cinema and epic (Bewes, "Against" 289)—with lethal violence also has an effect on the novel's media ecology: it means that the immediacy and integrity of other media do not become the objects of the novel's formal desire, and that *Eat the Document* will develop another mode of access to reality that it cannot simply adopt from the visual media, but that it will model on media that capture reality in a different way.

Such a more instructive medium is introduced immediately after the novel's first section, when it switches to the journal of Jason, Louise's son, who is obsessed with the music of the Beach Boys. Jason is listen-ing to the "three-disc *Smile* bootleg," which features "like ten versions of the same song," which "are usually just alternate takes that vary only slightly from the other versions" (21). Importantly, this bootleg does not feature *different* versions, with an occasional "extra verse, or a different person singing lead" (21); instead, it contains different "screwups" of the same song, with only the smallest of differences—someone saying "one, two, three, four," or someone starting laughing in the middle of a track. Jason's immersion in this music, that is, thrives on the fetishization of minimal differences. Crucially, these differences are dependent on the use of analog—as opposed to both digital and written—recording devices. As Friedrich Kittler has observed, there is a fundamental distinction between the (traditionally privileged) pro-cess of writing, on the one hand, and acoustic recording devices like the phonograph and the tape recorder on the other. In writing, only those data that make symbolic sense and that can be captured in avail-able codes are retained and noted down; in writing, data have to pass through "the bottleneck of the signifier" and all noise sequences are cat-egorically excluded as insignificant (3–4). Textual media, that is, enforce a strict division between significant and insignificant elements, as they record some things while leaving others unwritten. As I showed in my previous chapter, such a distinction between significance and noise is carefully erased in Cole's *Open City*. And if this difference is crucial for a program such as that of the late Lukács that celebrates the power of types to exemplify the ways of the world, *Eat the Document* develops an alternative conception of the novel form that leans on the capacity of phonographs and tape recorders to function as unselective inscription devices, which indiscriminately record intentional as well as unintentional acoustic events: unlike writing, these devices "can record and reproduce the very timeflow of acoustic and optical data" (Kittler 3); in Kittler's words, they "do not have to make do with the grid of the symbolic" (11), and can directly inscribe reality without first deciding what parts of reality will count as significant. They do not, to echo Lukács's words, think in terms of totality.

If we return to Spiotta's evocation of the *Smile* bootleg with Kittler's distinction in mind, it emerges as a testimony to the power of recording devices to capture the flow of time and to sidestep the inevitable belatedness of all forms that depend on the medium of writing: their inability to capture those moments that cannot pass through the bottleneck of the signifier, and their inevitable loss of the realities that novelistic notation cannot inscribe. In contrast, Jason describes the effect of listening to these analog recordings of minimal differences as an achieved immediacy:

> What happens is you jump to a new level in your obsession where even the most arcane detail becomes fascinating. You follow a course of minutiae and repetition, and you find yourself utterly enthralled. Listening deeply to this kind of music is mesmerizing in itself; the same song ten times in a row is like a meditation or a prayer. (22)

Listening for minute inscriptions of reality that a textual medium would have failed to pick up is a strategy to *sustain* a desire for reality: the "desire to listen is being satisfied but hasn't been entirely fulfilled" (22). This sustainable attraction is different from the fatal collision with reality that the novel figures through the lethal accident, as well as from the achieved connection with reality that Lukács sees condensed in the notion of the type. *Eat the Document* is less interested in definitive aesthetic achievements that it cannot hope to emulate than in experiences that sustain the desire for reality in the media ecology it inhabits, as these are experiences that it *can* hope to adopt as an alternative program for the novel. *Eat the Document* no longer thinks in terms of totality;

instead, it sustains a desire for a reality it knows it can only record, not transform into significance.

In the novel's media ecology, "[e]ventually all will be equally faint" (195), and only a deliberate return to pre-digital recording media can offer a palpable sense of reality. The analog, in Cary Wolfe's words, figures a resistance to the "digitalization-of-all-media" because it "depends on the interplay of material forces and bodies [...] it is not wholly subsumable or predictable by programs and schemata" (284, 292). This sense of an escape from fatal abstraction is also provided by lost albums—"legendary albums that never saw commercial release," or that "only saw a brief initial release and are now out of print," and can therefore not be recoded into digital form (80). The lost album featured in the novel is an unreleased solo album by Dennis Wilson, the drummer for the Beach Boys. Like the earlier Beach Boys bootleg, the encounter with this record triggers a reaction in Louise that reveals a strange intimacy with the music and sets Jason on the trail of her hidden past. This past is finally uncovered when Jason spots his mother (under her old name) in the *Lost Love Movie*, a film he acquires from a "neo-Luddite Web ring" that "only sold original-format items: Super 8 films, 16-millimeter film, reel-to-reel audio" (248), without "digital remastering or video transferring" (216). Here again, analog media figure a palpable connection to history that digital culture has failed to erase.[8]

The *Lost Love Movie* turns out to have been made by Bobby Desoto, Louise's former lover. The parts of the novel that do not deal with Louise's and Jason's story focus on a loosely related set of characters centered around an alternative Seattle bookstore, and they present the novel's underlying media dynamic as a pervasive cultural condition. Jason's obsession with obsolete formats is not unique: he spots a broad cultural trend to have "the most advanced technology" imitate "inferior technology," movies "being made to look like a video game or, rather, a computer game" (123–24). Elsewhere, the novel remarks on a recent vogue for tapes: "outdated technology for young kids who already saw the vanguard in the past, the recent past, and not just in content but in format" (52). While the novel's insistence on the commodification of media nostalgia may compromise the power of the analog to serve as a viable aesthetic model, it at the same time generalizes that desire as a broad cultural need. The same ambiguity besets the attempts by Henry and Nash, who respectively finance and run the bookstore, to organize mock protest groups. They argue that, after all, "there are worse ways for these kids to expend their anger and energy" (43). Activism, that is, survives as anger management, but that does not make the need for it any less real. Nash reasons that "the actions were about keeping their own resistance vital. Direct action to keep you from being absorbed and destroyed" (131). Nash, who at the end of the novel turns out to be the same person as Bobby Desoto (although readers might have guessed this earlier), knows that mock protests, like obsolete media, are ways to keep the memory of the possibility of a significant engagement with reality alive, and to continue a desire for such an engagement, even if it cannot be actualized in the present. This, then, is the particular anachronistic operation through which *Eat the Document* disjoints itself from the present in order to achieve its contemporaneity: by bracketing the possibility of an aesthetics of the type, and through an extended confrontation with the powers of analog media, it dismantles the novelistic mandate to articulate the particular and the general, the private and the public, and reformulates its contemporary task as the work of preserving desire for action and hope for change. Like *Open City*, *Eat the Document* discovers that it can remember the past and salvage the future by recording, rather than transforming, reality.

Adam Kelly has remarked that *Eat the Document* evokes the late 1960s as "an era when political agency still seemed possible, when individual acts of protest could make a difference in the public sphere, and when notions of responsibility, while difficult and pressing, seemed comparatively well-defined" (220). These certainties are gone in the late 1990s, and this means that "the manner in which events can signify in unanticipated ways over time" becomes one of the novel's main themes (Kelly 221). The difficulty of identifying the origins of suffering and the effects of activism—and thus of finding a vantage for action—are most clearly illustrated in the story of Henry. Henry suffers from extremely vivid hallucinatory flashbacks in which he finds himself in a B-52 dropping bombs over Vietnam, and later experiences the Napalm jelling to his skin and burrowing into his flesh (128). His symptoms also include insomnia, depression, and suicidal ideation (70), which clearly identify his condition as post-traumatic stress disorder. Yet Henry was not in Vietnam: these are "proxy memories" of someone who "knew all about that war, and [...] never did a thing to stop it" (163). The symptoms are not an effect of his involvement in the war, but, it seems, of a failure to act against it. Yet the blurring of the clear boundaries between victims, activists, perpetrators, and bystanders does not stop there. In order to combat his symptoms, Henry takes a drug that is made by the same corporation that put dioxin in Agent Orange. The drug finally kills Henry, and so by some perverse, unpredictable logic, his non-involvement in the war indirectly still makes him a casualty of Agent Orange, and his hallucinations become accurate predictions rather than inaccurate memories.

The understated, suggestive way in which Spiotta's novel clusters these events in order to render legible the very real effects of an intangible (non-)act of (non-)resistance is an essential aspect of its aesthetic program, and affirms the importance of the analog as a model for the ways in which the novel aims to restore and maintain a desire for political agency. Without delivering a full account of the interactions between politics, the military, industry, and people's private lives, it still records—without pre-packaging into articulated significance—what would otherwise remain illegible. Events and connections are *neither* forced to pass "through the bottleneck of the signifier," as in traditional regimes of writing, except in the hardly trivial sense that they are rendered in language, *nor* surrendered to a "fully incorporated future of media sameness" in which we can "leave the materiality of the book behind" (Tabbi and Wutz 1, 19). Counteracting both the logic of writing and the drive for digitalization, *Eat the Document* insists on what we can call an *analog* aesthetic: a form that, even if it cannot compose events, connections, and characters into meaningful totalities (the lesson learned from the *Theory of the Novel*), still records them and renders their unpredictable interactions legible. Indeed, analog devices, unlike novels, "do not have to make do with the grid of the symbolic" (Kittler 11), and this gives them their paradoxical capacity to record reality. *Eat the Document* is a sustained attempt to test to what extent an inevitably symbolic form can yet adopt an *analog* aesthetic.

If *Eat the Document* aims to preserve the desire for political agency, this also means that it has few illusions about the present possibilities for political intervention. It carefully chastises Louise's initial desire for "tangible, unequivocal action" (188). Instead, in a much more minimal gesture, it keeps the desire for decisive action *legible* by encrypting it in the media ecology that underlies the novel. Like Spiotta's later novel *Stone Arabia*, *Eat the Document* invests much of its stylistic bravado in ekphrases of visual and auditory works. By featuring extensive descriptions of music and cinema, it makes the absence of and the desire for these forms part of the novel's texture, without feeding the illusion that their immediacy can somehow be achieved in novelistic form. The novel invites its readers to adopt this attitude through its very title: *Eat the Document* is the title of an obscure documentary about Bob Dylan, which is even today only available as a bootleg and screened on very rare occasions. The title only activates a desire that it perpetuates but does not satisfy. Just as the specters of epic and cinema kept the question of the (im)possibility of the novel rigorously open for Lukács, this novel's media nostalgia allows it to sustain an examination of the residual powers of the form, and to draw on the ontology of analog media to rethink novelistic notation in a way that does not aim at an impossible totality, but merely renders reality legible.

Rendering and keeping things legible: we already encountered the trope of legibility in the austere aesthetics of Teju Cole's *Open City*, where it indicated a refusal of conclusive interpretation and sensual immediacy, and an insistence on the dutiful recording of historical time. I have imported it in my discussion of *Eat the Document* from an interview with Spiotta following the publication of her novel, in which she uses the term to describe the way she, as a novelist, engages reality: "I'm interested in relationships, in character, but within a specific social context. Which is kind of a political thing—I admit that. But it's what I'm interested in, and it's how I believe human behavior is legible" (qtd. in Johnson). Making life legible is, for Spiotta, a matter of tracing the interrelations between the self and its social contexts, a commitment that comes close enough to the job description of the traditional novel, yet takes on a more minimalist tenor here: the different unintegrated strands of the novel do not achieve a significant interpenetration of personal fates and public meanings, but only map out a set of trajectories and encounters that are recorded even if they cannot pass through the "bottleneck of the signifier." The novel awakens and preserves a desire for a significant connection with the real that it cannot achieve.

Spiotta uses the "legibility" trope a second time in the interview, when she notes that, at the beginning of the twenty-first century, "it's harder than ever to engage the idea of revolutionary violence [...] It's hard to make it legible" (qtd. in Johnson). Spiotta here draws attention to a conspicuous absence in *Eat the Document* that I already remarked on: the events of 9/11, which have altered the parameters within which the question of the (im)possibility of the novel can be approached. *Eat the Document* ends in Seattle in 2000, the year after the protests against the World Trade Organization that, at the time Spiotta was writing, had already become a receding memory rather than the onset of a widespread repoliticization of contemporary life that they had initially seemed to be. The novel only records this lost future in passing, when it notes that scarves like those "the anarchist blac bloc kids used" are on sale in "a large, trendy clothing store called Suburban Guerilla" (255–57). Suspended between Seattle in 1999 and New York in 2001, and barely registering either, the ending of the novel indicates that it is concerned with a consideration of the (im)possibility of the novel that is not primarily determined by present events, but rather achieved by updating the endemic untimeliness that Lukács's *Theory of the Novel* makes available. I now turn directly to the issue of the post-9/11 novel—an issue that, like Kunzru and Spiotta, I have bracketed for as long as possible—in order to read a novel that adopts the same central conceit as *My Revolutions* and *Eat the Document* while declining to problematize its relation to the present; the result, as we will see, is a surfeit of presence that preempts an enabling contemporaneity.

Russell Banks's *The Darling* and the worlding of the post-9/11 novel

In a widely noted essay from 2009, Richard Gray diagnoses American literature in the wake of 9/11 with a failure of the imagination. While most fictions duly acknowledge that "the cataclysmic events of 9/11" are "a defining element in our contemporary structure of feeling" ("Open Doors" 129), their assessment of that impact rarely moves beyond "the preliminary stages of traumas" (130). And while much fiction after 9/11 indulges in a "[r]ecognition that the old mindset has been destroyed," it lacks "a fictional measure of the new world view" (132). However attentive it is to the impact of disastrous events on the lives of its protagonists, canonical post-9/11 fiction—Gray, like many critics, mentions DeLillo's *Falling Man*, Jay McInerney's *The Good Life*, and Claire Messud's *The Emperor's Children*—suffers from a tendency to "retreat into domestic detail" (134); time and again, "cataclysmic public events are measured purely and simply in terms of their impact on the emotional entanglements of their protagonists" (134). The problem, in other words, is a failure of imaginative nerve: while these novels' routine references to the events and to the paradigm of trauma duly "recognize that some kind of alteration of imaginative structures is required," they lack "the ability and the willingness imaginatively to act on that recognition" (134).[9]

For Gray, this lack of nerve leads to a double limitation. First, these novels do not translate the perceived need for "new forms of consciousness" and "new structures of ideology and the imagination" (133–34) into a questioning of the limits of traditional realism and a search for innovative forms: instead, they "simply assimilate the unfamiliar into familiar structures" (134). Rachel Greenwald Smith echoes this assessment when she points out that canonical post-9/11 novels lack a sufficient "exposure to the transfiguring effect of the catastrophe," as they fail to reflect "the breaking of the world in the breaking of form" ("Organic Shrapnel" 153–54). This responds to a more pervasive sense that the old protocols of realism no longer suffice to capture the ethical complexities and affective recalibrations of early twenty-first-century life (Davis Wood, DeRosa, Randall). When studies of post-9/11 fiction unproblematically assert that novelists are taking on an "ongoing mission to interpret the culture and to provide points of view from which to approach it" (Versluys 12), they overlook the fact that the epistemic privilege of the novel form is itself at issue; they forget that the novel form, which has historically sustained particular structures of feeling and perception, cannot remain unaffected by the recalibration of belief and feeling that is underway in contemporary life, whether we periodize the present as post-9/11 or not. Gray's intervention strongly suggests that overcoming the formal impasses of contemporary fiction requires a willingness to question the self-evident ability of representations of domestic life to figure larger social constellations. As I showed in the previous sections, Spiotta's and Kunzru's examination of the necessarily private afterlife of activism amounts to just such an interrogation. Even if they are not centrally concerned with the events of 9/11, they take up formal challenges that mainstream post-9/11 fiction tends to sidestep. Indeed, these novels' decision to only reference 9/11 in an oblique way is entirely consonant with their readiness to question the mandate of traditional realisms; as novels that do not mention 9/11 and yet confront the main ethical, political, and aesthetic challenges that surface in the wake of those events, they help expand the category of post-9/11 fiction beyond those works that address 9/11 itself (Davis Wood 135).

The pervasive domestication of change in mainstream post-9/11 novels is not only visible in a lack of *formal* innovation, but also in a failure to imagine the *global* dimensions of that change—and this is a second limitation that Gray identifies. These novels are so excessively occupied with domestic trauma that "their encounters with strangeness" are often stalled in "a kind of imaginative paralysis" (Gray, "Open Doors" 135). While Gray himself notes that recent immigrant fictions have begun to "open up and hybridize American culture," Michael Rothberg, in his response to Gray, calls for "a supplementary form of deterritorialization" ("Failure of the Imagination" 153). Rothberg proposes to supplement Gray's advocation of the "centripetal" globalization on display in immigrant fiction with "a complementary centrifugal mapping that charts the outward movement of American power" and that explores "the prosthetic reach of [the U.S.] empire into other worlds" (153). For Rothberg, this entails "mapping America's extraterritorial expansion; exploring the epistemology, phenomenology, and impact of America's global reach; and revealing the cracks in its necessarily incomplete hegemony" (158). For Gray and Rothberg, contemporary fiction must do more than cultivate "an ethics of disturbance" with regard to mainstream fiction's tendency toward domestication (Irom 520): it must supplement its questioning of the forms and functions of the novel with a deterritorializing exploration of global fissures and alterities.

In a wide-ranging study of the narrative ethics of literature after 9/11, which demonstrates that the fallout of 9/11 is encrypted in many novels that are not thematically dedicated to it, Georgiana Banita has illustrated that recent fiction—what she calls the "second wave" of 9/11 fiction (166) has begun to heed Gray's and Rothberg's calls. This wave of novels "clearly attempts to deal with America's liminal position between historical borders and cultures" (166), and it has moved away from introspective accounts toward "a vivid interest in the human impact of the War on Terror on diasporic communities and in the larger implications of the wars in Afghanistan and Iraq" (56). But we may well ask what has happened to the other challenge that Gray identified—the need for formal recalibration? Banita seems to sidestep this issue, when she notes that "formal strategies" are, in the final analysis, "merely an envelope for rhetorical tropes" that do the actual work of generating "a productive and aesthetically experimental ethical disorientation" (110). Indeed, for Banita the move toward the domestic, or what she calls "the transference of the public into the personal" (110), is itself such a mildly unsettling trope, and can have an innovative, defamiliarizing effect.

The formal innovation Gray calls for and the unsettling of the relations between the public and the personal that Banita advocates have at least one thing in common: they are both strategies through which contemporary fiction can interrogate the kind of realism that I have identified with Lukács's notion of the type. In the previous sections, I have shown how Kunzru and Spiotta formulate fractured responses to the challenges facing contemporary fiction, as they start from such an unhinging of the private and the public through the conceit of the inactive afterlife of activism. As they filter their negotiations of the viability of the novel form through an affective media ecology, rather than through a direct engagement with 9/11, they underline that the challenges facing the contemporary novel are part of a formal dynamic that is not reducible to the post-9/11 context.

In both these novels, the interrogation of the (im)possibilities of the novel form is not complemented by an increased worldliness of the kind that Gray, Rothberg, and Banita all call for.[10] *Eat the Document* stays on domestic soil, while Kunzru's protagonist's time in Asia is less a global engagement than a means to fill up narrative time between the early 1970s and the late 90s. In the remainder of this chapter, I focus on a novel that, like the ones discussed before, adopts the conceit of the underground afterlife of a political activist, but that is, in contrast to these, a thoroughly *worldly* novel that, as Gray recommends, "pivot[s] away from the American homeland and direct[s] all our attention to America's extraterritorial expansion through trade, tourism, war, cultural or political or even military invasion" (*After the Fall* 124).[11] Russell Banks's *The Darling* (2004) brings into relief the projects of Kunzru and Spiotta; in contrast to them, it embraces a worldliness that allows it to criticize U.S. involvement around the globe. Still, its rendering of the historical present does not disjoint itself from that present by addressing the formal questions that Spiotta and Kunzru do take up. *The Darling* is a confidently imagined historical novel and an unproblematic first-person narrative, yet its refusal of formal complexity ends up foregrounding the limitations of a project that explores the global dimensions of contemporary life without broaching the question of the novel's viability. The result, I argue, is a novel that, in Agamben's terms, "coincide[s] too well with the epoch" to be contemporaneous with it (41). It demonstrates what I already anticipated in my reading of *Open City*: that an imagining of worldly or cosmopolitan encounters does not automatically amount to a significant engagement with reality.

The Darling tells the story of Hannah Musgrave, a child of 1960s' privilege, who has to flee the United States after her involvement with the Weather Underground. Yet unlike the other activist protagonists we have encountered, she only disappears from the public domain to end up in Liberia, where she works for an American university in a position sponsored by a pharmaceutical company, and becomes an unwitting accomplice of the United States' dramatic involvement in devastations abroad. She will ultimately end up (unwittingly) helping Charles Taylor escape from his American prison, which will eventually lead to the murder of her husband—a Liberian official—and the transformation of her sons into child soldiers and revenge killers in Liberia's atrocious civil war. The novel rather unproblematically situates its protagonist in close proximity to actual historical events; it features long digressions on Liberian history, and contains detailed accounts of Samuel Doe's 1980 coup and the escalation of the civil war in the following two decades. Like *Eat the Document* and *My Revolutions*, *The Darling* aims to "reinvigorate debates concerning identity and the agency of the subject" in the "culturally sensitive post-9/11 climate" (Varvogli 658, 660); in stark contrast to these novels, however, Banks's protagonist is a privileged witness as well as a reluctant participant in the mainstream of national history, albeit the national history of a country that is not hers; *The Darling*, in other words, mobilizes (rather than problematizes) a traditional critical realist template for its worldly concerns (Wegner).

Hannah's inability to extract her (American) self from worldly affairs informs one of the novel's main themes. That most of the novel is set in Liberia, a country founded as a colony for freed African Americans in the nineteenth century, underlines this compulsive involvement (Birnbaum). Yet Hannah's *factual* implication in foreign affairs— through the liberation of Charles Taylor and her work for American businesses abroad—contrasts sharply with her *psychological* distance from real-world events. During her times in the Weather Underground, she appears as an "anomic revolutionary" (Gordon); when living in Liberia, she appears "empty of purpose but full of unfocused goodwill" (Phillips), initially living happily in a bubble of privilege and failing to be affected by the cascade of events around her. Hannah's story is, as she realizes in the novel's last sentence, "the story of an American darling" (408), a description in which the adjective indexes her nearly automatic involvement in foreign affairs and the noun an equally representative sense of naivety and carelessness. The novel foregrounds the similarities between Hannah's activism and the United States' entanglement in other countries' affairs; they appear as two forms of the same undirected involvement. In Hannah's retrospective narration, "the bombings, the robberies, the terrorist campaign against the war, against colonialism and U.S. Imperialism" (114) in which she participated in her youth are merely symptoms of the same frenetic yet indifferent mindset that also fuels the colonialism and imperialism she opposes. She almost absent-mindedly drifts into activism as "a newly minted rebel, fresh faced and romantic" (13), and notes how in the new century, that mindset might predispose someone like her to become "a born-again Christian fundamentalist, dark and judgmental" (8).

In *The Darling*, youthful activism is cut from the same cloth that underlies American involvement abroad. Its protagonist's lack of commitment to either of these phenomena makes her an ideal vehicle for affirming this continuity and for blotting out the contradictions between them. Indeed, Hannah functions as a traditional typical character, who stands "for something larger and more meaningful than [herself]" (Jameson, *Marxism and Form* 191); she stands for America, and her exile and compulsive worldliness are Banks's way of asserting the need for contemporary fiction to leave the American homeland and take stock of America's extraterritorial entanglements.[12] The novel takes this structure of typicality for granted; unlike other fictions of the afterlife of activism, it does not evoke a dissociation between private life and public meaning. Therefore, Hannah's (or America's) actions are inescapably *significant*; they cannot but have resonances—for the reader, but also in the world of the novel: her forced escape from American life only ends up engulfing her in global guilt. The insistent demands of historical and political contexts are not suspended; and while such a suspension creates the imaginative room to interrogate the novel's epistemic and ethical mandate for Kunzru and Spiotta, its absence here is reflected in a refusal of formal complication. *The Darling* is an eerily perfect counterpart to the other fictions of the afterlife of activism that I have discussed; together, these novels' shared as well as their diametrically opposed strategies trace the contours of a particular subgenre of post-9/11 fiction.

The Darling insistently refuses to question its own possibility conditions until its very last paragraph. Here, Hannah notes that, in the wake of 9/11, she "saw that the story of [her] life could have no significance in the larger world" (408). Hers is "the story of an American darling, and had been from the beginning" (408). This belated recognition of its residual provincialism retroactively qualifies the novel as a prolonged exercise in denial, as the undead remainder of a formal tradition that knows, and ultimately acknowledges, that it will no longer quite do. This gesture is comparable to the one Richard Gray observes in Claire Messud's *The Emperor's Children*, one of the canonical post-9/11 novels: it acknowledges the need for a different literary practice "by suggesting how 'forlorn' texts written prior to the crisis appear to be. But it does not enact it" (*After the Fall* 30). *The Darling* ends up testifying to the insufficiency of its attempt to map "America's extraterritorial expansion (the global reach of American culture and power)" (Gray, *After the Fall* 17) without interrogating its own formal parameters, even as it is these parameters that condition its access to the world.

As *The Darling* approaches the afterlife of activism from a direction that is directly opposed to that of *Eat the Document* and *My Revolutions*, it is unsurprising that it also constellates the fascination with immediacy and the focus on different media, which are intricately connected in those two novels, in a radically different way. Hannah only achieves moments of perfect intimacy and insight when she is among "the dreamers"—the name she gives to the chimpanzees she takes care of in her lab in Liberia. Contact with the chimps allows her to momentarily sidestep the fundamental dissonance of human existence: when she "penetrate[s] their consciousness," she discovers minds "behaving as if they were free to look at every single thing as if it had never been seen before, as if everything, a leaf, an ant, a human ear, were of terrible and wondrous significance" (20). In this state of mind, there is "only the immediate present" (20). This state is not linked to epic or cinema, as we might have come to expect, but rather to a simian dream state. The chimps allow Hannah to transcend what the novel theorizes as a state of empathy and exercise real sympathy—to experience the difference between "feeling *for* the other and feeling *with* the other" (340). Empathy is, for Hannah, merely a variant of narcissism, as it indexes a relation with someone or something "that's as real as yourself" (341). In the logic of the novel, empathy characterizes the *psychological* distance and indifference besetting Hannah's—and America's, and the novel's—*factual* involvement in the world, while the immediate connection that the novel calls sympathy figures a withdrawal from the world into the realm of the merely private interaction between man and chimp, or the life on the farm to which Hannah turns after 9/11, when she has come to realize the meaninglessness of her story for the larger world.[13] Immediacy, for Banks, is not an object of the novel's formal desire, but the mark of an ultimate insignificance it works hard to deny.

In spite of the novel's tendency to resist the problematization of its own formal status, Hannah's only true act of unconditional commitment—as opposed to the marriage, the motherhood, the bombing plots, and the liberation scheme she seems to stumble into—does articulate the specter of immediacy (figured by the chimps) and the powers of visual media. In order to solicit support for the chimps, Hannah uses a camera intended for family films to record the deprivation of the chimps, "dead and dying of hunger and thirst and neglect" (344):

> I flipped the switch of the video camera and slowly, back and forth in front of the cages, from one foul end of the Quonset hut to the other, I shot close-ups of the dreamers' flaccid faces, their emaciated, scab-covered bodies, their sores and self-inflicted abrasions and wounds, and I took lingering footage of the dead. Then I stepped to the center of the hut and panned the length of it, filming a slow, sweeping medium shot of the rack of cages. Doc lifted his huge head, and when he looked at me, I switched to zoom and closed on his blank gaze and held it for a full minute. (342)

The emphatic attention to technical detail in this passage is a rare recognition of the limits of the novel's own procedures, and it indicates Hannah's own total absorption in the moment. The phrase "lingering footage" points to a peculiar temporality that seems to outlive human perception. This desire returns when she mentions her recurrent fantasy "to survive [her] own death so [she] could overhear the postmortem" (58). In this way, this passage points to a mode of perception that is not accessible to the novel. By registering the animals' suffering in a medium that is appropriate for that task and transmitting it to others, Hannah will try to move others—specifically, president Doe, with whom she watches the footage—beyond the limits of sympathy into the folds of a companionship that is both intimate and transformative. Here, the power of visual media and the promise of immediacy are finally connected.

The unedited footage is described as being "as shocking and indicting as footage of the hold of a slave ship" (344). It is here, I want to suggest, that *The Darling*, in spite of its sustained profession of self-confidence, registers an otherwise unacknowledged desire for a more immediate access to the nerve center of American guilt, figured in this sentence by the unsolicited comparison to a slave ship. In this one moment, the novel realizes what it manages to repress until its last paragraph: that an effective reengagement with a world beyond national self-satisfaction requires a thorough interrogation of the validity of the templates of the traditional novel. Near the end of the novel, we learn that it is Hannah's ultimate failure to save the lives of the chimps during the Liberian civil war that motivates her telling of the story: "their curses rained down on me, and my long remorse and secret shame were replaced that day by the *permanent mournfulness* that has given rise to the telling of this story" (402). The novel is, in short, an act of penance for a barely acknowledged failure to find, or to even recognize the need to find, a fitting form.

My readings of *My Revolutions* and *Eat the Document* have shown that these other fictions of the afterlife of activism are crucially occupied with such formal hesitations, to the extent that they entirely bracket the issue of worldliness and rather focus on the formal interrogation that, as *The Darling* realizes with a vengeance, precedes the imagining of a worldliness that matters. In the early twenty-first century, when the end of history has decidedly failed to materialize, a suspension of all-too-present concerns and a staging of the end of the novel seem surprisingly powerful strategies for tackling the question of the politics and ethics of form. The suspension of the present makes it possible for the novel to exercise its paradoxical contemporaneity—its relevance for a present with which it cannot coincide.

Coda: The Descent of the Novel (James Meek)

The earth, after humans, will offer "a reading" of a species'
history, just as we might say that Robinson Crusoe *offers*
"a reading" of race, empire and capitalism, even if neither
Defoe nor his readers actually actualized the sense of the
reading.
—Claire Colebrook, *The Death of the PostHuman*

This book has interrogated the ethics and politics of contemporary
fiction by foregrounding one particular cluster of literary strategies.
While the novels in this study draw on very diverse tonal and narrative
repertoires, they all set out to provoke a crisis in the emotive scenarios
through which the novel form has traditionally done its cultural work.
As I emphasized especially in my readings of McCarthy (in the first
chapter) and Coetzee (in the second), such an evacuation of familiar emotive experiences generates a space for less tractable and more
awkward feelings—what Sianne Ngai has described as "meta-feeling[s]
in which one feels confused about what one is feeling," or as "dysphoric
affect[s] of affective disorientation—of being lost on one's own 'cognitive
map' of available affects" (Ngai 14). While Ngai emphasizes the sense of
disappointment besetting this shift from codified emotion to trackless
affect, this book has shown that the production of such "after-affects"
makes room for a very broad set of emotive registers: Coetzee's work,
for instance, delivers a sense of embodied, creatural excess, while in
both *Open City* and *Eat the Document*, a sense of disconnection displaces
political hope from contemporary subjects to imagined communities of
posthumous readers. Affective disorientation, then, not only informs
negative experiences; by generating encounters that escape consciously
codified emotions, it cuts across the boundaries of the individual and

the collective that the novel has traditionally drawn and policed, and intuits possibilities for ethical and political connections that disturb extant social categories and divisions. In this way, these novels' formal strategies signal an open-ended potentiality for transformation; they provide what Rachel Greenwald Smith has described as "a wealth of feeling that is poised for connection, for recombination, attachment, and eventual codification" ("Postmodernism" 438).

I want to insist on the capacities of "after-affects" to cut across the customary categories to which the novel has traditionally referred the lives that it imagines—categories such as the subject, the individual, the nation, and (as I will underline in this coda) even the human. For Nancy Armstrong, for instance, the modern novel is essentially a cultural technology for resolving the unavoidable tensions between the asocial interests of individuals and the demands of a society that can only accommodate individuals' rights to self-expression to the extent that they do not threaten the liberties of others ("Fiction of Bourgeois Morality" 350–51). Reconciling these concerns requires a careful calibration of autonomy and flexibility that has taken different shapes in the history of the form. Yet the novel does more than navigate the relations between the individual and the collective: as Mario Ortiz-Robles has emphasized, the constitution of novel characters relies on processes in which non-subjective affects and textual events are transcoded as individual emotions. For Ortiz-Robles, the project of the traditional novel consists in "the narrative elaboration of an emotional subject or a subject of emotion" (193); the novelistic subject, that is, is the effect of the "formalization of multiple [affective] events whose material singularity is suppressed in a process of sedimentation that gives the illusion of a whole, totalized, or totalizable experience" (167). If the traditional novel has managed to codify the relations between individuals, subjects, and collectives, it has done so through a massive effort to capture, contain, and map affective events. The novels in this study self-consciously inhabit the zone between non-subjective affect and subjective emotion in order to reconfigure the ethics and politics of fiction.

The second half of *Contemporary Literature and the End of the Novel* recognizes that the Anglophone novel has, in the past few decades, been less interested in suturing subjects to their national contexts than in exploring the ways in which subjects increasingly inhabit transnational and cosmopolitan domains. My discussions of *Open City* and of post-9/11 fiction more generally have shown that contemporary fiction also disturbs prevalent transnational and cosmopolitan models. Especially *Open City* intimates that such models, in their reliance on empathy, curiosity, and the transformative powers of the imagination, continue to rely on assumptions customarily linked to the traditional novel. The result is that they constrain the capacity of fiction to engage radically different affective modalities and realities that cannot be captured under the rubrics of the transnational or the cosmopolitan. The question of the ethics and politics of fiction is not exhausted by the choice between the domestic and the worldly, as such divisions are crossed through by radically inappropriable dimensions. McCarthy's secondary affects, Coetzee's creatural life, Cole's fugue state, and Spiotta's analog aesthetics are so many placeholders for a difference that even the extended scope of a more worldly fiction does not register.

I conclude this book by tightening the connections between fiction's emotive operations across the boundaries of the individual and the collective, on the one hand, and its occupation with a dimension that a cosmopolitan extension of scope cannot contain, on the other. I bring the overlapping issues of the human, of form, and of scale in dialogue with two contemporary critical discourses that powerfully suggest the productivity of imagining a *shift in scale* rather than an *extension of scope* for confronting contemporary ethical and political challenges. Contemporary critical thinking on the anthropocene and on the geological ramifications of the literary imagination—the two discussions with which I engage below—show that the emphasis on *interhuman* connectedness in cosmopolitan and transnational frameworks can fruitfully be supplemented with a recognition of a more excessive otherness; to the extent that such an overwhelming difference does not fit existing social categories, it calls for the kind of formal and affective innovations that this book has examined. After introducing these perspectives, I turn to James Meek's understudied post-9/11 novel *We Are Now Beginning Our Descent* (2008) in order to illustrate how contemporary fiction provides formal possibilities that discussions of cultural geology and the anthropocene have not yet considered. Meek's novel, like many other post-9/11 fictions, begins with an attempt to position itself along the continuum between the domestic and the transnational, only to shift its scale to a dimension that is radically exterior to that spectrum, and that calls forth a form of life that is not merely human, but instead what I have earlier theorized, in relation to the work of Coetzee, as creatural life. *We Are Now Beginning Our Descent* occupies the same uncharted territory that the other novels in this study also inhabit; as it does so in the name of concerns that implicate the very category of the human, it underscores the ethical and political stakes of contemporary fiction's unsettling affective operations.

The scales of literature

In an article entitled "The Posthuman Comedy," Mark McGurl commends Wai-Chee Dimock's influential work on the "deep time" of literary history for relating American literature to other times and continents. Dimock's daring juxtapositions of Thoreau and the Hindu *Bhagavad Gita*, for instance, or of Henry James and the *Odyssey*, expand "the tracts of space-time across which literary scholars might draw valid links between author and author" (533). For McGurl, Dimock instantiates the "transnational turn" that I have also observed, in my previous chapter, in Richard Gray's and Michael Rothberg's interventions on post-9/11 fiction: for her, as for those critics, an extension of space-time somehow reinvigorates "our very sense of the connectedness among human beings" across the globe (533); for Dimock and the commitments she exemplifies, literature operates as "a remarkably frictionless conduit of transnational sympathy and identification" (534). As my previous two chapters have shown, contemporary fiction's affective work unsettles these assumptions and points to a dimension that transnational circulation cannot capture; what interests me in McGurl's work is that he gives that dimension some of its names (the posthuman, geology, deep time), and that he restates this imaginative challenge in genre-theoretical terms.

McGurl argues for the need to supplement the transnational exploration of different locales and temporalities with the more encompassing perspective of a "new cultural geology." This approach would "position culture in a time-frame large enough to crack open the carapace of human self-concern, exposing it to the idea, and maybe even the fact, of its external ontological preconditions, its ground" ("New Cultural" 380). Transnationalism, even in its most adventurous forms (as in the work of Dimock), fails to factor in "scientific knowledge of the spatiotemporal vastness and numerousness of the nonhuman world" ("Posthuman" 537). McGurl envisions a literature in which this nonhuman vastness "becomes visible as a formal, representational, and finally existential problem" (537). He does not find these more capacious spatiotemporal parameters in the realist novel, which typically "eddies in an unheroic present" ("Critical" 632), but rather in the genres of science fiction and horror. Unlike the literary novel, these genres are "willing to risk artistic ludicrousness in their representation of the inhumanly large and long" ("Posthuman" 539). For McGurl, "those rare works of literature that set themselves the task of scaling our vision dramatically up or down or both" (541) define what he calls the "posthuman comedy"—his term for "the appearance of the problem of scale in modern literary history" ("Critical" 632).

McGurl's term "posthuman comedy" usefully foregrounds questions of genre and of the role that literary form plays in intimating nonhuman forces.[1] Yet even if McGurl explicitly excludes the literary novel—as opposed to genre fiction—from the category of posthuman comedy, it persists in a less conspicuous form in his intervention. For one thing, McGurl's expectation that genre fiction make the challenges of scale "visible as a formal, representational, and finally existential problem" voices a markedly *novelistic* conception of literature: as I explained in my introduction, the expectation that literature can recode historical and ontological challenges as existential concerns is traditionally directed at the literary novel, as the main modern literary technology for the management of empathy and desire. To put this differently, if genre fiction has the means to *evoke* nonhuman otherness, it cannot therefore do the cultural work of making it *matter* as a formal and existential *problem*; indeed, McGurl's case would be better served by recording the breakdown of the human in the face of the nonhuman in the very form through which the human has traditionally been imagined—in the literary novel. Even if the impact of nonhuman otherness on human life requires that the narrative repertoire of the traditional novel be revised, this shift can be made palpable by confronting the limits of that repertoire in the very form in which the reader expects it to be operative.[2] As I show below, this is precisely what happens in *We Are Now Beginning Our Descent*, as the gradual intrusion of nonhuman dimensions forces it to abandon the novelistic techniques that it initially, if only reluctantly, adopts. Meek's novel tests the form's "elastic powers" only to radicalize these to breaking point through their confrontation with an "excessive otherness" that finally overwhelms them—a condition that David Palumbo-Liu has identified as a consequence of the demand on contemporary literature to deliver ever more otherness (15, 29).

The overlap between questions of scale, form, and the human is also explored in discourses on the anthropocene—and this is the second critical domain on which I will draw to fine-tune my account of contemporary fiction's ethics and politics of form. The notion of the anthropocene has gained a wide currency in the last few years, as its relevance for the study of literature and culture has begun to be assessed.[3] Coined by the Dutch chemist Paul Crutzen and the biologist Eugene Stoermer in 2000, the term captures the influence of human activity on the world's geological and ecological make-up, and proposes that man's dramatic impact on the globe's chemical composition and climate since James Watt's development of a practical steam engine in 1784 be recognized as a geochronological unit in its own right.[4] Capturing the realization that "in terms of key environmental parameters, the Earth System has recently moved well outside the range of natural variability exhibited over at least the last half million years" (Crutzen and Steffen 251), the anthropocene underlines the urgency of learning to think of humanity "as a geological force" (Chakrabarty, "Postcolonial" 2). The anthropocene, in other words, demands an imaginative change of scale; it requires that we "scale up our imagination of the human" (Chakrabarty, "Climate" 206), as the human now at once participates in "differently-scaled histories of the planet, of life and species, and of human societies" ("Postcolonial" 14).

While the anthropocene opens up the same sublime vistas as McGurl's posthuman comedy, the conception of human agency that it entails is very different. If McGurl wants to acknowledge the vanity of human striving in the face of "an absolutely indifferent, starkly inhuman universe" ("Posthuman" 548), the anthropocene inserts the human into geological deep time as a responsible agent. Deep time, in the anthropocene, is not the human's other, but rather another plane on which it cannot but exert agency. If anything, it further augments human responsibility and agency: the human is the force that has decisively contributed to global warming, mass extinction of species, and rising sea levels, but it is also the only power that can consciously intervene in the destructive movements it has unleashed. In the anthropocene, the human needs to think of itself not only as a "human human" (human life as we think we know it), but also as a particularly "nonhuman human" (Chakrabarty, "Postcolonial"12), as a force that is of the same order as nonhuman agencies such as rocks, meteors, and volcanoes. The anthropocene does not require—indeed, it does not even allow—that we abandon our customary conceptions of human life for a geological one, but rather that we imagine "human agency over multiple and incommensurable scales at once" (1) and think "disjunctively about the human" (2). Human life, that is, must be figured as both a geological force and a conscious agent. The crucial imaginative task is not that of *evoking* nonhuman dimensions, but that of figuring the fissure that cultural geology and the anthropocene locate at the heart of human life.

In the case of the anthropocene, a disjunction at the heart of human life; in the case of cultural geology, a confrontation with the limits of the human scale: both these critical contexts point to the unsettling of codified emotion by intractable affect as a strategy for responding to the reorganization of human life that, they remind us, is currently underway. The form that has traditionally sustained the categories of the human and the individual offers a privileged site to stage the collapse of the "age-old humanist distinction between human history and natural history" (Chakrabarty, "Climate" 201) and to explore the "affect and knowledge about collective human pasts and futures" that this collapse unleashes (221). Ian Baucom has remarked that the anthropocene "seems to wreak havoc on [...] key principles of historical understanding and political commitment" (3); Claire Colebrook, for her part, notes that it calls for a rethinking of "the terms of our ethical vocabulary—justice, fairness, respect, forgiveness, hospitality or virtue" ("Not Symbiosis, Not Now" 185). All of which means that the anthropocene positions human life in the emotive and conceptual *terra incognita* where all of the novels in this study operate: in the aftermath of the breakdown of categories such as the human, the subject, and the individual that can neither be perpetuated nor abandoned, and that require innovative affective efforts in order to reconfigure the ethics and politics of fiction.

On creatural war

The disfigurement of human life by the anthropocene and the posthuman comedy echoes tonalities and dissonances that this book has addressed before. If McGurl applauds genre fiction for its willingness to "risk ludicrousness" ("Posthuman" 539), Lars Iyer's staging of farcical life and Coetzee's evocation of creatural life explore tonal and affective possibilities that make ludicrousness part of the repertoire of contemporary fiction. For Iyer and Coetzee, farcical and creatural life name a condition in which an outworn form of life (such as the novel) can no longer be comfortably inhabited, but cannot for all that simply be abandoned. This powerless persistence of disgraced forms of life also marks human life in the anthropocene: customary models of intention and agency, of responsibility and chance, are thrown into crisis as human life needs to think of itself as *also* a geological force, without that new designation cancelling its former attachments. The anthropocene reminds the human that it can never simply coincide with a particular form of life. The questions of the human, of form, and of scale come together in the close affinity between the anthropocene, on the one hand, and the novelistic elaboration of creatural—or farcical, or ludicrous—life on the other.

Before I show how *We Are Now Beginning Our Descent* explores this overlap, I want to briefly return to the account of the relation between the rise of the novel and the domestication of creatural life in my second chapter. I showed there that Ian Watt's influential account of the rise of novelistic individualism suppresses the twitches and spasms of creatural life that overwhelm Watt's source text, Auerbach's *Mimesis*, when it evokes the wake of Dante's *Divina Commedia*. What can it mean, then, that these creatural twists emerge again in contemporary fiction as the domestic union of the novel and the individual unravels? What, in other words, connects the period post-*Divina Commedia* to the present posthuman comedy? Recall that Auerbach discusses "creatural realism" in the tenth chapter of *Mimesis*, which deals with *Le réconfort de Madame de Fresne* (232), a late work by the fifteenth-century writer Antoine de la Sale, on whom Auerbach had already extensively written in his 1921 dissertation. The work relates "an episode from the Hundred Years' War," and it evokes the realities of war through "unconcealed creatural realism" with "symptoms of excess and crude degeneracy" (*Mimesis* 246–48). Ian Watt's domestication of creatural life is then also a suppression of the realities of war—a reality that Auerbach famously acknowledges in his epilogue to *Mimesis* (557) and, I am suggesting, in its little-discussed tenth chapter.

The distinction between Watt's suppression of war and Auerbach's explicit as well as oblique acknowledgments of it are consistent with their different autobiographical trajectories. Watt read the work of Auerbach, like that of Lukács, after his return to England and the United States, where he arrived after he spent the time between February 1942 and August 1945 as a prisoner of war doing forced labor in the East. Marina MacKay has shown that these traumatic experiences resonate throughout *The Rise of the Novel*, even if these resonances only rarely crystallize into explicit references to war. MacKay's account of the enabling role of Watt's "formative exposure to the sheer fragility of the solitary self" (139) for his famous account of the rise of individuality is especially surprising in light of the smoothness of Watt's prose, which conceals "the existential dread that underlies the rise of the novel" (Carnochan qtd. in MacKay 141n9) as much as the traumas of its author. This reluctance to recognize the horrors of war—both in literary history and in his life story—is reflected in Watt's decision to assert an unproblematic continuity between "the Christian view of man," which "founds its greatest expression in Dante's *Divina Commedia*," and "the serious literary portrayal of ordinary people and of common life" in the novel (*Rise of the Novel* 79).

This is the only moment in *The Rise of the Novel* where Watt explicitly mentions Auerbach, which makes it all the more remarkable that he here overwrites Auerbach's registration of war in the chapter on Antoine de la Sale. This chapter emphatically records the uncontainable force of war in history as well as in Auerbach's life at the time he was writing *Mimesis*. This becomes clear when we compare *Mimesis* to Auerbach's 1929 book *Dante als Dichter der irdischen Welt*. Written before the war, the Dante book offers a smooth literary historical narrative of untraumatized continuity that anticipates that of Watt: Auerbach sums up Dante's achievement as the "discovery of the historical world" (179), which enables the achievements of Petrarch and Boccaccio, in whose work "the historical world acquired a fully immanent autonomy" (178); this in its turn leads seamlessly to the modern age, in which the "sense of the self-sufficiency of earthly life spread like a fructifying stream to the rest of Europe" (177–78). It is only one and a half decades later, when writing *Mimesis*, that Auerbach will insert the "radically creatural picture of man" in wartime (*Mimesis* 249) as an essential force in keeping European literature on the track of realism (261).[5] Creatural life, that is, begins to disturb the continuities of literary history through the force of war.

The divergence between Watt's and Auerbach's mediations of war shows that the novel's domestication of creatural life, post-*Divina Commedia*, is much more tenuous than the imperturbability of Watt's account initially seems to suggest. And it is no coincidence that this domestication becomes undone—as *posthuman comedy*—in the war climate that marks the early twenty-first century. Like the anthropocene, war confronts contemporary life with a force that is undeniably more-than-human as well as irrevocably man-made.[6] This disjunction makes the novel, as the form that has done more than any other to institute the individual subject, burst at the seams and admit more unruly forms of life and affect. If war and the anthropocene are only two forces that currently bend human life in the direction of farcical, ludicrous, and creatural life, *We Are Now Beginning Our Descent* makes a compelling case for their centrality, as well as for the close affinities between them. As I show, it channels these forces into a staging of the end of novel; in this way, it offers a last example of the particular formal and emotive operation that is at the heart of this book.

Worldliness and creatural shame

My account of *The Rise of the Novel* has suggested that it could only declare the power of the novel to animate the individual by burying the disturbing forces of creatural life under the smooth path leading from

Dante to the novel. In a subsequent moment, this half-buried creature resurfaces when nonhuman forces come to break open the fateful domestic union of human life and the novel form. This double movement also accurately describes what happens in *We Are Now Beginning Our Descent*. Published in 2008, *We Are Now Beginning Our Descent* is James Meek's fourth novel; informed by Meek's own experiences as a war reporter, the novel derives much of its energy and urgency from its gradual discovery that its plot—the story of one man, the war reporter Kellas, chased by his demons from Afghanistan over London and the United States to Iraq— can hardly contain its momentous intellectual and formal ambitions: not just tackling questions of global responsibility, but also, in the words of Meek's later novel *The Heart Broke In* (2012), making its characters' lives part of "the same narrative as the billion-year past and future of life and earth" (311). The book opens as a work of genre fiction: the first pages present a Tom Clancy-style thriller set in Afghanistan at the time of the American invasion in the immediate aftermath of September 11. This opening soon turns out to be an excerpt from a manuscript, rather grandiosely called *Rogue Eagle Rising*, that Kellas is writing in order to cash in on his embedded experience of the Afghan campaign (which is described in the book's first half) and on the rising international tide of Anti-Americanism. This opening immediately introduces two of the novel's animating concerns: finding an adequate literary form in which to register the complexities of early twenty-first-century globalized life, and finding a way to relate to global others in the disabling knowledge that these relations are irrevocably contaminated by one's uneasy complicity in the continued violence of war and colonialism.

The novel dramatizes the question of form throughout—and even if after its first few pages, it reluctantly settles for the reflexiveness, the psychologically motivated interweaving of plot and flashbacks, and the allusive density of literary fiction, it only manages to remain settled in the patterns and trajectories of the literary novel in its first half. There is not only Kellas's attempt at a thriller; the novel also foregrounds the rivalry between Kellas and his childhood friend M'Gurgan, a poet who at the opening of the story is writing the first part of a fantasy trilogy for teenagers, but who later in the novel abandons this project—"I realised I'd spent two days coming up with names for elves" (34)—and achieves critical and commercial success with a "dazzling, lovely" "poet's novel" entitled *The Book of Form* (34). So much, then, for commercial calculation: *Rogue Eagle Rising* will never be published, while M'Gurgan beats all odds to reach a large audience with a book composed of "burnished parts of a flying machine that hadn't been put together because they'd never been designed to be, couldn't fit, and would never fly" (35); so much, also, for books that aim for a wider scope than a concentration on mere form— books that, continuing the "flight"-imagery that this last quote and the novel's title introduce, aim to "fly." This formal anxiety also implicates Meek's novel, major parts of which are narrated from an airplane bringing Kellas from London to the United States.

The novel further recycles the popular notion that the events of 9/11 stole the novel's thunder (12), only to complicate it through the life story of the character Bastian. Bastian recounts how he was recruited in the late 1970s to teach in "the CIA's first Creative Writing Program," in which writers learned "how to harness a writer's imagination in the service of intelligence" (222–23). Bastian teaches his students to imagine what "[their] organisation, or [their] country, might be capable of, and then [they] went and did it" (224). It seems that the literary imagination has provided the blueprints for U.S. foreign policy since the late 70s, even if the effects of that policy (9/11), in the logic of Kellas's writerly anxieties, end up undoing the powers of literature. A literature that seeks to be more than an exercise in form, Meek's novel suggests, cannot avoid complicity in the terror that threatens to abolish it.

These bleak prospects for the novel form resonate with Kellas's inability to connect to the Afghan reality he is meant to report on. All attempts to reach out to the local population are blocked by an overriding sense of shame—the novel's one affective keyword (42, 58, 63)—and by uncontrollable bursts of violence that end up perpetuating the dynamic of shame. At one point, Kellas and a group of other journalists interview (with the help of interpreters) one Jalaluddin, a man who has just lost his wife and seen the rest of his family severely wounded after the Americans bombed their house. Acutely aware of the shamefulness of this scene, Kellas tries a different approach: "Kellas took a million in the local currency out of his pocket, about twenty-five dollars, and gave it to [the interpreter] to give to Jalaluddin. He shook Jalaluddin's hand and told [the interpreter] to tell him that he hoped life would become good again" (75). Predictably, this gesture only exacerbates Kellas's sense of shame and disconnection, as it underlines disparities of power that a gratuitous ethical gesture cannot begin to undo. Kellas's repeated experiences of shame firmly anchor him in what Timothy Bewes has called "a global conjuncture in which the very expression of ethical solidarity displays and enacts unprecedented disparities of power" (*Event of Postcolonial Shame* 11), and only confirms the "inherent shamefulness" of the colonial situation that the war on terror perpetuates (12). Good intentions alone will not stop Kellas from being perceived as complicit in this violence.

For Bewes, "[s]hame arises from an incommensurability between my own experience and myself as reflected back to me in the eyes of an other" (41). This description brings shame very close to creatural life, which similarly thrives in the rift between exposed lives and the forms with which they can never fully coincide; shame is, in other words, one of the affects through which human life is riveted to its creatural dimension. In the case of Kellas, the pervasiveness of shame leads to a desire to sidestep this disjunction between being and perception by fleeing the gaze of the other. The day after the shameful encounter with Jalaluddin, Kellas loses his temper with a boy he hits and screams at—"one of those moments of rage that seemed to come from nowhere" (76). Kellas analyzes his actions as an impossible attempt at intimacy, as an expression of a desire to cut through the complexities of shame and somehow connect directly with others: it was "[l]ike a man in a mask and helmet and goggles looking down through a Perspex canopy at something far away he doesn't understand, and the only way he can try to understand it is to hit it" (77). Creatural shame generates a desire to escape shame, and this desire manifests itself in actions that exacerbate the disconnections that give rise to shame. It fuels a destructive cycle that no cosmopolitan intentions can hope to interrupt.

The dynamic of an intimacy that passes through distance in order to (wishfully) sidestep the dynamics of shame recurs when Kellas looks down from his airplane window, and his perspective shifts to that of the F-18 pilots bombing Afghanistan. As I noted before, this aerial perspective is also part of the novel's sustained meditation on the possibilities of the novel form.

> The pilots had left the air-conditioned cabins of their aircraft carriers flown over Pakistan into Afghanistan and tattooed the earth with bombs, then flown home for a meal and a shower [...] Hitting was also a kind of touching. But if hitting was the only kind of touching you did you would damage the one you touched so badly that, by the time you came to embrace them, they would recoil from you [...] America reached out for thousands of miles and its sense of touch stopped three miles short [...] There was curiosity in that reach, and a kind of regret. In any act of hurting there remained the ghost of intimacy. (65)

In passages like these, the novel makes clear that a decision to abandon the domestic sphere ("home for a meal and a shower") and to aim for transnational or cosmopolitan connection does not begin to address the complexities besetting global ethics and politics. Attempts to connect either get tangled up in shame or only ever seem to extricate themselves from shame through (inevitably, shameful) acts of violence. Meek's novel consistently associates the perspective from the plane with the epistemic and cultural powers traditionally ascribed to the novel to combine "depth psychology and social expansiveness" (Woloch 19)—a combination that the dynamics of shame preempts. For Bewes, shame also conditions contemporary literature, as a responsible mode of writing is necessarily "aware of its reflection in the eyes of the other," and is caught in the double bind of "an obligation to write" and "the impossibility of doing so innocently" (42). This awareness of the need for the novel to confront others, and to assume a shameful exposure to their gaze, is also encrypted in the passage above. The passage conveys a sense that, if writing can only hope to record the intimate lives of others by violating them, the only thing that is left for it to do is, precisely, *descend*—renounce its epistemic privilege and come down to a position where it is itself exposed to both the proximate and distant designs of others.

After his tenure in Afghanistan, Kellas continues this shift out of the comforts of the domestic to the shame of exposure when he alienates his London friends during a disastrous dinner party that ends with him destroying the living room of his host's Georgian house and throwing a bust of Lenin through the front window (110–11).[7] This leaves Kellas out in the street, without friends and without a purpose—"full of the sense of lonely cheatedness that comes when all the favourite characters in a drama are dead, yet the drama continues" (56). For Kellas, it continues for 180 more pages, in which he descends from embarrassment over deeper shame to ever more humiliation. Left without the comforts of plot or plan, the goal he adopts in order to orient his movements is a desperate and arbitrary one: he decides to travel to the United States to visit Astrid, a reporter with whom he had a brief affair in Afghanistan and who has just sent him an email out of the blue inviting him over— an email that, he will learn, has been sent by a computer virus to her whole address book. After hearing in New York that he has lost his book deal for *Rogue Eagle Rising*, he finds himself without money, without friends, without means of transportation, and with only the awkward illusion of a love interest. Kellas's shift is very comparable to that underlying Coetzee's *Slow Man*—from novel character to needy creature.[8]

Not sinking but descending: the affect of the present

Nor is this the end of Kellas's descent. He takes a Greyhound bus to the small island and nature resort of Chincoteague, only to discover that his visit there upsets the tenuous equilibrium in the household of Astrid, a man named Bastian, and her small baby. Soon enough, a sexual rendezvous with Astrid triggers her relapse into alcoholism, a condition to which Kellas had thus far remained conveniently blind, and the discovery of which removes his last illusions of human connectedness and his exposure to a different, nonhuman order of life: facing a drunk Astrid, he encounters "the container of a familiar human being when the human was not present" (252). He is struck by "[t]he cold, lizardish emptiness of the eyes," "the reptile stare and the slackness of her jaw" (252). The setting of this confrontation confirms Kellas's slide down an evolutionary scale, as it returns him to the swamps in which reptile life emerged, hundreds of millions of years before the rise of man: they are "two fools fighting over nothing in a dark, freezing marsh" (255), a marsh that keeps sucking him down: "His feet were clasped in cold black pap and he sank till the water came to just over his knees" (253). At this point, the "descent" in the novel's title acquires its full biological meaning.

The novel offers glimpses of a radically nonhuman scale before. During the pivotal dinner party, Kellas's erratic behavior is neither intentional nor controlled, but compelled by forces both below and beyond him: making inappropriate remarks "was like finding that the rock between you and the lava below was infinitely thinner than you had thought, inches thin" (91); a bit later, "[h]is soul was being driven down, into some deeper place than he had known of, while his body tingled and felt strong and light and cold" (107).[9] During his time in Afganistan, the spectacle of reporters "murmuring into their satellite phones" conjures the image of people "sitting on the shore of the cosmos listening to the roar of time" (43). If this last image hovers between a bleak vision of geological deep time and a promise of cosmic release, the downward slant of the other images clearly connects his fate to a geological dimension in which domestic—or even cosmopolitan—concerns count for very little.

The morning after the disastrous confrontation with Astrid, Kellas faces up to the depths of his descent. He walks out to the beach at dawn. Since the ending of Foucault's *The Order of Things*, we know that beaches are the place where the human goes to be erased, "like a face drawn in sand at the edge of the sea" (422), or, in this case, to confront the limits of its humanity. He "had to be the first man out," ready to confront "the continent's eastern edge," which promises "great wonders, in its own time, for the patient among the species"—and emphatically not in *this* time for *this* particular human being (267–68). The setting is significant: although the novel does not tell us so, Chincoteague is also a wildlife refuge that is increasingly under threat from rising sea levels, which may endanger the habitat of several species of shorebirds; so much for the *Rogue Eagle Rising*, then, in the anthropocene. Walking across the shoreline, amid the shells, Kellas notices "a soldier's helmet [that] had been washed up and partly buried in the sand," a material reminder of war that has somehow "floated and not sunk" (270).

An upturned helmet that refuses to be buried and that recalls a war that resists domestication: this is not just a moment of posthuman comedy, but also an unmistakable echo of the poet who guided Dante through the *Divina Commedia*. Of course, Virgil is not only the author of epic wars, but also of the *Georgics*, a work in which the fields of war are cultivated as fertile soil, and in which epic excess is buried in pastoral composure. Or so it seems. Near the end of the first *Georgic*, Virgil notes the transformation of past wars into a plenteous future in a passage from which Meek's helmet might as well be lifted:

> [...] Macedonia
> And the broad Balkan plains were twice made fertile by our blood.
> And a time shall surely come that, in those countries,
> The farmer working the soil with his curved plow
> Shall discover javelins corroded and scabrous with rust
> Or clank on empty helmets with his heavy hoe
> And wonder at the huge bones found in uncovered graves.
> (Lembke 19)

The *Georgics* here intimate that remnants of a more violent order will always threaten the illusory domesticity of the human scale, and that cultural forms of domestication, such as the georgic, or indeed the novel, are bound to be ruptured by forces of a grander scale.

In the *Georgics*, as in *We Are Now Beginning Our Descent*, this larger scale is linked to war, which is traditionally the provenance of the epic rather than the novel. Kellas initially tries to identify the helmet as the kind that "Russians and Chechens [are] wearing in Grozny," or "Azerbaijani marines, or Ethiopian sailors" (270). This display of worldly knowledge is immediately interrupted by a forceful reminder of man's creatural condition as Kellas looks inside the helmet and finds that "[h]is guts were pinched by a spasm of fear and he took a brisk step back, baring his teeth" (270). Unlike Virgil's helmet, Meek's helmet is not empty, nor is it linked to "huge bones," but to a natural history of boneless vulnerability:

> Occupying the helmet, and fused to it, was the remains of an arthropod, a jointed beast eight inches long, like a headless scorpion, with ten or twelve jointed legs and a demon's tail. The vision that came to Kellas's mind in the instant was of a wounded soldier's head becoming stuck to the material of his helmet with his own blood, and some battlefield scavenger creeping out and feeding off it from the inside, till the head was entirely consumed. (270)

This encounter with a radically nonhuman scale inspires a vision of warring men being eaten by the technologies they have invented to protect them, and human life being reclaimed by the natural history it has tried to master. If, as Mark McGurl writes, the "first act" in the posthuman comedy is the one "in which we realize that we cannot be understood apart from our technological prostheses" ("Posthuman" 549), then this is the second act, in which "nature, far from being dominated by technology, *reclaims* technology as a human *secretion*" (550).

This situation, in which human life experiences its non-coincidence with the forms of life that shape it and its exposure to a nonhuman order in which it cannot disappear, is also the moment in which the creatural dimension of life typically asserts itself. For Eric Santner, the sense of creatural life is especially acute when we encounter nature "as a piece of human history"—say, a helmet that refuses to sink—"that has become an enigmatic ruin beyond our capacity to endow it with meaning, to integrate it into our symbolic universe" (*On Creaturely Life* xv). "[S]uch natural historical fissures or caesuras in the space of meaning" (xv) open up a creatural dimension, which is in this novel emphatically linked to a nonhuman scale, as Kellas, when seeing the arthropod, realizes that "[t]his creature had been coming to these shores for longer than humans, and would be here when the humans were gone" (270–71).

We Are Now Beginning Our Descent registers this natural historical insistence through its gradual abandoning of novelistic composure, through its protagonist's exposure to a destructive vortex of shame, and through this climactic scene in which it ties the themes of war, scale, and the creatural together. It is significant that it echoes the *Georgics* at the moment when its disruptions of the novel form become most apparent. In her book on georgic verse, Kevis Goodman counters the prevalent understanding of the georgic mode as a studied evasion of history. As Goodman shows, and as Virgil's "empty helmets" confirm, history is never successfully buried in georgic verse, and these verse can more productively be read as "complexly communicative sites for certain kinds of history" (3). This is especially the case for experiences that have not yet found a stable form and that, in the terms I have drawn on throughout this book, can as yet only register as provisional, non-emotional affects, and often emerge "as *unpleasurable* feeling: as sensory discomfort, as disturbance in affect" (3–4). And yet, Goodman writes, "these moments of excess and dissonance" are the only way for "an otherwise unknowable history" to register and potentially make a difference (9). Goodman's revision of the georgic mode dovetails with the account of contemporary fiction that I have developed in this book: instead of a form that domesticates the affective forces it mobilizes and the modes of life it presents, contemporary fiction stages the end of the novel in order to make room to record as yet uncodified historical changes through its affective operations.

After the irruption of deep time, *We Are Now Beginning Our Descent* speeds to a resolution, and seems to end with a scene of domestic reconciliation between Kellas and M'Gurgan's family, in a chapter that closes with Kellas beginning "with great care to lay the table for dinner" (292), as if the disasters of the earlier dinner party could be undone. Yet the story offers one last surprise, as the short coda fast forwards to March 2003, when Astrid and Kellas again find themselves together, reporting on the planned liberation of Basra in Iraq. Instead of domestic bliss, Kellas and Astrid find themselves caught in the repetitive rhythms of war. This war is not unique, as Kellas imagines it as a replay of former wars, and as part of a loop in which fiction also plays its part: "It was easy to imagine because it was not really imagining, but remembering; and not even remembering something he had seen, but remembering newsreel clips of British tanks liberating Europe in 1944, except for the man in the white suit, who was from *Casablanca*" (297). These are forces that the novel cannot control, as it acknowledges when, in its very last paragraph, it abandons the mind of Kellas, and zooms out to an external perspective on Kellas and Astrid:

> Gradually the watcher drew back, until Kellas and Astrid could no longer be distinguished as individuals; they were two dark, generic figures in the car. The watcher continued to extend his distance. The two cars became smaller and smaller, shrinking into the landscape, and seemed to move more and more slowly, until in the black-and-white glow of his reticulated screen the watcher saw nothing but two dark spots, crawling like lice through the desert along the empty road. (299)

The shift from distinguishable individuals over generic figures to creatures that are barely human confirms the general movement of the novel, as does the passage's modulation through changes of scale. The watcher and his "reticulated screen" cannot but recall the figure we encountered before of the "man in a mask and helmet and goggles looking down through a Perspex canopy" (77) to which Kellas compared himself when he hit the Afghan boy. The difference is, of course, that now Kellas himself has descended to the role of the target. This turning of the tables is all the more emphatic when we note that the concluding paragraph echoes another scene earlier in the book. In this earlier passage, set in Afghanistan, Kellas is on the phone with his mother, absentmindedly chatting about her garden, while a tank driver who has misunderstood Kellas's words as a request to shoot a Taliban truck does exactly that and ends up killing two people. Kellas observes this from a distance: "He lifted the binoculars. Now he could see that the two dots were burning. They were men on fire, burning like candles [...] Kellas couldn't make out the features, only the black lengths of his body and limbs and head" (162–63).

"Two dots" then, "two dark spots" now: the parallels between the two passages suggest that Kellas is about to become the victim of a violence with which he is fatally, if reluctantly, complicit. This sense of imminent death becomes even more palpable when we realize that Kellas and Astrid are travelling on the road that leads to the place where the ITN correspondent Terry Lloyd, his Lebanese interpreter Hussein Osman and the French cameraman Frédéric Nérac were killed by friendly fire in March 2003 (Raban). Yet the novel does not offer the satisfying sense of closure it seems to anticipate. The parallelism between the two scenes is complicated when we note that the last paragraph introduces the "watcher" as follows: "After a while [...] he felt his consciousness dividing; he was still Adam Kellas at the wheel of the car, watching the road ahead, and at the same time he was another, estranged version of himself, watching Kellas and Astrid as they drove" (298). This suggests that the watcher and her target are really metaphors for the two parts of a "consciousness dividing" to the point where it morphs into a condition of full dissociation: human life is split into a pure, sovereign, weirdly disembodied point of observation, on the one hand, and a life "crawling like lice" that is at the mercy of this and other forces on the other.

While it is perfectly possible to read the relation between these two poles as that between a sniper and her target, I want to suggest that such a reading avoids the real challenge of this paragraph by recasting the scene in *human* terms, as a relation of *interhuman* violence. Instead, it is also possible to read the disjunction between a distant observer and a remainder of life as an exercise in what Chakrabarty calls "thinking disjunctively about the human" ("Postcolonial" 2), in imagining "human agency over multiple and incommensurable scales at once" (1). On this reading, *We Are Now Beginning Our Descent* does not close with the imminent end of human life, but rather leaves it suspended, simultaneously *implicated* in a power that cannot be captured in customary social or psychological categories and *exposed* to the effects of that power. The spectacle of human life morphing into a lice life exposed to the gaze of others that will survive it offers another version of the imagined posthumous readers that we encountered in the discussions of *Eat the Document* and *Open City*. In these novels, these readers figure a future perspective on a present that it is too soon to comprehend, and that can as yet only be made "legible" for these imagined future readers. In the case of Meek's novel, it reminds contemporary human life that, in the anthropocene, the human is also a geological object "to be contemplated by the geologist-to-come" (Szerszynski 179). This is an unsettling, awkward position to abandon human life to; and if it is, as I submit, a moment of posthuman comedy, it also gives us a sense of what it means to be human in the anthropocene, even if that sense does not crystallize into anything as substantial as a firm ethical or political position. Like the other novels in this study, *We Are Now Beginning Our Descent* affirms the novel form as one site where the reorganization of human life that is underway in the early twenty-first century is being registered as an affect that remains to be captured.

Notes

Introduction: After-Affects

1. See the first chapter in Huber for an acute and wide-ranging discussion of different accounts of literature after postmodernism.
2. James and Seshagiri refer to the twenty-first aesthetic informed by modernism as "metamodernism." They are seemingly unaware of the alternative career of that term managed by Timotheus Vermeulen and Robin van den Akker. See Vermeulen and van den Akker for a definition of metamodernism as a structure of feeling that oscillates between modernism and postmodernism, and Eve 10–11 for a trenchant critique.
3. That postmodernism is a less conspicuous reference point for my argument than modernism does not mean that there are no significant continuities between postmodern fictions and the novels I read. Most importantly for my argument, Rachel Greenwald Smith has shown that the notion of non-emotional affect can be retrofitted into postmodern fiction. Against Fredric Jameson's influential thesis that postmodernism was marked by a "waning of affect," postmodern tactics—"metafictional strategies, skepticism toward subjective consistency, and deferral of narrative closure" (Greenwald Smith, "Postmodernism" 424)—in fact enable the decoupling of feeling and subjectivity that in its turn allows contemporary fiction to do its affective work. Jameson's thesis presupposes that only traditional subjects with their "psychopathologies" (*Postmodernism* 15) can have feelings and emotions. See Abel 49–50, Beasley-Murray 125–26, Ngai 4, and Terada 2.

1 Persistent Affect (Tom McCarthy, David Shields, Lars Iyer)

1. For an analysis of the genre of "narratives proclaiming the death of something," see Phelan.
2. For the consolidation of "trauma fiction" and the "trauma novel" as distinctive genres, see Craps and Buelens, Luckhurst, *Trauma Question* 87–116, and Whitehead.
3. This is even more apparent in McCarthy's third novel *C*: as Amanda Claybaugh notes, Serge, the novel's protagonist, "endures the traumas of war, in addition to those of incest and the primal scene, but he does not register any of them as traumatic" (178).
4. See Luckhurst, *Trauma Question* 87–90 for the (strongly ethicized) "trauma aesthetic" that characterizes "an emergent international canon of writers and works."
5. Justus Nieland has accurately described the hermeneutical difficulty that McCarthy's work poses: "Part of the challenge of writing on McCarthy is escaping the gravitational pull of his own avowed theoretical investments

while also taking seriously the intellectual traces of this conceptual archive in his work" (578). My reading focuses on the notion of affect that, while sharing the poststructuralist wing of McCarthy's conceptual archive, still constitutes an element that his self-interpretations do not fully control.

6. While the phrase "traumatic realism" captures the idea that the rendering of a traumatized psyche often relies on the conventions of psychological realism, Michael Rothberg's book of that title problematizes the tendency to recuperate the formal features of trauma literature as, in the final analysis, a mimesis of the effects of trauma on the psyche. Rothberg underlines that he does not understand traumatic realism as a "passive mimesis" of the traumatic event, but rather as "an attempt to produce the traumatic event as an object of knowledge and to program and thus transform its readers so that they are forced to acknowledge their relationship to posttraumatic culture" (*Traumatic Realism* 103).

7. I use the term "mimesis" to refer to the power of literature to represent reality. While this may seem self-evident to literary scholars, it is not in the study of trauma, where Ruth Leys has defined the mimesis of trauma as "an experience of hypnotic imitation or identification" (*Trauma* 8), as an embodied reenactment of the traumatic event. On Leys's account, a reaction to trauma that manages to incorporate it in an adequate representation is precisely antimimetic. See Ingham for an illuminating sketch of the tensions between Leys's account and literary theoretical approaches to trauma.

8. In the study of trauma literature, Dominick LaCapra's notion of "empathic unsettlement" has been extremely influential. In its reliance on the kind of empathy (rather than fully fledged identification [78, 102]) that is crucial to the cultural work that the novel has traditionally done, this notion still belongs to the novelistic paradigm from which *Remainder* departs. In LaCapra, the proximity between empathic unsettlement and more traditional notions of empathy becomes clear in casual juxtapositions such as "empathy (or what I term empathic unsettlement)" (97n10).

9. Such a perceptible elision of an expected emotion has also been associated with the form of late twentieth-century fiction that James Annesley has labeled "blank fiction." Associated with authors like Dennis Cooper and Bret Easton Ellis, blank fiction tends to focus on extreme violence and sexuality without providing the proper psychological and emotional framing for such events. Here is Annesley on one of Cooper's stories: "The text's blank response to corporeality compels the reader to reflect on this blankness and encourages a search for the elements that have been displaced in the narrative's attempt to appear empty" (34). While *Remainder* does end in mindless violence and killing, one notable difference is that McCarthy also manages to stage "blank" emotive scenarios *without* needing extreme events; his main interest is in the link between form and affect, rather than violence. Annesley's study does not uncouple literary violence from scenes that are *about* violence, and it does not attend to the affective charge of literary form as such. For a necessary corrective, see Abel.

10. Even while Zadie Smith calls McCarthy's novel the "strong refusal" of lyrical realism, her account intermittently suggests that it is precisely the superimposition of two traditions that makes *Remainder* truly distinctive. Smith keeps insisting on the separation between realism and the French

connection, but her own account tends toward the idea that novels in the latter tradition *subsume* the realist tradition they criticize. In what amounts to a crypto-Hegelian hierarchy, they simply inhabit a higher degree of self-consciousness than even an embarrassed and self-critical realist novel such as *Netherland*: if "*Netherland* plants inside itself its own partial critique," it remains "a novel only partially aware of the ideas that underpin it, [while] *Remainder* is fully conscious of its own." McCarthy's "brutal excision of psychology," in its turn, only makes sense against the background of a less self-conscious tradition for which psychological depth is both an assumption and a goal. Far from remaining indifferent to the tradition it departs from, *Remainder* "meticulously [...] works through the things we expect of a novel, gleefully taking them apart, brick by brick." Smith's "two traditions" can more fruitfully be understood as two opposing forces at work in the same novel; her remark that "[f]riction, fear, and outright hatred spring up often between these two traditions" acknowledges the affective yield of that encounter in McCarthy's work.

11. Of course, the experience that spontaneous actions feel "second-hand" (26) and have stopped being self-evident has little to do with the symptomatology of trauma. It is another indication of McCarthy's indifference to the psychology of trauma that he couples the grammar of trauma with the thematics of inauthenticity by adding the symptoms of deafferentation (the destruction of sensory nerve fibers) to the narrator's injury (see, for instance, 19–20).

12. McCarthy has himself launched the idea that "failed transcendence" is at the heart of his work. Especially *Men In Space*, a novel written before but published after *Remainder*, draws on this idea through the central image of an astronaut who keeps orbiting the earth and is unable to land, as the country that launched him into space (the Soviet Union) has ceased to exist during the time of his trip. Also see the International Necronautical Society's "Declaration on Inauthenticity."

13. See Lea for a more encompassing discussion of the "unresolved tension between the expressivist ethic and the horizon of the postdeconstructive subject" in contemporary literature. Lea locates "a residual belief in the transtemporal, self-identical subject" in *Remainder* (461). This interpretation depends on a misreading of non-subjective affect as subjective emotion, which allows Lea to understand the sensations that afflict the narrator as "micromoments of perfect convergence," as conduits to "a form of authenticity" (466). See Huber and Seita for a different reading of authenticity that traces *Remainder*'s decision to locate authenticity neither in the subject nor the object, but to instead present "authenticity as a quality of experience" (263).

14. At times, Shields seems to acknowledge the potential of the novel, as when he notes that writers like Naipaul and Sebald make "a necessary postmodern return to the roots of the novel as an essentially Creole form, in which 'nonfiction' material is ordered, shaped, and imagined as 'fiction'" (14).

15. One rhetorical tic that Shields shares with McCarthy is a tendency to present insights such as these, which one can assume to be rather old news to most of their audience, as if they were cutting-edge ideas that might still shock the faint-hearted and naive. Amanda Claybaugh's remark that McCarthy's reports

for the International Necronautical Society "read like the seminar papers of a graduate student who has gotten in over his head" also applies to *Reality Hunger* (172). Shields has remarked on the book's origin as a coursepack (Albanese 30).

16. In one of the most perceptive responses to Shields' text, Donald Brown formulates the crucial problem with Shields' position in terms congenial to mine. Brown notes that while "the great modernist challenges" to the traditional novel were "challenges within the form of the novel," "Shields wants to step out of that form and find another," which begs the question whether "there [is] enough 'there there.'" I argue that Shields' text only produces the sense of reality it is after by by remaining stuck on the threshold between the novel form and its illusory other.

17. In an interview, Shields provides further evidence for such a reading. Commenting on the unattributed quotations in the text, he notes: "I just lived with these passages so fully, they seemed so much a part of my brain, that I somewhat vaingloriously came to think of them as mine. I had lived inside of them, and I had rewritten almost all of them considerably" (qtd. in Albanese 30).

2   Abandoned Creatures (J.M. Coetzee)

1. We only learn about the character's initials, which I will use in this chapter, when he uses them to sign a letter (123). Two other characters in the novel refer to him as Señor C and Juan.

2. I am taking my cue here from Arne De Boever's reading of the novel, which also mines the resonances of the phrase "biologico-literary experiment." Relying on Foucault's account of pastoral power, De Boever shows how *Slow Man* reveals the modern history of the novel to be a sustained biopolitical experiment "in the governance of the present" (45)—a literary history that dovetails with my emphasis later in this chapter on the novel's role in "domesticating" creatural life.

3. In support of the *idée reçue* that the traditional novel affords a significant emotional experience, we need look no further than the critical literature on *Slow Man*. Indeed, it is remarkable to what extent the criticism on the novel has combined the observation that Coetzee's late fiction fails to generate a meaningful emotional experience with the notion that these works are somehow not fully fledged novels. Especially the character of Paul Rayment has been called "obdurately unnovelistic or unnovelizable" (McDonald 493). This resistance to novelization is often seen as a motivation for the unceremonious introduction of Elizabeth Costello in *Slow Man*'s thirteenth chapter: Gareth Cornwell writes that Costello intervenes because Paul "has simply not turned out to be as interesting or promising a subject for novelistic treatment as his creator would have liked" (100); according to Zoë Wicomb, Costello is introduced to "move on a story that threatens either to go in an unsuitable direction or to grind to a halt" (219). Barbara Dancygier, for her part, links her observation that Costello is introduced in order to "prompt Paul into a narratologically useful direction" (244) to the novel's seeming lack of emotional engagement: "*Slow Man* is not as complex as other works by Coetzee, and the impact on the reader seems less daring [... Paul] leaves the rest of the story wanting in the power to reach our deepest selves" (245). Kenneth C. Pellow echoes this assessment when he notes that *Slow Man* is

"a novel notably short on anything like pathos, and Rayment, often stoic, sometimes bathetic, evokes but little emotion in us—or in himself" (550). These observations confirm the main premise of this book: that the novel form is intricately connected to the expectation of a significant emotional experience, and that the refusal to deliver such an experience allows contemporary fiction to explore less familiar territory.

4. See the chapter on *Slow Man* in De Boever for a reading of the novel as a novel of care. See Danta, "Janus Face" (xix) for a congenial reading of this scene as a moment of exposure where the conventions of fiction are turned inside out, and where we find ourselves "pinioned between reality and its metamorphic shadow."

5. The observation that it is vital to factor in Coetzee's relation to the tradition of the novel for a proper understanding of his work has been commonplace in Coetzee studies already since the publication of *Foe*. In recent Coetzee criticism, his relation to that tradition has become a key concern. For this emerging critical tendency, see especially De Boever, Hayes, Ogden, McDonald, and Mukherjee.

6. The figure of the gaze is linked to desire in most of Coetzee's fiction. For the image of the "imperial gaze" in Coetzee, see Marais 71. For Coetzee's own most extended discussion of the gaze, see *White Writing* 163–67.

7. See Nethersole and Klopper for extensive discussions of the postscript. Alyda Faber has already noted the affinities between Coetzee's ethical sensibility and Santner's work, especially the poetics of exposure Santner develops in his book on Benjamin, Rilke, and Sebald. For a concise statement of these affinities, see Faber 303–304. A recent volume of essays on Coetzee locates "a form of controlled exposure" at the heart of Coetzee's practice. The introduction to the volume notes that Coetzee's "scrupulous eschewal of authority" is especially acute when he mercilessly "pillor[ies]" his characters" (Danta, "Janus Face" xii, xvi)—when he, on my terms, exposes them as abandoned creatures.

8. Hofmannsthal's text famously describes the agony of death of a mob of poisoned rats as an occasion for such a response. This sight inspires an emotion that is, in Lord Chandos's words, "far more and far less than pity: an immense sympathy, a flowing over into these creatures, or a feeling that an aura of life and death, of dream and wakefulness, had flowed for a moment into them" (76). As in Coetzee's description, we encounter an affect that cannot be reduced to available templates (it is "far more and far less") and that exposes human life to animals from which it is no longer clearly separated.

9. The emphasis on creatural life makes it possible to understand the remarkable attention to the divine in Coetzee's late fiction together with the increasingly explicit exploration of the affinities between human and animal life. The challenge of mapping the relations between humans, animals, and gods in Coetzee was formulated by Michael Valdez Moses (see also Danta, "Melancholy Ape" 128–29).

10. Watt elsewhere acknowledges that the influence of *Mimesis* (and of Lukács's *Theory of the Novel*) was far more important for him than "the few references in the text suggest" ("Flat-Footed" 150–51). Watt read both works in the original German. See Frank for a discussion.

11. Marina Mackay has shown that Ian Watt's account of individualism was decisively inflected by his experience as a prisoner of war—by what she calls "his formative exposure to the sheer fragility of the solitary self"

(139); indeed, "*The Rise of the Novel* is itself a universalizing of a traumatic experience" (137). She explicitly connects *The Rise of the Novel* to *Mimesis*, which was famously written in Auerbach's wartime exile, in order to argue for the decisive role of World War II in the theorization of the novel (137). I explicitly return to the relation between the end of the novel, creatural life, and the experience of war in my coda.

12. In his translation of *Mimesis*, Willard Trask glosses the first occurrence of the term "creatural" [*Kreatürliches*] as follows: "The word, a neologism of the 1920's, implies the suffering to which man is subject as a mortal creature" (246n1). Luiz Costa Lima has suggested that the logic of Auerbach's argument makes it possible to apply the label of "creatural realism" to "post-Flaubertian and post-Baudelairian literature" (138). The notion of the "creatural" or the "creaturely" in the oeuvre of Walter Benjamin (where it emerges in response to the work of Karl Kraus and Franz Kafka) has been discussed extensively by, for instance, Beatrice Hansen, Eric Santner, and Sigrid Weigel.

13. The pun on "flesh" and "flash" returns later in the novel: "That is how it happens. In a flash, in a flesh. If there were any clouds, they have fled" (174). The connection between the "flash" and "the clouds" recalls the crossing of the Alps in the sixth book of Wordsworth's *The Prelude*. In this canonical passage, the imagination transcends nature and rises up "Like an unfathered vapour," "in such strength/Of usurpation, when the light of sense/Goes out, but with a flash that has revealed/The invisible world" (VI 594–601). This is not a random reference: it is the very passage that David Lurie teaches near the beginning of *Disgrace*, where he mobilizes it as a covered defense for his affair with one of his students in the name of desire. The word "flash" recurs at important moments in *Disgrace*, and, as in the Wordsworth passage, it is generally connected to a weightless moment of (wishful) transcendence over material resistance (see, for instance, *Disgrace* 13, 21). That *Slow Man* fills in the afterlife of this idea of the "flash" by linking it to the "flesh" supports my thesis about the intricate relation between *Disgrace* and Coetzee's later "biologico-literary experiments."

14. It is no coincidence that Lukács's book and Hofmannsthal's *Letter* were published only a few years apart in the same cultural realm. Their attempts to cope with the inaccessibility of a blissful state in which "the spiritual and physical worlds seemed to form no contrast" (Hofmannsthal 71–72) respond to the particular intensity with which the question of modernity asserted itself in German-speaking Europe around the time of World War I. Coetzee's explicit engagement with Hofmannsthal in *Elizabeth Costello* makes Lukács's work a relevant reference point for Coetzee's interrogation of the historical fate of the novel.

15. A scenario in which the threat of infinite regress ("second thoughts to the power of n") is countered by the authority of the physical recalls one of the touchstones of Coetzee criticism, his long essay "Confession and Double Thoughts." In this essay, Coetzee discusses the work of Rousseau, Dostoevsky, and Tolstoy in order to explore "the impasses of secular confession" (*Doubling* 291). Lacking faith in the intervention of grace, secular confession is open to the disabling possibility of "a potentially infinite regression of self-recognition and self-abasement in which the self-satisfied candor of each level of confession of impure motive becomes a new source of shame and each twinge of shame a new source of self-congratulation"

(282). In the interview preceding the essay in the volume *Doubling the Point,* Coetzee notes that when there is no grace in a secular world, there is "at least the body," and that "[t]he body with its pain" can serve as "a counter to the endless trials of doubt" (248).

16. Rebecca Walkowitz has noted the productive role of translation in *Diary.* The book's peculiar layout offers "a visual juxtaposition that matches classic modes of interlineal and facing-page translation" ("Comparison Literature" 567); in this way, the book "anticipates its own future as a work of world literature" (569). Walkowitz's observation that Coetzee's late work, like a number of other contemporary Anglophone oeuvres, seems to be "written for translation" and eschews using vernacular elements resonates with the widespread observation of the abstractness of this part of his oeuvre, or what Melinda Harvey calls these novels' "escape from place."

3 Cosmopolitan Dissociation (Teju Cole)

1. Apart from many nominations, the book won the 2012 PEN/Hemingway award, the 2011 New York City Book Award for Fiction, and a Rosenthal Award from the American Academy of Arts and Letters.

2. To name only a handful of monographs that invoke the signifiers in their title, we can think of *Modernist Fiction, Cosmopolitanism, and The Politics of Community* (Berman), *Cosmopolitanism in Contemporary British Fiction* (McCullough), *The Cosmopolitan Novel* (Schoene), *Cosmopolitan Fictions* (K. Stanton), and *Cosmopolitan Style* (Walkowitz). The first four of these titles explicitly signal the privileged role of fiction and the novel. Rebecca Walkowitz's *Cosmopolitan Style,* for its part, almost exclusively deals with novels, and only with authors who are known primarily as novelists, while its introduction displays an (apparently untheorized) emphasis on narrative rather than style.

3. In his plea for aesthetic cosmopolitanism, Nikos Papastergiadis underplays the vital need for such an aesthetic complement in Kant's cosmopolitanism in order to argue for a turn from Kant to the Stoics. Kant, Papastergiadis writes, emphasized "political reasoning and rational deduction, rather than subjective feeling and aesthetic experience" (83), while the Stoics "believed that cosmopolitanism could develop through the aesthetic dimension of imagination" (88).

4. For Kant, the novel genre answers the need to "represent an otherwise unplanned aggregate of human actions [*ein sonst planloses Aggregat menschlicher Handlungen*] at least in general as a system" (14). What the novel is implicitly called upon to do, then, is to articulate the particular with universal reason, and save the latter from its fatal abstractness. This position is echoed in many contemporary cases for the cosmopolitan reach of the novel form. For Jessica Berman, for instance, narratives do their cultural work "in their transposition of this question of community from the domain of public citizenship and the state to a liminal zone where community is both intimate and political, both local and worldly" (6–7).

5. This is the strategy that Kant's remarks on the novel seem to envision. As Jan Plug has noted, Kant turns to the novel because, on the terms of Kant's own system, an Idea (in this case, the Idea of universal history) cannot possibly find a referent in the historical realm. The novel genre then "tak[es] the

place of the absent referent"; it acts "*as if* it were the referent" (13–14). See also Juengel 69. Christian Thorne has brilliantly interrogated the apparent absence of truly "planetary novels" (Thorne 71).

6. In the humanities, there is a notable tendency to underplay the tension between the cosmopolitan and the universal, and to focus instead on the opposition between the cosmopolitan on the one hand and the "parochial" and the "chauvinistic" on the other (D. Stanton 629). This is a continuation of the traditional opposition between cosmopolitanism and nationalism (influentially updated in the 1990s by Martha Nussbaum), in which the latter is invariably cast as the negative term. One effect of this near-automatic coding is a tendency to consider all things that "transcend national or ethnic boundaries" as cosmopolitan by default (Levy and Sznaider, "Memory Unbound" 88). See especially Berman, Levy and Sznaider, and Schoene, *The Cosmopolitan Novel* for this tendency. Compare Amanda Anderson's more careful definition, in which the universal horizon is maintained: "cosmopolitanism endorses reflective distance from one's cultural affiliations, a broad understanding of other cultures and customs, and a belief in universal humanity" (72).

7. If, as Pheng Cheah writes, "cosmopolitanism and human rights are the two primary ways of figuring the global as the human" (*Inhuman Conditions* 3), it is unsurprising that human rights discourse, like cosmopolitanism, is conceptually and historically linked to the novel form. Joseph Slaughter has demonstrated that human rights are constrained and energized by an essentially "novelistic" way of looking at "human personality and its sociality" (50). Invested in concurrent accounts of human flourishing, human rights and the novel are, for Slaughter, not merely homologous, but they are "mutually ratifying" (52), as human rights discourse, through its dependence on cultural forms to give its precepts moral force, has historically relied on a cultural imagery that was sustained by the conditions of social inclusion and exclusion that were codified in the genre of the *Bildungsroman*.

8. See especially Spencer, who argues that criticism must attend to "the extraordinarily violent and unequal conflicts inaugurated over the past several centuries by the project of imperialism"; it needs to focus on "literature concerned with these conflicts [...] and also with the no less fascinating and sometimes rather auspicious forms of contact and communication that have sometimes resulted from them" (1). A comparable investment in the nexus of the memory of violence and the dynamics of intercultural encounter is apparent in the field of memory studies, where this interface has been studied under such labels as "prosthetic" (Landsberg), "multidirectional" (Rothberg), and, most tellingly, "cosmopolitan memory" (Levy and Sznaider, "Memory Unbound").

9. And obviously, the fact that the novel's main movements are already formulated in its very first sections only to be reworked throughout the rest of the novel further connects it to the fugue form, which is precisely defined by the recurrence of its opening theme(s) throughout the composition. For a musicological perspective on the tensions between fugue and noise, see Dineen 52–53.

10. In one of the foundational texts in the field of trauma studies, Kathy Caruth holds that, in a catastrophic age, "trauma itself may provide the very link

between cultures: not as a simple understanding of the pasts of others but rather, within the traumas of contemporary history, as our ability to listen through the departures we have all taken from ourselves" (11). *Open City's* decision to devote so much space to traumatic memories and, at the same time, to question the possibility of translating such memory work into inter- cultural connectedness brings it in line with recent assessments of trauma studies' failure to live up to its intercultural promises. See especially Craps.

11. Rita Barnard has coined the term "hyperlinking" to describe the seemingly uncontrolled and fortuitous linkages between characters and stories in a film like Alejandro Iñárritu's *Babel* or a novel like David Mitchell's *Ghostwritten* (210). *Open City's* descent into the tonality of a Wikipedia entry seems to point to the threat that such a principled openness can always flip over into indifferent accumulation. For another account of this threat to "multi- directional" or "cosmopolitan" models of memory, see Vermeulen, "Video Testimony" 557–62.

12. I have my student Eva Mebius to thank for drawing my attention to the close parallels between the character of Julius and the figure of the *fugueur*. Caren Irr has shown that the fugue serves as a privileged trope and an organ- izing device in what she identifies as the emergent genre of the "peace corps fugue" (70–72).

13. Bruce Robbins uses the term "extraterrestrial" to characterize (and criti- cize) the cosmopolitanisms of Noam Chomsky and Immanuel Wallerstein (*Perpetual War* 64, 84). For Robbins, the problem with a cosmopolitanism that abandons the dynamic of detachment and (re)attachment for a princi- pled disconnect is that "it exists on a time scale utterly divorced from our own," which leads to "the deferral or dilution of political agency" (84, 87). For a defense of a theoretical perspective that explodes the all-too-human bounds of cosmopolitanism in a way congenial to Szendy, or indeed Cole, see Colebrook, *Death of the PostHuman* 96–115.

14. While I have not touched on the theme of cosmopolitanism in my discus- sion of Coetzee in my second chapter, Katherine Hallemeier has shown that Coetzee's late fiction, like Cole's *Open City*, offers a sustained engagement with the limits of rational and affective cosmopolitanisms that tend to cel- ebrate cross-cultural feelings as cosmopolitan achievements.

4   Epic Failures (Dana Spiotta, Hari Kunzru, Russell Banks)

1. Both Rüdiger Campe and Eva Geulen have emphasized that the very exist- ence of the epic "already presupposes the loss of totality and a rupture between subject and object," without which there would be no reason to write an epic *affirming* that totality (Geulen, "Response" 20; Campe 62). Yet even if for Homer "life has lost its immanent significance," creating epics "was just a matter of lifting the meaningful forms of life to consciousness" (Geulen, "Response" 20), an option that the novel lacks, as it has no access to such meaningful forms.

2. The tension between the end as an *empirical fact* and the sense of an end- ing as a *constitutive dimension* of a particular phenomenon (in this case, the novel) has been extensively explored in the case of Hegel's thesis of "the end

of art." For excellent discussions of what Eva Geulen calls this "rumor" (as opposed to a fully fledged "thesis") as more than an empirical observation that can be disproven by pointing to the continued existence of art works and artists, see Geulen, *The End of Art*, and Horowitz, especially 56–90. Horowitz glosses Hegel's rumor by noting that, in an age when spirit and nature are fatefully separated, "art looks like a reconciliation that is unavailable to us" (72). Just as Lukács's novel testifies to the unavailability of the immediacy and wholeness associated with the epic, "[a]rt is modernity's privileged bearer of what it had to sacrifice to attain spiritual maturity" (72).

3. The recent work of Timothy Bewes argues for (and exemplifies) the productivity of extending this non-chronological approach to Lukács's oeuvre itself: "The challenge is to avoid differentiating between an early, pre-ideological Lukács, who 'sees' clearly, and a later Lukács who 'fails' to see [...] Better would be to grasp the necessity of the connection between these stages in his thinking" ("How to Escape" 38). I adopt this approach in this chapter by considering the *Theory of the Novel* and Lukács's later notion of the type as two available positions that are negotiated in contemporary fiction. For an excellent account of the shift from the *Theory of the Novel* (where totality is lost) to Lukács's work after *History and Class Consciousness* (where dialectical materialism lays the basis for a new totality), see Fredric Jameson's chapter on Lukács in *Marxism and Form*, especially pages 190–92. For the compelling argument that Balzacian realism functions in the later Lukács in much the same way that the epic does in the *Theory of the Novel*, see Sorensen 69–70.

4. Bewes adduces Lukács's short essay "Thoughts Toward an Aesthetic of the Cinema" as evidence that cinema and epic attract comparable associations in Lukács's aesthetic thought ("Against" 274; "How to Escape" 41–44). Lukács's fairly extensive writing on cinema has recently become available in Aitken.

5. In *The Anxiety of Obsolescence*, her widely noted study of the ways in which the novel's terminal anxieties are featured in postmodern fiction, Kathleen Fitzpatrick interprets negative depictions of electronic media, and especially television, as a cover for a conservative, even sexist and racist, agenda. For Fitzpatrick, the postmodern novel's engagement with electronic media needs to be decoded twice in order to reduce it to a struggle between a set of novelists and other social agents: first, as a reflection of "a cluster of anxieties" about being displaced from a position of cultural authority; and second, these anxieties themselves "are in certain ways a pose" that obscure "other, unspeakable anxieties about shifts in contemporary *social* life" (201–202). This perspective, which mobilizes a popular zero-sum logic for a reading of literary texts, obscures the fact that novels' evocations of other media often crystallize their concerns about the very possibility of relating literary form to social life. Studies of the place of the book in the new media ecology tend to focus on the materialities of communication and explicitly aim to move beyond interpretation. Still, as Joseph Tabbi and Michael Wutz note, their volume *Reading Matters* attempts to "come up with new ways of engaging with narrative" in which "the sense of an ending" plays a crucial role (3). The novel, for them, "remains the one medium that allows the historical effects of media differentiation to be remarked" (18). For a celebration of (mostly postmodern) novels that abandon a sense of belatedness for an embrace of "information multiplicity" or "media assemblages," see Johnston.

6. For a discussion that touches on Banks, Choi, Gordon, Sorrentino, and Spiotta, see the fourth chapter in M. Ryan; for the same names without Sorrentino, see Wiener. Especially Gordon's *The Company You Keep* brings together almost all the elements that I observe in Kunzru and Spiotta: a complex temporal structure that sidesteps 9/11, a concern with new media (the novel is written as a series of emails), and a preoccupation with the demise of the "novelistic" tension between private and public.

7. Both Dave Gunning (809) and Matthew Hart (1066) read the ending of the novel more positively as Michael's decision to reconcile with society. For Hart, Michael's decision to phone his wife shows that "the nuclear family mediates Chris' self-willed transformation from outlaw back to citizen" (1066). What complicates this reading is that this phone call also marks the moment when Chris stops being the author of his own story, and when his transformation is, in a sense, no longer his to will. Hart's assertion that the novel ends on the insight that "the choice between individualism and community [is] a false one" (1066) underestimates the novel's investment in the rupture between the public and the private.

8. Florence Dore argues that *Eat the Document* can be considered what she calls "a rock novel." According to Dore, "[o]ver the decade or so after 2000, novel after novel takes some feature of rock and roll as basic to its project." Dore's reading of contemporary fiction in general, and *Eat the Document* in particular, is different from mine in that she sees the recourse to rock as a strategy to reaffirm the centrality of the "private subject" that is threatened by impersonal media, while I emphasize that the novels I analyze revise the project of the novel in a way that also implicates the human individual.

9. One novel that is indisputably part of the post-9/11 canon and that might seem to contradict Gray's assessment is Safran Foer's *Extremely Loud and Incredibly Close*. Gray acknowledges that "the novel seems experimental, disruptive, responsive to the strange," yet concludes that the seemingly experimental elements (especially its typographical and visual features) in the end are "not so much disruptive as illustrative" of "a deeply traditional narrative" (*After the Fall* 52–53). See Robbins, "Worlding" for a broader perspective on the ethical implications of the worlding of American fiction; Morley for a reminder that American fiction was already moving toward the domestic before 9/11; and Duvall and Marzec for a defense of the worldliness of DeLillo's *Falling Man*—one of Gray's main targets—and for discussions of Jess Walter's *The Zero* and Salman Rushdie's *Shalimar the Clown* that unsettle Gray's and Rothberg's encompassing critiques of post-9/11 fiction (384–93).

10. Lee Konstantinou nominates David Foster Wallace as another writer for whom worldliness is not only a representational choice but first of all a formal challenge. Konstantinou uses William T. Vollmann rather than Russell Banks as an example of a "representational" worldliness. Wallace, for Konstantinou, "wants to find a literary form that demonstrates (rather than represents) the limited bounds of his own imagination [...] which he regards as constitutionally unable to see on a planetary scale. Wallace's fiction arguably highlights these lacunae, without pretending to overcome them, far more forcefully that the writing of those, such as Vollmann, who often try to escape their limited perspectives by getting on a plane and traveling to another country" (84).

11. While *The Darling* embraces a more worldly perspective by moving away from American territory, it does not take the next step that Gray's exemplary post-9/11 fictions perform: inhabiting the space between cultures "by means of a mixture of voices, a free play of languages and even genres" (*After the Fall* 19), "responding to intercultural exchange in terms that are themselves genuinely intercultural, that hybridize" (114). Martin Randall's *9/11 and the Literature of Terror*, like Gray, valorizes "a hybrid form that is sufficiently open to self-questioning, irony, self-reflection and that possesses an awareness of its own limitations" (76). For another important indictment of the parochialism of most post-9/11 fictions, which explicitly commends Banks's work for piercing the "climate of political conformity" during the Cold War, see Mishra. In the rest of this chapter, I link *The Darling*'s disinterest in hybridity to the novel's nearly consistent confidence in its aesthetic project.
12. In his reading of *The Darling*, Phillip Wegner also underlines the epistemic significance of the character of Hannah. Wegner notes Banks's recurrent use of "major characters in circulation within and across national borders" as a strategy to "think the world system as such" (95), and to enable the cognitive mapping of "the often obscure political and economic flows constituting U.S. global power in the Cold War period" (97). While Wegner reads *The Darling* as a "critical realist novel" that successfully extends the terms of pre-9/11 realism, I argue that the novel's realist epistemology finds itself afflicted by challenges that it cannot incorporate into a revised project. The difference between these two readings hinges on the interpretation of the novel's last few paragraphs.
13. For other readings of the distinction between empathy and sympathy in the novel, see Varvogli and Wegner.

Coda: The Descent of the Novel (James Meek)

1. In her response to McGurl, Dimock continues the conversation in genre-theoretical terms, even if she seems to miss the radicality of McGurl's proposals. Dimock introduces the notion of "low epic," which emphasizes the role of literature in domesticating "the quintessential epic encounter with alien orders of magnitude" (617); she proposes "a lyricization of epic—our brain's way of telescoping in reverse, turning unthinkable orders of magnitude into thinkable ones" (619), which is quite different from McGurl's interest in a direct confrontation that does not reduce the scales it faces.
2. McGurl recognizes the potential of the breakdown of form to evoke the irruption of the nonhuman, even if he again attributes this potential to genre fiction, rather than to the literary novel: that works that aim to scale our visions up or down "fail to transcend their historical and medial conditions of possibility testifies to the limits of the human imagination [...] but those limits are also what allow us to know and feel our presence in the world as something in particular" ("Posthuman Comedy" 541–42). I argue that the impact of such a confrontation with the limits of the imagination is potentially greater when readers expect to find imaginative resolutions, which is more typically the case when reading a literary novel.

3. A section devoted to "The Ecological Humanities" in the *Australian Humanities Review* in 2009 is an early example of this attempt to reposition the humanities in light of this new concept. One of the most remarkable manifestations of this attempt is the effort to retrieve the relevance of deconstruction, and especially the work of Jacques Derrida, for an engagement with climate change and the anthropocene. See especially an issue of the *Oxford Literary Review* from 2012 on "Deconstruction in the Anthropocene" and the *Critical Climate Change* book series that Tom Cohen and Claire Colebrook edit for Open Humanities Press.

4. Dating the start of the anthropocene to the eighteenth century is not uncontroversial, and this date will remain contested as the term awaits official recognition as a distinctive stratigraphic unit. Crutzen's and others' idea that the anthropocene was inaugurated around 1800 is challenged by William Ruddiman's contention that it began with the mass clearing of forests for agriculture about 8,000 years earlier. For a good sketch of these and other issues surrounding the use of the term, including the option of subdividing the period into different stages, see Szerszynski. For a concise response to Ruddiman, see Crutzen and Steffen.

5. In an unpublished lecture entitled "Auerbach Theologicus," Jane Newman also links the conclusion of Auerbach's 1929 book to the narrative of *Mimesis*. Newman shows that while the earlier text merely registers that the literary direction taken by Boccaccio created "grave dangers" for realism, *Mimesis* presents de la Sale's creatural realism as a paradoxically more productive successor to Dante's achievement. Newman also notes that the opposition between Boccaccio and de la Sale already shows up in Auerbach's 1921 dissertation. For the intellectual and political contexts of Auerbach's different accounts of Dante and his successors, see also Newman, "Auerbach's Dante."

6. Another way to think together the anthropocene and war as related challenges for the novel form is by underlining their association with epic. The scale of geological events is routinely called "epic" (for instance, Zalasiewicz et al. 2228), while the epic form is of course historically linked to the representation of war. In his response to Dimock's defense of the epic as a laudably transnational form, Mark McGurl notes that she overlooks the problem of the genre's "booming, war-mongering braggadocio" ("Critical" 636).

7. It is hard not to read this dinner party as an allusion to Ian McEwan's *Saturday*, which is also set in a Georgian townhouse, and which infamously reduces the scale of the post-9/11 world to the size of the family. In *Saturday*'s climactic scene, the irruption of the external world into the domestic sphere is figured by a couple of lowlifes interrupting a family party, only to be overpowered—and later operated on—by the brain surgeon who serves as the novel's self-confident and controlled narrator. Meek's dinner scene suggests a very different geopolitics than *Saturday*'s picture of punctured domestic bliss: while in *Saturday*, the domestic sphere seems to be in need of protection from foreign threats, in *We Are Now Beginning Our Descent*, domesticity is itself riven by affective charges that it cannot contain and that Meek's novel refuses to project onto foreign intruders.

8. In his review of Meek's book, Jonathan Raban notes a shift in the quality of the writing after the moment in the story when Kellas loses everything. In the first two-thirds of the novel, Meek manages to make "recent memory and

present experience mingle on equal terms," and we see "scene disssolving into scene with great naturalness and fluency"; in the novel's latter part, "the texture of his writing thins," newly introduced characters "are little more than functional cut-outs," and the story "returns to conventional and-then-and-then chronology." If we realize that the interweaving of flashbacks and action is a far more conventional novelistic device than mere chronology, this shift resembles nothing so much as the shift from novelistic composure to the less substantial and rewarding kind of writing we already encountered in Coetzee.

9. Kellas's erratic behavior during the dinner party is not only the result of bio-logical urges; indeed, the passage weaves this layer of meaning together with an element that directly overlaps with my earlier account of creatural shame, understood as "the incommensurability between my own experience and myself as reflected back to me in the eyes of an other" (Bewes 41). One of the things that make the situation unbearable for Kellas is that the other guests suspect him of having gone out and had sex with one of the guests, while he knows that it was in fact his married friend and literary rival M'Gurgan who did this. Out of loyalty to his friend, and out of affection for his friend's wife, Kellas cannot correct the image of himself reflected back to him from around the table, and instead remains caught in a shameful exposure that, as elsewhere in the novel, can only find intermittent relief through violence.

Works Cited

Abbott, H. Porter. "Time, Narrative, Life, Death, & Text-Type Distinctions: The Example of Coetzee's *Diary of a Bad Year*." *Narrative* 19.2 (2011): 187–200.

Abel, Marco. *Violent Affect: Literature, Cinema, and Critique after Representation*. Lincoln, NE: University of Nebraska Press, 2007.

Agamben, Giorgio. "What is the Contemporary?" *"What is an Apparatus?" And Other Essays*. trans. David Kishik and Stefan Pedatella. Stanford, CA: Stanford University Press, 2009. 39–54.

Aitken, Ian. *Lukácsian Film Theory and Cinema: A Study of Georg Lukács' Writing on Film 1913–1971*. Manchester: Manchester University Press, 2012.

Albanese, Andrew Richard. "Make Mine Yours." *Publishers Weekly* 15 March 2010: 29–32.

Alter, Robert. *Partial Magic: The Novel as a Self-Conscious Genre*. Berkeley, CA: University of California Press, 1975.

American Psychiatric Association. *Diagnostic and Statistical Manual of Mental Disorders*. 4th ed. Washington: American Psychiatric Association, 2000.

Anderson, Amanda. *The Way We Argue Now: A Study in the Cultures of Theory*. Princeton, NJ: Princeton University Press, 2005.

Annesley, James. *Blank Fictions: Consumerism, Culture, and the Contemporary Novel*. New York: St. Martin's Press, 1998.

Appiah, Kwane Anthony. *The Ethics of Identity*. Princeton, NJ: Princeton University Press, 2004.

Armstrong, Nancy. *How Novels Think: The Limits of British Individualism from 1719–1900*. New York: Columbia University Press, 2006.

———. "The Fiction of Bourgeois Morality and the Paradox of Individualism." *The Novel, Volume 2*. Ed. Franco Moretti. Princeton, NJ: Princeton University Press, 2007. 344–389.

Attwell, David. *J.M. Coetzee: South Africa and the Politics of Writing*. Berkeley, CA: University of California Press, 1993.

———. "Mastering Authority: J.M. Coetzee's *Diary of a Bad Year*." *Social Dynamics* 36.1 (2010): 214–221.

Auerbach, Erich. *Mimesis: Dargestellte Wirklichkeit in der abendländischen Literatur*. Bern: Francke Verlag, 1946.

———. "Figura." *Scenes from the Drama of European Literature*. Trans. Ralph Manheim. Minneapolis, MN: University of Minnesota Press, 1984. 11–79.

———. *Mimesis: The Representation of Reality in Western Literature*. Trans. Willard Trask. Princeton, NJ: Princeton University Press, 2003.

———. *Dante: Poet of the Secular World*. Trans. Ralph Manheim. New York: New York Review Books, 2007.

Balaev, Michelle. "Trends in Literary Trauma Theory." *Mosaic* 41.2 (2008): 149–166.

Banita, Georgiana. *Plotting Justice: Narrative Ethics and Literary Culture after 9/11*. Lincoln, NE: University of Nebraska Press, 2012.

Banks, Russell. *The Darling*. London: Bloomsbury, 2006.

Barnard, Rita. "Fictions of the Global." *Novel: A Forum on Fiction* 42.2 (2009): 207–215.

Barth, John. "The Literature of Exhaustion." *The Friday Book: Essays and Other Nonfiction*. Baltimore, MD: Johns Hopkins University Press, 1984. 62–76.

———. "The Literature of Replenishment." *The Friday Book: Essays and Other Nonfiction*. Baltimore, MD: Johns Hopkins University Press, 1984. 193–206.

Baucom, Ian. "The Human Shore: Postcolonial Studies in an Age of Natural Science." *History of the Present: A Journal of Critical History* 2.1 (2012): 1–23.

Baudrillard, Jean. "Simulacra and Simulations." *Selected Writings*. Ed. Mark Poster. Stanford, CA: Stanford University Press, 1998. 166–184.

Beasley-Murray, Jon. *Posthegemony: Political Theory and Latin America*. Minneapolis, MN: University of Minnesota Press, 2011.

Benhabib, Seyla. "The Philosophical Foundations of Cosmopolitan Norms." *Another Cosmopolitanism*. Seyla Benhabib and Robert Post. New York: Oxford University Press, 2006. 13–44.

Berlant, Lauren. *The Female Complaint: The Unfinished Business of Sentimentality in American Culture*. Durham: Duke University Press, 2008.

———. "Intuitionists: History and the Affective Event." *American Literary History* 20.4 (2008): 845–860.

Berman, Jessica. *Modernist Fiction, Cosmopolitanism, and the Politics of Community*. Cambridge: Cambridge University Press, 2007.

Bewes, Timothy. "Against the Ontology of the Present: Paul Auster's Cinematographic Fictions." *Twentieth Century Literature* 53.3 (2007): 273–297.

———. *The Event of Postcolonial Shame*. Princeton, NJ: Princeton University Press, 2011.

———. "How to Escape from Literature? Lukács, Cinema, and *The Theory of the Novel*." *Georg Lukács: The Fundamental Dissonance of Existence*. Ed. Timothy Bewes and Timothy Hall. London: Continuum, 2011. 36–48.

Birnbaum, Robert. "Author Interview: Russell Banks." *Identity Theory* 18 January 2005. Web. 21 May 2014.

Boehmer, Elleke. "J.M. Coetzee's Australian Realism." *Strong Opinions: J.M. Coetzee and the Authority of Contemporary Fiction*. Ed. Chris Danta, Sue Kossew, and Julian Murphet. London: Continuum, 2011. 3–17.

Boxall, Peter. "Late: Fictional Time in the Twenty-First Century." *Contemporary Literature* 53.4 (2012): 681–712.

———. *Twenty-First-Century Fiction: An Introduction*. Cambridge: Cambridge University Press, 2013.

Brennan, Timothy. "Cosmo-Theory." *South Atlantic Quarterly* 100.3 (2001): 659–691.

Brooks, Peter. *Reading for the Plot: Design and Intention in Narrative*. Cambridge, MA: Harvard University Press, 1992.

Brown, Donald. "Novel Ideas? Problems with *Reality Hunger* by David Shields." *The Quarterly Conversation* 6 September 2010. Web. 21 May 2014.

Buck-Morss, Susan. "The Flaneur, the Sandwichman, and the Whore: The Politics of Loitering." *New German Critique* 39 (1986): 99–140.

Campe, Rüdiger. "Form and Life in the Theory of the Novel." *Constellations* 18.1 (2011): 53–66.

Caruth, Kathy. "Trauma and Experience: Introduction." *Trauma: Explorations in Memory*. Ed. Kathy Caruth. Baltimore, MD: Johns Hopkins University Press, 1995. 3–12.

Chakrabarty, Dipesh. "The Climate of History: Four Theses." *Critical Inquiry* 35.2 (2009): 197–222.

———. "Postcolonial Studies and the Challenge of Climate Change." *New Literary History* 43.2 (2012): 1–18.

Cheah, Pheng. "Cosmopolitanism." *Theory, Culture and Society* 23.2–3 (2006): 486–496.

———. *Inhuman Conditions: On Cosmopolitanism and Human Rights*. Cambridge, MA: Harvard University Press, 2007.

Claybaugh, Amanda. "McC." *N+1 Magazine* 11 (2011): 169–180.

Clayton, Jay. "Narrative and Theories of Desire." *Critical Inquiry* 16.1 (1989): 33–53.

Clune, Michael. *Writing against Time*. Stanford, CA: Stanford University Press, 2013.

Coetzee, J.M. *White Writing: On the Culture of Letters in South Africa*. New Haven, CT: Yale University Press, 1988.

———. *Doubling the Point: Essays and Interviews*. Ed. David Attwell. Cambridge, MA: Harvard University Press, 1992.

———. *Disgrace*. London: Vintage, 1999.

———. *Elizabeth Costello*. London: Secker & Warburg, 2003.

———. *Slow Man*. London: Secker & Warburg, 2005.

———. *Diary of A Bad Year*. London: Vintage Books, 2008.

Cole, Teju. *Open City*. London: Faber & Faber, 2011.

Colebrook, Claire. "The Calculus of Individual Worth." *Theory and the Disappearing Future: On de Man, On Benjamin*. Tom Cohen, Claire Colebrook, and J. Hillis Miller. Abingdon: Routledge, 2012. 130–152.

———. "Not Symbiosis, Not Now: Why Anthropogenic Change is Not Really Human." *Oxford Literary Review* 34.2 (2012): 185–210.

———. *Death of the PostHuman: Essays on Extinction, Vol. 1*. Ann Arbor, MI: Open Humanities Press, 2014.

Cooppan, Vilashini. "Memory's Future: Affect, History, and New Narrative in South Africa." *Concentric: Literary and Cultural Studies* 35.1 (2009): 51–75.

Cornwell, Gareth. "'He and His Man': Allegory and Catachresis in J.M. Coetzee's Nobel Lecture." *English in Africa* 34.1 (2007): 97–114.

Costa Lima, Luiz. "Between Realism and Figuration: Auerbach's Decentered Realism." *Crossroads* 2.2 (2008): 133–140.

Craps, Stef. *Postcolonial Witnessing: Trauma out of Bounds*. Basingstoke: Palgrave Macmillan, 2012.

Craps, Stef and Gert Buelens. "Introduction: Postcolonial Trauma Novels." *Studies in the Novel* 40.1–2 (2008): 1–12.

Crutzen, Paul and Will Steffen. "How Long Have We Been in the Anthropocene Era?" *Climatic Change* 61.3 (2003): 251–257.

Dancygier, Barbara. "Close Encounters: The Author and the Character in *Elizabeth Costello, Slow Man*, and *Diary of a Bad Year*." *J.M. Coetzee's Austerities*. Ed. Graham Bradshaw and Michael Neill. Surrey: Ashgate, 2010. 215–230.

Danta, Chris. "J.M. Coetzee: The Janus Face of Authority." *Strong Opinions: J.M. Coetzee and the Authority of Contemporary Fiction*. Ed. Chris Danta, Sue Kossew, and Julian Murphet. London: Continuum, 2011. xi–xx.

————. "The Melancholy Ape: Coetzee's Fables of Animal Finitude." *Strong Opinions: J.M. Coetzee and the Authority of Contemporary Fiction*. Ed. Chris Danta, Sue Kossew, and Julian Murphet. London: Continuum, 2011. 125–140.

Davis Wood, Daniel. "Rebirth of the Nouveau Roman: 9/11 as a Crisis of Confidence in American Literary Aesthetics." *9/11*. Spec. issue of *Other Modernities* (2011): 134–145.

De Boever, Arne. *Narrative Care: Biopolitics and the Novel*. London: Bloomsbury, 2013.

De Lauretis, Teresa. "Desire in Narrative." *Alice Doesn't: Feminism, Semiotics, Cinema*. Bloomington, IN: Indiana University Press, 1984. 103–157.

DeRosa, Aaron. "Analyzing Literature after 9/11." *Modern Fiction Studies* 57.3 (2011): 607–618.

Dimock, Wai Chee. "Critical Response I: Low Epic." *Critical Inquiry* 39.3 (2013): 614–631.

Dineen, Murray. "Fugue, Space, Noise, and Form." *International Studies in Philosophy* 36.1 (2004): 39–60.

Dore, Florence. "The Rock Novel and Jonathan Lethem's *The Fortress of Solitude*." *Nonsite.org* 8 (2013): n. pag. Web. 21 May 2014.

Duvall, John and Robert Marzec. "Narrating 9/11." *Modern Fiction Studies* 57.3 (2011): 381–400.

Egginton, William. "Affective Disorder." *Diacritics* 40.4 (2012): 25–43.

Eliot, T.S. *Selected Prose of T.S. Eliot*. Ed. Frank Kermode. London: Faber & Faber, 1975.

Eve, Martin. "Thomas Pynchon, David Foster Wallace, and the Problems of 'Metamodernism.'" *C21 Literature: Journal of 21st-Century Writings* 1.1 (2012): 7–25.

Faber, Alyda. "The Post-Secular Poetics and Ethics of Exposure in J.M. Coetzee's *Disgrace*." *Literature and Theology* 23.3 (2009): 303–316.

Fitzpatrick, Kathleen. *The Anxiety of Obsolescence: The American Novel in the Age of Television*. Nashville, TN: Vanderbilt University Press, 2006.

Foden, Giles. Rev. of *Open City*, by Teju Cole. *Guardian* 17 August 2011. Web. 21 May 2014.

Fojas, Camilla. *Cosmopolitanism in the Americas*. West Lafayette, IN: Purdue University Press, 2005.

Foucault, Michel. *The Order of Things: An Archeology of the Human Sciences*. Abingdon: Routledge, 2002.

Frank, Joseph. "The Consequence of Ian Watt: A Call for Papers on Diminished Reputations." *Common Knowledge* 13.2–3 (2007): 497–511.

Freud, Sigmund. "Mourning and Melancholia." *The Standard Edition of the Complete Psychological Works of Sigmund Freud, Volume XIV*. Ed. James Strachey. London: Hogarth Press, 1957. 243–258.

Gasiorek, Andrzej and David James. "Introduction: Fiction since 2000: Postmillennial Commitments." *Contemporary Literature* 53.4 (2012): 609–627.

Genette, Gérard. *The Architext: An Introduction*. Trans. Jane E. Lewin. Berkeley: University of California Press, 1992.

Geulen, Eva. *The End of Art: Readings in a Rumor after Hegel*. Trans. James McFarland. Stanford, CA: Stanford University Press, 2006.

————. "Response and Commentary." *Romanticism and Biopolitics*. Ed. Alastair Hunt and Matthias Rudolf. College Park, MD: University of Maryland Press, 2012. n. pag. Romantic Circles Praxis Series. Web. 21 May 2014.

Goodman, Kevis. *Georgic Modernity and British Romanticism: Poetry and the Mediation of History*. Cambridge: Cambridge University Press, 2004.

Gordon, Mary. "*The Darling*: Among the Dreamers." Rev. of *The Darling*, by Russell Banks. *New York Times* 24 October 2004. Web. 21 May 2014.

Gordon, Neil. *The Company You Keep*. New York: Penguin Books, 2003.

Gray, Richard. "Open Doors, Closed Minds: American Prose Writing at a Time of Crisis." *American Literary History* 21.1 (2009): 128–148.

———. *After the Fall: American Literature Since 9/11*. Chichester: Wiley-Blackwell, 2011.

Green, Jeremy. *Late Postmodernism: American Fiction at the Millennium*. New York: Palgrave Macmillan, 2005.

Greenwald Smith, Rachel. "Organic Shrapnel: Affect and Aesthetics in September 11 Fiction." *American Literature* 83.1 (2011): 153–174.

———. "Postmodernism and the Affective Turn." *Twentieth Century Literature* 57.3–4 (2011): 423–446.

Greif, Mark. "'The Death of the Novel' and its Afterlives: Toward a History of the 'Big, Ambitious Novel.'" *Boundary 2* 36.2 (2009): 11–30.

Gunning, Dave. "Ethnicity, Authenticity, and Empathy in the Realist Novel and Its Alternatives." *Contemporary Literature* 53.4 (2012): 779–813.

Hacking, Ian. *Mad Travelers: Reflections on the Reality of Transient Mental Illnesses*. Charlottesville, VA: University of Virginia Press, 1999.

Hallemeier, Katherine. *J.M. Coetzee and the Limits of Cosmopolitanism*. Basingstoke: Palgrave Macmillan, 2013.

Hart, Matthew. "The Politics of the State in Contemporary Literary Studies." *Literature Compass* 6.5 (2009): 1060–1070.

Hart, Matthew and Aaron Jaffe, with Jonathan Eburne. "An Interview with Tom McCarthy." *Contemporary Literature* 54.4 (2013): 656–682.

Harvey, Melinda. "'In Australia you start zero': The Escape from Place in J.M. Coetzee's Late Novels." *Strong Opinions: J.M. Coetzee and the Authority of Contemporary Fiction*. Ed. Chris Danta, Sue Kossew, and Julian Murphet. London: Continuum, 2011. 19–34.

Hayes, Patrick. *J.M. Coetzee and the Novel: Writing and Politics after Beckett*. Oxford: Oxford University Press, 2010.

Hofmannsthal, Hugo von. *The Whole Difference: Selected Writings of Hugo von Hofmannsthal*. Ed. J.D. McClatchy. Princeton, NJ: Princeton University Press, 2009.

Horowitz, Gregg. *Sustaining Loss: Art and Mournful Life*. Stanford, CA: Stanford University Press, 2002.

Huber, Irmtraud. *Literature after Postmodernism: Reconstructive Fantasies*. Basingstoke: Palgrave Macmillan, 2014.

Huber, Irmtraud and Sophie Seita. "Authentic Simulacra or The Aura of Repetition: Experiencing Authenticity in Tom McCarthy's *Remainder*." *Aesthetics of Authenticity*. Ed. Wolfgang Funk, Florian Groβ, and Irmtraud Huber. Bielefeld: Transcript, 2012. 261–280.

Huggan, Graham. *The Postcolonial Exotic: Marketing the Margins*. London: Routledge, 2001.

Hunt, Lynn. *Inventing Human Rights: A History*. New York: Norton, 2007.

Huyssen, Andreas. "International Human Rights and The Politics of Memory: Limits and Challenges." *Criticism* 53.4 (2011): 607–624.

Ingham, Patricia Clare. "Chaucer's Haunted Aesthetics: Mimesis and Trauma in *Troilus and Criseyde*." *College English* 72.3 (2010): 226–247.

International Necronautical Society. "INS Declaration on Inauthenticity." *Necronauts.org* 2007. Web. 21 May 2014.

Irom, Bimbisar. "Alterities in a Time of Terror: Notes on the Subgenre of the American 9/11 Novel." *Contemporary Literature* 53.3 (2012): 517–547.

Irr, Caren. *Toward the Geopolitical Novel: U.S. Fiction in the Twenty-First Century.* New York: Columbia University Press, 2013.

Iyer, Lars. *Spurious.* New York: Melville House, 2011.

———. *Dogma.* New York: Melville House, 2012.

———. *Exodus.* New York: Melville House, 2013.

———. "Nude in Your Hot Tub, Facing the Abyss (A Literary Manifesto after the End of Literature and Manifestos)." *The White Review* n.d. Web. 21 May 2014.

James, David and Urmila Seshagiri. "Metamodernism: Narratives of Continuity and Revolution." *PMLA* 129.1 (2014): 87–100.

James, Henry. *The Art of the Novel: Critical Prefaces.* Ed. R.P. Blackmur. New York: Charles Scribner's, 1962.

Jameson, Fredric. *Marxism and Form: Twentieth-Century Dialectical Theories of Literature.* Princeton, NJ: Princeton University Press, 1974.

———. *Postmodernism, or, The Cultural Logic of Late Capitalism.* London: Verso, 1992.

———. *The Antinomies of Realism.* London: Verso, 2013.

Johnson, Liza. "Interview with Dana Spiotta." *Believer* n.d. Web. 21 May 2014.

Johnston, John. *Information Multiplicity: American Fiction in the Age of Media Saturation.* Baltimore, MD: Johns Hopkins University Press, 1998.

Juengel, Scott. "The Novel of Universal Peace." *Cultural Critique* 73 (2011): 60–93.

Kant, Immanuel. "Idea for a Universal History with a Cosmopolitan Purpose." *"Toward Perpetual Peace" and Other Writings on Politics, Peace, and History.* Ed. Pauline Kleingeld. Trans. David L. Colclasure. New Haven, CT: Yale University Press, 2006. 3–16.

Kelly, Adam. "Who Is Responsible? Revisiting the Radical Years in Dana Spiotta's *Eat the Document.*" *Forever Young? The Changing Images of America.* Ed. Philip Coleman and Stephen Matterson. Heidelberg: Universitätsverlag, 2012. 219–230.

Keniston, Ann and Jeanne Follansbee Quinn. "Representing 9/11: Literature and Resistance." *Literature after 9/11.* Ed. Ann Keniston and Jeanne Follansbee Quinn. New York: Routledge, 2008. 1–15.

Kittler, Friedrich. *Gramophone, Film, Typewriter.* Trans. Geoffrey Winthrop-Young and Michael Wutz. Stanford, CA: Stanford University Press, 1999.

Klopper, Dirk. "'We are not made for revelation': Letters to Francis Bacon in the Postscript to *Elizabeth Costello.*" *English in Africa* 35.2 (2008): 119–132.

Konstantinou, Lee. "The World of David Foster Wallace." *Boundary 2* 40.3 (2013): 59–86.

Kuitenbrouwer, Kathryn. "Mise en abîme: An Interview with Tom McCarthy." *Bookninja Magazine* 2007. Web. 26 August 2011.

Kunzru, Hari. *My Revolutions.* London: Penguin, 2008.

Kurnick, David. "The Novel (in Theory)." *Literature Compass* 6.1 (2009): 228–243.

LaCapra, Dominick. *Writing History, Writing Trauma.* Baltimore, MD: Johns Hopkins University Press, 2001.

Landsberg, Alison. *Prosthetic Memory: The Transformation of American Remembrance in the Age of Mass Culture*. New York: Columbia University Press, 2004.

Lawrence, D.H. "The Future of the Novel (Surgery for the Novel—Or a Bomb)." *Study of Thomas Hardy and Other Essays*. Cambridge: Cambridge University Press, 1985. 149–156.

———. "Why the Novel Matters." *Study of Thomas Hardy and Other Essays*. Cambridge: Cambridge University Press, 1985. 191–198.

Lea, Daniel. "The Anxieties of Authenticity in Post-2000 British Fiction." *Modern Fiction Studies* 58.3 (2012): 459–476.

Lembke, Janet. *Virgil's Georgics: A New Verse Translation*. New Haven, CT: Yale University Press, 2005.

Levy, Daniel and Natan Sznaider. "Memory Unbound: The Holocaust and the Formation of Cosmopolitan Memory." *European Journal of Social Theory* 5.1 (2002): 87–106.

———. "Cosmopolitan Memory and Human Rights." *The Ashgate Research Companion to Cosmopolitanism*. Ed. Maria Rovisco and Magdalena Nowicka. Aldershot: Ashgate, 2011. 195–209.

Leys, Ruth. *Trauma: A Genealogy*. Chicago, IL: University of Chicago Press, 2000.
———. "The Turn to Affect: A Critique." *Critical Inquiry* 37.3 (2011): 434–473.

Luckhurst, Roger. *The Trauma Question*. London: Routledge, 2008.

———. "In War Times: Fictionalizing Iraq." *Contemporary Literature* 53.4 (2012): 713–737.

Lukács, Georg. *Studies in European Realism: A Sociological Survey of the Writings of Balzac, Stendhal, Zola, Gorky, and Others*. Trans. Edith Bone. London: Merlin Press, 1972.

———. "Art and Objective Truth." *"Writer and Critic" and Other Essays*. Trans. Arthur Kahn. London: Merlin Press, 1972. 25–60.

———. *The Theory of the Novel*. Trans. Anna Bostock. Cambridge, MA: MIT Press, 1974.

———. "Thoughts toward an Aesthetic of the Cinema." Trans. Janelle Blankenship. *Polygraph* 13 (2001): 13–18.

MacKay, Marina. "The Wartime Rise of *The Rise of the Novel*." *Representations* 119 (2012): 119–143.

Malik, Rachel. "We Are too Menny." Rev. of *The One vs. the Many*, by Alex Woloch. *New Left Review* 28 (2004): 139–149.

Marais, Michael. "The Hermeneutics of Empire: Coetzee's Post-Colonial Metafiction." *Critical Perspectives on J.M. Coetzee*. Ed. Graham Huggan and Steve Watson. London: Macmillan, 1996. 66–81.

Marcus, Ben. "The Genre Artist." *Believer* July 2003. Web. 21 May 2014.

Massumi, Brian. *Parables for the Virtual: Movement, Affect, Sensation*. Durham, NC: Duke University Press, 2012.

McCarthy, Tom. *Remainder*. London: Alma Books, 2007.
———. *Men In Space*. London: Alma Books, 2008.
———. *C*. London: Jonathan Cape, 2010.
———. "Stabbing the Olive." *London Review of Books* 11 February 2010. Web. 21 May 2014.
———. "Technology and the Novel: From Blake to Ballard." *Guardian* 24 July 2010. Web. 21 May 2014.

———. *Transmission and the Individual Remix*. London: Vintage Digital, 2012.

McDonald, Peter. "The Ethics of Reading and the Question of the Novel: The Challenge of J.M. Coetzee's *Diary of a Bad Year*." *Novel: A Forum on Fiction* 43.3 (2010): 483–499.

McEwan, Ian. *Saturday*. London: Jonathan Cape, 2005.

McGurl, Mark. "The Zombie Renaissance." *N+1 Magazine* 9 (2010): n. pag. Web. 21 May 2014.

———. "The New Cultural Geology." *Twentieth Century Literature* 57.3–4 (2011): 380–390.

———. "The Posthuman Comedy." *Critical Inquiry* 38.3 (2012): 533–553.

———. "Critical Response II: 'Neither indeed could I forebear smiling at my self.' A Reply to Wai Chee Dimock." *Critical Inquiry* 39.3 (2013): 632–638.

Meek, James. *We Are Now Beginning Our Descent*. Edinburgh: Canongate, 2009.

———. *The Heart Broke In*. Edinburgh: Canongate, 2012.

Messud, Claire. "The Secret Sharer." Rev. of *Open City*, by Teju Cole. *New York Review of Books* 14 July 2011. Web. 21 May 2014.

Mishra, Pankaj. "The End of Innocence." *Guardian* 19 May 2007. Web. 21 May 2014.

Morley, Catherine. "'How do we write about this?' The Domestic and the Global in the Post-9/11 Novel." *Journal of American Studies* 45.4 (2011): 717–731.

Mukherjee, Ankhi. "The Death of the Novel and Two Postcolonial Writers." *Modern Language Quarterly* 69.4 (2008): 533–556.

Nethersole, Reingard. "Reading in the In-Between: Pre-Scripting the 'Postscript' to *Elizabeth Costello*." *Journal of Literary Studies* 21.3–4 (2005): 254–276.

Newman, Jane. "Auerbach's Dante: Poetical Theology as a Point of Departure for a Philology of World Literature." *Approaches to World Literature*. Ed. Joachim Küpper. New York: De Gruyter, 2013. 39–58.

Ngai, Sianne. *Ugly Feelings*. Cambridge, MA: Harvard University Press, 2005.

Nieland, Justus. "Dirty Media: Tom McCarthy and the Afterlife of Modernism." *Modern Fiction Studies* 58.3 (2012): 569–599.

Ogden, Benjamin. "The Coming into Being of Literature: How J.M. Coetzee's *Diary of a Bad Year* Thinks through the Novel." *Novel: A Forum on Fiction* 43.3 (2010): 466–482.

Ortiz-Robles, Mario. *The Novel as Event*. Ann Arbor, MI: The University of Michigan Press, 2010.

Orwell, Roger. "What's Left Behind: An Interview with Tom McCarthy." *Catastrophe*. Spec. issue of *Static* 7 (2008): 4 pages. Web. 21 May 2014.

Palumbo-Liu, David. *The Deliverance of Others: Reading Literature in a Global Age*. Durham, NC: Duke University Press, 2012.

Papastergiadis, Nikos. *Cosmopolitanism and Culture*. Cambridge: Polity, 2012.

Pellow, C. Kenneth. "Intertextuality and Other Analogues in J.M. Coetzee's *Slow Man*." *Contemporary Literature* 50.3 (2009): 528–552.

Phelan, James. "Assessing Narratives Proclaiming the Death of Something." *Narrative* 6.1 (1998): 96–101.

Phillips, Mike. "Monkey Business." Rev. of *The Darling*, by Russell Banks. *Guardian* 2 April 2005. Web. 21 May 2014.

Plug, Jan. "Citizens of Modernity from a Cosmopolitan Point of View." *CR: The New Centennial Review* 1.1 (2001): 1–21.

Raban, Jonathan. "Planes, Trains, and SUVs." Rev. of *We Are Now Beginning Our Descent*, by James Meek. *London Review of Books* 7 February 2008. Web. 21 May 2014.

Rabinovitz, Lauren. *For the Love of Pleasure: Women, Movies, and Culture in Turn-of-the-Century Chicago*. New Brunswick, NJ: Rutgers University Press, 1998.

Randall, Martin. *9/11 And the Literature of Terror*. Edinburgh: Edinburgh University Press, 2009.

Reed, Walter. "*Don Quixote*: The Birth, Rise, and Death of the Novel." *Indiana Journal of Hispanic Literatures* 5 (1994): 263–278.

Robbins, Bruce. "Introduction I: Actually Existing Cosmopolitanism." *Cosmopolitics: Thinking and Feeling beyond the Nation*. Ed. Pheng Cheah and Bruce Robbins. Minneapolis, MN: University of Minnesota Press, 1998. 1–19.

———. "The Village of the Liberal Managerial Class." *Cosmopolitan Geographies: New Locations in Literature and Culture*. Ed. Vinay Dharwadker. New York and London: Routledge, 2001. 15–32.

———. "The Worlding of the American Novel." *The Cambridge History of the American Novel*. Ed. Leonard Cassuto. Cambridge: Cambridge University Press, 2011. 1096–1106.

———. *Perpetual War: Cosmopolitanism from the Viewpoint of Violence*. Durham, NC: Duke University Press, 2012.

Rothberg, Michael. *Traumatic Realism: The Demands of Holocaust Representation*. Minneapolis, MN: University of Minnesota Press, 2000.

———. *Multidirectional Memory: Remembering the Holocaust in the Age of Decolonization*. Stanford, CA: Stanford University Press, 2009.

———. "A Failure of the Imagination: Diagnosing the Post-9/11 Novel. A Response to Richard Gray." *American Literary History* 21.1 (2009): 152–158.

Rourke, Lee. "In Conversation: Lee Rourke and Tom McCarthy." *Guardian* 18 September 2010. Web. 21 May 2014.

Ryan, Judith. *Early Psychology and Literary Modernism*. Chicago, IL: University of Chicago Press, 1991.

Ryan, Maureen. *The Other Side of Grief: The Home Front and the Aftermath in American Narratives of the Vietnam War*. Amherst, MA: University of Massachusetts Press, 2008.

Sanders, Mark. Rev. of *J.M. Coetzee and the Ethics of Reading: Literature in the Event*, by Derek Attridge. *Modern Fiction Studies* 53.3 (2007): 641–645.

Santner, Eric. *On Creaturely Life: Rilke, Benjamin, Sebald*. Chicago, IL: University of Chicago Press, 2006.

———. *The Royal Remains: The People's Two Bodies and the Endgames of Sovereignty*. Chicago, IL: University of Chicago Press, 2011.

Sayeau, Michael. *Against the Event: The Everyday and the Evolution of Modernist Narrative*. Oxford: Oxford University Press, 2013.

Schmidt, Rachel. *Forms of Modernity:* Don Quixote *and Modern Theories of the Novel*. Toronto: University of Toronto Press, 2011.

Schoene, Berthold. *The Cosmopolitan Novel*. Edinburgh: Edinburgh University Press, 2009.

———. "*Tour Du Monde*: David Mitchell's *Ghostwritten* and the Cosmopolitan Imagination." *College Literature* 37.4 (2010): 42–60.

Shields, David. *Reality Hunger: A Manifesto*. London: Hamish Hamilton, 2010.

Shklovsky, Viktor. "The Novel as Parody: Sterne's *Tristram Shandy*." *Theory of Prose*. Trans. Benjamin Sher. Champaign, IL: Dalkey Archive Press, 1991. 147–170.

Siskind, Mariano. "The Globalization of the Novel and the Novelization of the Global: A Critique of World Literature." *Comparative Literature* 62.4 (2010): 336–360.

Slaughter, Joseph. *Human Rights Inc.: The World Novel, Narrative Form, and International Law*. New York: Fordham University Press, 2007.

Smith, Zadie. "Two Paths for the Novel." *New York Review of Books* 20 November 2008. Web. 21 May 2014.

Sorensen, Eli Park. "Novelistic Interpretation: The Traveling Theory of Lukács's *Theory of the Novel*." *Journal of Narrative Theory* 39.1 (2009): 57–85.

Spencer, Robert. *Cosmopolitan Criticism and Postcolonial Literature*. Basingstoke: Palgrave Macmillan, 2011.

Spiotta, Dana. *Eat the Document*. London: Picador, 2008.

———. *Stone Arabia*. New York: Scribner, 2011.

Stanton, Domna. "Presidential Address 2005: On Rooted Cosmopolitanism." *PMLA* 121.3 (2006): 627–640.

Stanton, Katherine. *Cosmopolitan Fictions: Ethics, Politics, and Global Change in the Works of Kazuo Ishiguro, Michael Ondaatje, Jamaica Kincaid, and J.M. Coetzee*. London: Routledge, 2009.

Szendy, Peter. *Kant in the Land of Extraterrestrials: Cosmopolitical Philosofictions*. New York: Fordham University Press, 2013.

Szerszynski, Bronislaw. "The End of the End of Nature: The Anthropocene and the Fate of the Human." *Oxford Literary Review* 34.2 (2012): 165–184.

Tabbi, Joseph and Michael Wutz. "Introduction." *Reading Matters: Narratives in the New Media Ecology*. Ed. Joseph Tabbi and Michael Wutz. Ithaca, NY, and London: Cornell University Press, 1997. 1–25.

Terada, Rei. *Feeling in Theory: Emotion after the Death of the Subject*. Cambridge, MA: Harvard University Press, 2001.

Thorne, Christian. "The Sea is Not a Place; or, Putting the World back into World Literature." *Boundary 2* 40.2 (2013): 53–79.

Timmer, Nicoline. *Do You Feel it Too? The Post-Postmodern Syndrome in American Fiction at the Turn of the Millennium*. Amsterdam: Rodopi, 2010.

Todorov, Tzvetan. "The Origin of Genres." *New Literary Histories* 8.1 (1976): 159–170.

Valdez Moses, Michael. "'King of the amphibians': *Elizabeth Costello* and Coetzee's Metamorphic Fictions." *Journal of Literary Studies* 25.4 (2009): 25–38.

Varvogli, Alike. "Radical Motherhood: Narcissism and Empathy in Russell Banks's *The Darling* and Dana Spiotta's *Eat the Document*." *Journal of American Studies* 44.4 (2010): 657–673.

Vermeulen, Pieter. "Video Testimony, Modernity, and the Claims of Melancholia." *Criticism* 53.4 (2011): 549–568.

———. "Posthuman Affect." *European Journal of English Studies* 18.2 (2014): 121–134.

Vermeulen, Timotheus and Robin van den Akker. "Notes on Metamodernism." *Journal of Aesthetics and Culture* 2 (2010): 14 pages.

Versluys, Kristiaan. *Out of the Blue: September 11 and the Novel*. New York: Columbia University Press, 2009.

Vickroy, Laurie. *Trauma and Survival in Contemporary Fiction*. Charlottesville, VA: University of Virginia Press, 2004.

Walkowitz, Rebecca. *Cosmopolitan Style: Modernism beyond the Nation.* New York: Columbia University Press, 2006.

———. "Comparison Literature." *New Literary History* 40.3 (2009): 567–582.

Walton, Heather. "Staging John Coetzee / Elizabeth Costello." *Literature and Theology* 22.3 (2008): 280–294.

Watt, Ian. *The Rise of the Novel: Studies in Defoe, Richardson, and Fielding.* London: Pimlico, 2000.

———. "Flat-Footed and Fly-Blown: The Realities of Realism." *Eighteenth-Century Fiction* 12.2–3 (2000): 147–166.

Wegner, Phillip. "Things as They Were or Are: On Russell Banks's Global Realisms." *Reading Capitalist Realism.* Ed. Alison Shonkwiler and Leigh Claire La Berge. Iowa City, IA: University of Iowa Press, 2014. 89–112.

Whitehead, Anne. *Trauma Fiction.* Edinburgh: Edinburgh University Press, 2004.

Wicomb, Zoë. "*Slow Man* and the Real: A Lesson in Reading and Writing." *J.M. Coetzee's Austerities.* Ed. Graham Bradshaw and Michael Neill. Surrey: Ashgate, 2010. 215–230.

Wiener, Jon. "The Weatherman Temptation." *Dissent* 54.2 (2007): 100–104.

Wilson, Elizabeth. "The Invisible Flâneur." *New Left Review I* 191 (1992): 90–110.

Wolfe, Carry. *What is Posthumanism?* Minneapolis, MN: University of Minnesota Press, 2010.

Woloch, Alex. *The One vs. The Many: Minor Characters and the Space of the Protagonist in the Novel.* Princeton, NJ: Princeton University Press, 2003.

Wood, James. "The Arrival of Enigmas." Rev. of *Open City*, by Teju Cole. *New Yorker* 28 February 2011. Web. 21 May 2014.

Wordsworth, William. *The Fourteen-Book Prelude.* Ed. W.J.B. Owen. Ithaca, NY: Cornell University Press, 1985.

Zalasiewicz, Jan et al. "The New World of the Anthropocene." *Environmental Science and Technology* 44.7 (2010): 2228–2231.

Index

stance, definition of, 91
tradition, 83
Costello, Elizabeth, 44, 50, 63–5, 71,
    156
  see also Coetzee, J. M.
creatural/creaturely, 158*n*11
  abandon/abandonment, 49, 54–8,
    156–9
  life, 11, 18, 22, 44, 46, 55, 74, 107,
    136, 140, 149
    domestication of, *see* domestication
      of creatural life
  realism, 11, 18, 141, 158*n*11
  shame, 142–6, 166*n*9
  suffering, 56
  vulnerability, 55
  war, 140–2
cultural power of the novel, 2–4, 6–8,
    10, 146

D

Darling, The (Russell Banks), 4, 16,
    109, 126–33, 164*n*11
desire, 7, 50–4, 57
Diary of a Bad Year (J.M. Coetzee), 4,
    6, 15, 48–52, 57, 63, 73–80
digitalization-of-all-media, 122
Disgrace (J. M. Coetzee), 48, 50–4
Divina Commedia (Dante), 141–2,
    148
domestication of creaturely life, 59–63
Don Quixote (Cervantes), 1
dysphoric emotion, 30

E

earthly life, 60–1
Eat the Document (Dana Spiotta), 4–5,
    15, 18, 98, 109, 111–12, 116–26,
    128–9, 131, 133–4, 152, 163*n*8
Eliot, T.S., 19–22, 39, 43
Elizabeth Costello, 48–49, 56–8, 158
emotion, 7–11, 30–1
  see also affect(s)
emotional codifications, 9–11
emotive disorientation, 10
empathic unsettlement, 154*n*8
empathy, 16, 23, 28, 30, 32, 51–3, 56,
    75, 85, 132, 136, 138, 154*n*8,
    164*n*13

Emperor's Children, The (Claire
    Messud), 131
epic, 18, 72–3, 106, 108, 114, 120,
    124, 132
  folk, 69
  low, *see* low epic
  poetry, 21
  wars, 148
extraterrestrial cosmopolitics, 104,
    161*n*13

F

farcical life, 11, 23, 43–6, 107, 140
feeling(s), 8, 24, 30
  impersonal, see impersonal feelings
  neutral, *see* neutral feeling
  non-neutral, *see* non-neutral feeling
  second-order, *see* second-order
    feeling
  vocabulary dealing with, 31
flâneur, 83–4, 100–4
flash, 66–7, 158*n*12
flesh, 56, 62, 67–8, 71, 123, 158*n*12
flights of memory, 82–5
formal realism, 60
fugue state, 136
fugueurs, 84, 100–4

G

genre(s)
  definition of, 6
  dying into form, 1–4
  function, 7
geopolitical novel, 13
Georgics, 148–9
globalization process, 86
Greenwald Smith, Rachel, 8, 9, 10, 15,
    126, 135, 153n3

H

Heart Broke In, The (James Meek), 143
Hofmannsthal, Hugo von, 14, 49,
    56–8, 61–3, 157*n*7, 158*n*13
human
  agency(ies), 139, 152
  consciousness, 9
  life, 11–12, 17, 31, 46, 61, 140, 142
  realities, 61
  rights, 82, 84–91, 160*n*7

Printed in Great Britain
by Amazon